JESUS
and the four Gospels

Jesus Christ is a crucial figure of history. Today he is worshipped as God by millions, and his teaching continues to influence individuals, even whole societies. His life has been dramatized and written about many times; he is the star of film and musical.

John Drane does not simply retell the familiar story. He asks searching questions. How does Jesus fit into the time in which he lived? Did he really make great claims for himself or did the church later make them for him? Why did he teach in parables? What was the point of his miracles? And who recorded all the events of his life? Are those records accurate or embellished with legend? And why did he die . . .?

This book is both faithful to the New Testament evidence and fully aware of modern scholarship. The approach is popular and not over-technical; it is also thorough and well-informed. Subjects of more technical interest are tackled in special articles separate from the main text; photographs and line illustrations are informative and stimulating. The fresh presentation of the book makes it suitable not only for the general reader but also for use in schools and colleges.

Dr John Drane is Lecturer in Religious Studies at Stirling University. *Paul*, his companion volume to this book, has been published in several editions, and received outstanding reviews in the religious and educational press.

To William Lillie
with gratitude and affection

Jesus

and the four Gospels

John W. Drane

Published in San Francisco by
Harper & Row, Publishers
New York, Hagerstown, San Francisco, London

JESUS AND THE FOUR GOSPELS.
Copyright © 1979 by John W. Drane.
All rights reserved. Printed in Great
Britain. No part of this book may be
used or reproduced in any manner
whatsoever without written permission
except in the case of brief quotations
embodied in critical articles and reviews.
For information address Harper & Row,
Publishers, Inc., 10 East 53rd Street,
New York, NY 10022. Published
simultaneously in Canada by
Fitzhenry & Whiteside, Limited,
Toronto.

FIRST UNITED STATES EDITION

Designed by Tony Cantale

**Library of Congress Cataloging in
Publication Data**

Drane, John William.
  Jesus and the four Gospels.

  1. Jesus Christ – Biography.
2. Christian biography – Palestine.
3. Bible. N.T. Gospels – Criticism,
interpretation, etc. I. Title. Jesus and
the four Gospels.
BT301.2.D7 1978   232.9'01   77-20448
ISBN 0-06-062066-8

79 80 81 82 83 10 9 8 7 6 5 4 3 2 1

Picture credits:
David Alexander: 14, 15, 31, 61, 81, 87, 93, 114 (loaves and fish), 136, 139,
155, 165, 167, 170, 174 (both), 180.
American School of Classical Studies, Athens: 79.
Barnaby's: 42, 59, 67, 130 (background), 141.
British Museum: 27, 153.
Camera Press: 69, 118.
J. Allan Cash: 17, 32, 41, 53, 77, 120, 132 (mill), 142, 144, 148.
K. W. Coates: 97, 124.
Bruce Coleman: 126.
Fritz Fankhauser: 35 (soldier), 47, 91, 113, 161, 184.
Haifa Maritime Museum: 71.
Sonia Halliday Photographs: 22, 25, 35 (desert), 37, 41 (view), 54 (wall), 74,
84–85, 103, 104, 117, 122, 133 (flowers), 147, 157, 171; Jane Taylor 9, 11,
51, 111, 125; Laura Lushington 109, 173.
Phil Manning: 54 (dish).
Mansell Collection: 26, 168 (both), 169 (both).
Middle East Photographic Archive: 21, 38–39, 83, 98.
Popperfoto: 30, 35 (stuntman), 41 (jars and fragments), 46, 49, 54 (top and
right), 95, 96, 101, 130 (both), 131 (both), 179, 183.
Radio Times Hulton Picture Library: 41 (cave entrance), 106, 129.
John Ryland's Library: 177.
Tear Fund: 35 (distribution), 114, 163.

Line drawings by Vic Mitchell.
Maps and diagrams by Tony Cantale.

Contents

Section two God's new society

Section three Knowing about Jesus

Introduction

This book is about Jesus. It is also about the four New Testament Gospels which tell the story of his remarkable life and teaching.

We begin by examining the historical setting of Jesus' work, and then we go on to look at some important parts of his teaching. In the final section of the book we deal with the Gospels themselves. Who wrote them? Why did the authors write them as they did? And can we believe what they tell us about Jesus?

This book concentrates on particular themes, rather than providing either a biography of Jesus or a commentary on the text of the Gospels. So it is important to read the Gospels as well. They provide the essential framework for understanding the story and the arguments presented here.

Many people are reluctant to read the Bible for themselves. They think it dull, or find its language is too difficult to understand. But read in a modern translation the Gospels are no more difficult to get through than the average newspaper. Quotations in this book have been taken mainly from the Revised Standard Version and the Good News Bible, both easy to read.

The importance of actually reading the Gospels cannot be overemphasized. For if these stories are true, they present a person of such stupendous importance that we cannot simply accept a second-hand verdict from someone else. It is essential that we get at the facts for ourselves.

Section One
God's promised deliverer

Chapter 1 The world of Jesus

WHAT WAS Jesus really like? We have all asked that question at some time. Probably most of us have in our mind's eye a picture of what Jesus may have looked like. If our only encounter with Christianity has been through a visit to one of the great cathedrals, or even to the church on the street corner, we may picture him as a haloed figure in a stained-glass window. Or he may seem some kind of shadowy nonentity, important to the beliefs of Christians but more or less irrelevant to the real concerns of everyday life.

Mark 6:3
If, on the other hand, we have opened the New Testament out of curiosity and read there that Jesus was a carpenter, we may have quite a different impression of him. For according to the Gospels, Jesus spent most of his adult life as an ordinary working man. He was probably more than simply a wood-worker. The stories about him were written down by people who spoke in Greek, and the word they use to describe his job could just as easily suggest that he was a builder and stone-mason as well.

A slightly different picture emerges when we look further on in the New Testament stories of Jesus' life. We discover, for example, that he was a man who disliked violence of all kinds, and even told his followers: 'Do not take revenge on someone who wrongs you. If anyone slaps you on the right cheek, let him slap your left cheek too.' Yet he was also a man of great courage, and he suffered unflinchingly one of the most horrible forms of torture and execution that has ever been invented by the human mind.

Matthew 5:39

The fact is that if we are thinking of Jesus' physical appearance, we know nothing at all about what he looked like. If we are thinking of his personal qualities, then it very much depends on what parts of his life we are talking about as to what kind of person we think he was. But there is one thing we can be sure of. His background and way of life cannot have been very different from those of anyone else living at that time in what we now call the Middle East. So before we go any further, we need to ask a few questions about the kind of world he lived in. Since some of the countries in the Middle East had different names in Jesus' day from the ones we now use, we should first look at a map and compare it with a modern map.

The names have changed, but most of us would feel quite at home in the world of Jesus' day. Violence. Oppression. Racial discrimination. Totalitarianism. Exploitation. Dictatorship. Social injustice. All these problems were as familiar to the people of the Roman Empire 2,000 years ago as they are to us today, except that for most of us these things are just ideas and concepts that we talk about but do not experience ourselves. In the Palestine of Jesus' day they were the harsh realities of everyday life.

Herod the Great

Matthew 2:16

The Herodium is a fortress 7 m/12 km south of Jerusalem. Built by Herod the Great between 24 and 15 BC, it stands on the spot where he achieved one of his most important victories over the Hasmoneans in 40 BC.

When Jesus was born, Herod the Great was the ruler of Palestine, a small though strategically important state on the eastern boundary of the Roman Empire. He had been appointed king of Judea by the Romans in 37 BC. The story of his rise to power, and indeed of the rest of his reign, is a classic tale of intrigue and ruthlessness. As a king he combined a strange mixture of diplomatic brilliance with almost unbelievable stupidity. The story of how he murdered the children of Bethlehem after Jesus was born (although we have no record of it in any other documents) fits in perfectly well with all that we know of his character and behaviour. Anyone who opposed his policies could expect a violent death. Like many other tyrants, he never thought twice about killing even his own family. One of his wives, Mariamne, was executed on his orders; and he was involved in the murder of two of his own sons, Alexander and Aristobulus. Only five days before he died in 4 BC, he ordered the execution of yet another of his sons, Antipater, who was expected to succeed him.

The land of Jesus and the Gospels

Many of the places associated with Jesus were not very large or important, and some names have changed since the first century. No indication is given here of the relative sizes of towns and villages. Sites not definitely known are indicated with a question mark (?) and alternative names are in brackets. Some of the places here are not directly associated with Jesus but are known from other parts of the New Testament.

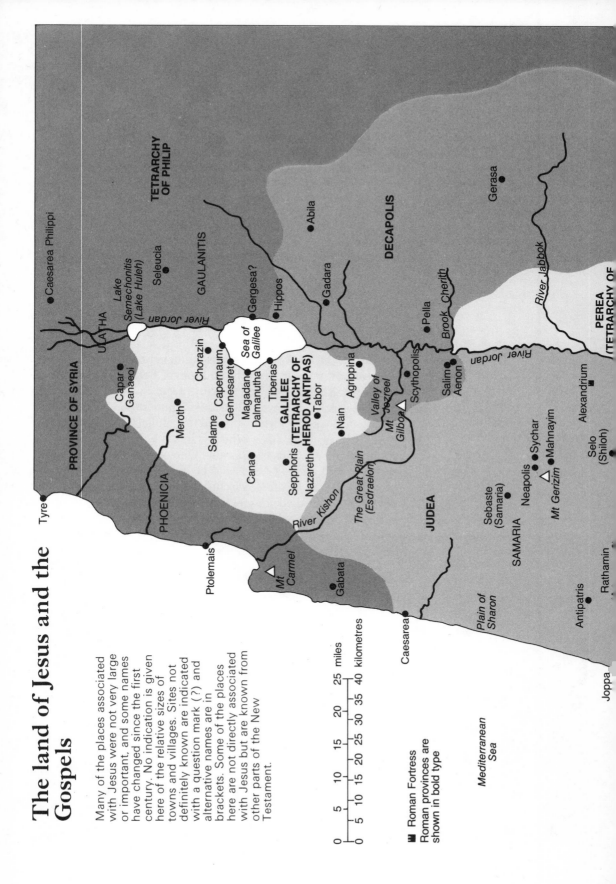

▥ Roman Fortress
Roman provinces are shown in bold type

Tyre

PROVINCE OF SYRIA

Caesarea Philippi

Lake Semechonitis (Lake Huleh)

Seleucia

River Jordan

ULATHA

TETRARCHY OF PHILIP

GAULANITIS

Abila

Gadara

Gergesa?

Hippos

DECAPOLIS

Gerasa

River Jabbok

Capar Ganaeoi

Chorazin

Capernaum

Gennesaret

Magadan
Dalmanutha

Sea of Galilee

Meroth

Selame

Tiberias

GALILEE
(TETRARCHY OF
HEROD ANTIPAS)

Agrippina

Tabor

Nain

Valley of
Jezreel

Pella

Brook Cherith

Scythopolis

Salim
Aenon

River Jordan

PEREA
(TETRARCHY OF

PHOENICIA

Cana

Sepphoris
Nazareth

Mt
Gilboa

Alexandrium

Kishon

River Kishon

The Great Plain
(Esdraelon)

Sychar

Mahnayim

Ptolemais

Mt
Carmel

Gabata

Neapolis

Mt Gerizim

Selo
(Shiloh)

Sebaste
(Samaria)

SAMARIA

JUDEA

Plain of
Sharon

Antipatris

Rathamin

Caesarea

Mediterranean
Sea

Joppa

0   5   10   15   20   25 miles

0   5   10   15   20   25   30   35   40 kilometres

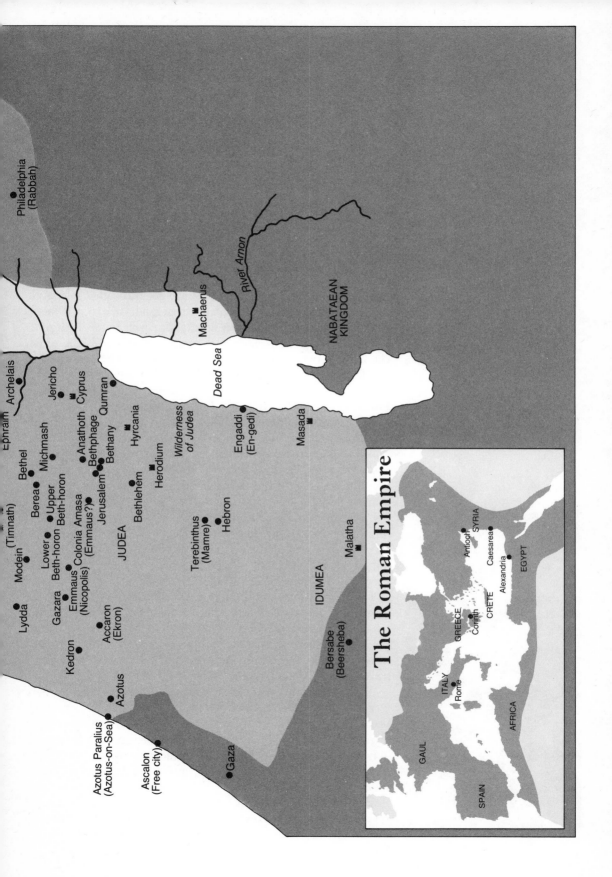

Philadelphia
(Rabbah)

River Arnon

Machaerus

Dead Sea

NABATAEAN
KINGDOM

Ephraim
Archelais
Jericho
Michmash
Bethel
Cyprus
Anathoth
Qumran
Berea
Bethphage
Bethany
Hyrcania
Upper
Beth-horon
Jerusalem
Herodium
Wilderness
of Judea
Engaddi
(En-gedi)
Lower
Beth-horon
Colonia Amasa
(Emmaus?)
Bethlehem
Masada
Modein
(Timnath)
JUDEA
Gazara
Emmaus
(Nicopolis)
Terebinthus
(Mamre)
Hebron
Lydda
Accaron
(Ekron)
Malatha
Kedron
IDUMEA
Azotus
Azotus Paralius
(Azotus-on-Sea)
Bersabe
(Beersheba)
Ascalon
(Free city)
Gaza

The Roman Empire

GAUL

SPAIN

ITALY
Rome

AFRICA

GREECE
Corinth
CRETE

Antioch
SYRIA
Caesarea
Alexandria
EGYPT

Yet Herod the Great was not called 'Great' for nothing. In contrast to previous rulers Herod maintained peace and order throughout his territory. He was also responsible for a massive building programme. It was Herod the Great who began building the temple at Jerusalem, which was still not finished during the lifetime of Jesus. He also built many other magnificent buildings in Jerusalem and Caesarea, and even in other Roman cities outside his own territory.

The three Herods

When Herod the Great died in 4 BC the Romans divided his kingdom among his three remaining sons. With one possible exception, none of them was any better than his father.

● Judea, the part of Palestine that included Jerusalem, was given to his son Archelaus. He was not allowed to call himself 'king' of Judea, as his father had been, but was called 'ethnarch' instead. He lasted for only ten years, and then the Romans removed him from office. In AD 6 Judea became a third-grade province of the Roman Empire, under an officer of the upper class equestrian rank, who was himself under the command of the Roman governor of Syria. These Roman rulers of Judea were later called 'procurators'. The one best-known to us is Pontius Pilate, who governed Judea from AD 26 to 36.

● The northern part of Palestine was given to Antipas, another son of Herod. He was known as the 'tetrarch' of Galilee and Perea. His territory included the village of Nazareth where Jesus grew up. Antipas was very much like his father. He was a crafty man who liked living in luxury. To make a name for himself he took great pride in erecting public buildings. One of his projects was the rebuilding of Sepphoris, a town only four miles from Nazareth. He also built the new town of Tiberias by Lake Galilee, and named it in honour of the Roman Emperor Tiberius. It was Herod Antipas who had John the Baptist executed and who was involved in the trials of Jesus.

● A third brother, Philip, was given some territory to the north-east of Palestine when his father died. He founded the town of Caesarea Philippi at the foot of Mt Hermon. Of all the sons of Herod the Great, Philip was the only one who proved to be a balanced and humane ruler. He survived as 'tetrarch of Iturea and Trachonitis' until the year AD 34.

After Archelaus was replaced by a Roman governor, there were many revolts against the Romans in Judea. The Jews became more and more frustrated at not having control of their own affairs. The Romans for their part became less interested in trying to understand the special problems of the Jewish people. As a result the oppression and corruption of many of the Roman rulers, encouraged by a rising tide of Jewish nationalism, continued to increase until eventually in the year AD 66 a general revolt broke out. This revolt was finally crushed when Jerusalem was largely destroyed by the Roman general Titus in AD 70.

The ruins of Masada, the last Jewish stronghold to resist the Romans in AD 70. It is near the southern end of the Dead Sea.

Mark 6:17–29
Luke 23:6–12

Jews and Romans

It was natural enough for the Jews of Palestine to resent being dominated by Rome. Anyone who has ever known freedom finds it hard to accept a totalitarian dictatorship. But with the Jewish people there was much more to it than that. The whole outlook of the Jewish people was based on their religion, and their religion was rather special. Unlike many other religions, the Jewish religion (Judaism) was not just concerned with the individual worshipper and his or her relationship to God. Judaism was the religion of a nation. To be a Jew had political as well as religious importance.

As the Jews read their sacred writings (what Christians call the Old Testament) they believed that they had been specially chosen by God. Some day they would rule the world, led by God's promised deliverer, whom they called the 'Messiah'. At one time it had been possible for them to expect that this would happen in the normal course of history. In the days of King David and King Solomon, almost a thousand years before the birth of Jesus, they had been one of the great world powers. And even more recently than that they had at times been a force to be reckoned with. But it was obvious to most Jews living in Palestine in Jesus' day that something of almost supernatural proportions would have to take place if they were ever to be released from the iron grip of Rome.

At the same time, not all Jews wanted to be freed from Roman rule. There were some sections of society in Palestine who found it was comfortable to be friendly with the Romans; and even among those who saw freedom as a desirable thing there were not many who were dedicated enough to do anything about it.

It is also important to remember that not all the Jews lived in Palestine itself. In fact there were far more Jews living in all the major cities of the Roman Empire than there were in the homeland. Not more than one fifth of all Jews in the Empire lived in Palestine; and even Jerusalem itself probably had fewer Jews than the city of Alexandria, in Egypt.

Most of the Jewish people must have been well accustomed to all aspects of Roman life and society. Certainly most of them living outside Palestine, the Dispersion (*Diaspora*), adapted their own style of life to suit their environment. To be sure, they were always conscious of being Jews, and they tried to preserve those parts of their own native culture that would distinguish them most clearly from their non-Jewish neighbours. Circumcision, the keeping of the sabbath day and the food laws of the Old Testament – these, and many other things, told the Roman world that the Jews were different. But for all their distinctiveness, not many of them really wanted to exchange the comfortable life of a respected class in a Roman city for the less prosperous, if more exciting, life of Palestine itself.

So when we talk about the Jews of Palestine we are in fact talking about a relatively small proportion of the Jewish people as a whole. Yet even among this small proportion there were

The Romans ruled Israel in the first century, and stationed armies there to keep control.

many different attitudes on matters affecting their religion and their relationship to the Romans who occupied their lands.

Palestine and its people

The Jewish historian Josephus, who lived towards the end of the first century AD, and who was a friend of the Romans, tells us that three main opinions were common among the Jews in Palestine: 'Jewish philosophy takes three forms. The followers of the first school are called Pharisees, of the second Sadducees, and the third sect, which has a reputation for being more *Jewish Wars* 2.8.2 disciplined, is the Essenes.' He also mentions a fourth group, called Zealots. But since he does not always include these among the philosophical sects, they must have formed a much looser *Jewish Wars* 4.3.9 kind of association. Obviously not all the Jewish people were members of one group or another, just as not everyone in our own society is a member of a political party. Each of the four groups probably had quite a small membership, though the ordinary person in the street would look to one of them for leadership. We meet three of these groups in the stories of Jesus' life: the Sadducees, the Pharisees and the Zealots.

● **The Sadducees** are often mentioned in the New Testament along with the Pharisees, but in fact the two groups were quite separate and held opposite opinions on almost everything. The Sadducees were only a small group, but they were very influential. They consisted mainly of the more important priests in the temple at Jerusalem, and included only the most well-to-do classes of Jewish society. They were extreme conservatives in everything and disliked changes of any kind, especially changes which could affect their own dominant position in society. Even if they believed theoretically in the coming of a Messiah, they generally had nothing to do with political protests. That would only cause trouble with the Romans.

The name 'Sadducee' probably means 'son of Zadok', although the Sadducees were certainly not direct descendants of the Zadok *2 Samuel* 15:24–29 mentioned in the Old Testament. Other meanings for the name have also been suggested: either from a Hebrew word that means 'moral integrity' or 'righteousness' (*sadiq*); or from the Greek word *syndicoi*, which could mean 'members of the council' – and it is certainly true that the Jewish council of seventy (the Sanhedrin) had many Sadducees among its members.

If the Sadducees are to be regarded as political conservatives, their understanding of the Jewish religion can only be called reactionary. They held that the only religious teaching with any authority was the Law given by Moses in the first five books of the Old Testament (the Pentateuch or *Torah*). They had no time either for the rest of the Old Testament, or for anyone who tried to reinterpret it or to apply it in a more direct way to their own situation. This meant that they did not share with other Jews some of the beliefs of Judaism that were not very explicit in the *Torah*. Sadducees did not believe that God had a purpose behind the events of history, and matters such as belief in a future life, resurrection, or a final judgement were to them simply irrelevant.

● **The Pharisees** were a much larger group; there may have been as many as 6,000 of them at the time of Jesus. Many of them were professional students of the Old Testament, but others had ordinary jobs. They were a national organization, with a large number of local groups. Each group had its own officials and rules, and groups were to be found in most towns and villages throughout Palestine. Religiously, they were probably the most important people in Judaism during Jesus' lifetime. The Sadducees disliked them because they believed and did things that a literal understanding of the Law of Moses could not really allow. But most ordinary people had a great respect for them.

The Sadducees' chief complaint against the Pharisees was that they had amassed a whole lot of rules and regulations to explain the Law of the Old Testament. Though the Pharisees regarded the Old Testament as their supreme rule of life and belief, they also realized that it had no direct application to the kind of society they lived in. To be relevant, it needed to be explained in new ways. For example, the Ten Commandments instructed people to keep the sabbath day holy. But what did that really mean in everyday terms? What should the pious Jew

Exodus 20:8

A street scene in present-day Bethlehem. While things have changed in the Middle East, as everywhere else, since Jesus' time, many customs and clothes remain very similar to those he would have known or worn.

Herod's Temple

Herod the Great began building the temple in Jerusalem in 19 BC. The main building was complete by AD 9 but work continued on it for many years. It was twice as high as Solomon's temple had been, and shone with gold decoration. This is an artist's impression of what it looked like.

The Holy of Holies, divided from the Holy Place by a curtain which Matthew's Gospel says split from top to bottom when Jesus died. The ark of the covenant stood here in Solomon's day but no longer existed in Jesus' time

The Holy Place, where the priests regularly burnt incense

A bowl for ritual washings

The altar where animals were sacrificed. Jesus was described by John the Baptist as being 'the lamb of God that takes away the sin of the world'

The court of the Gentiles. This was the only part in which non-Jews were allowed. The traders and money-changers worked here, and were turned out by Jesus

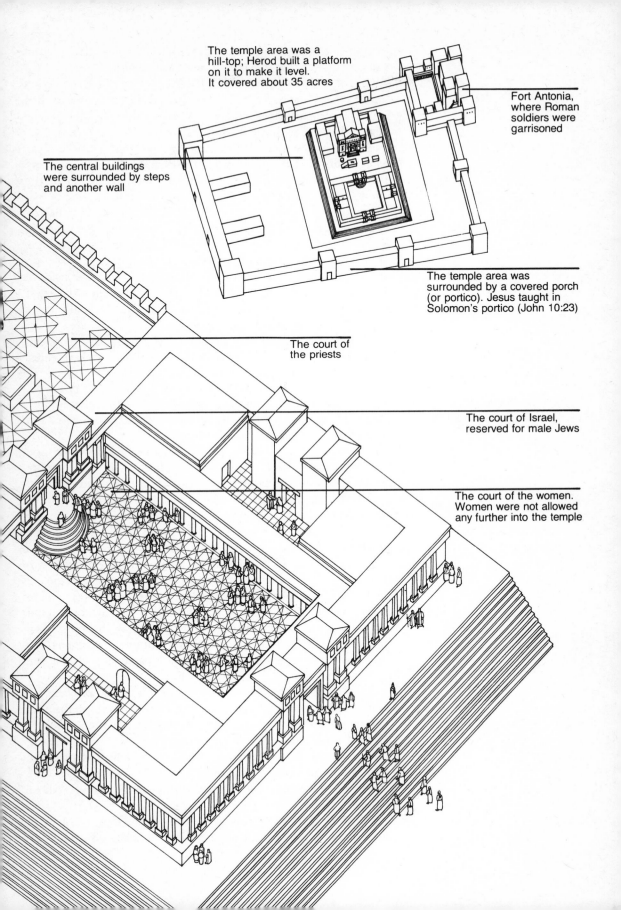

The temple area was a hill-top; Herod built a platform on it to make it level. It covered about 35 acres

Fort Antonia, where Roman soldiers were garrisoned

The central buildings were surrounded by steps and another wall

The temple area was surrounded by a covered porch (or portico). Jesus taught in Solomon's portico (John 10:23)

The court of the priests

The court of Israel, reserved for male Jews

The court of the women. Women were not allowed any further into the temple do and not do on the sabbath day? The Pharisees had a list of rules to answer that question in practical terms.

One of their writings, the *Pirke Aboth*, opens with the saying 'make a fence for the Law'. This meant 'protect it by surrounding it with cautionary rules to act as a warning notice to stop people before they get within breaking distance of the God-given Law itself'. This intention was praiseworthy enough. But there can be no doubt that eventually it led the Pharisees to make so many absurd rules that the Law became a moral millstone to the pious, rather than a gift from God. And to unbelievers much of it was simply nonsense. A tailor, for example, was not allowed to go out carrying his needle late in the day before the sabbath, in case it was still in his pocket when the sabbath began. But he, like everyone else, could go for a walk on the sabbath day – though not further than 2,000 cubits, two-thirds of a mile, the distance between the people of Israel and their holy ark when they first entered Canaan! This became known as the 'sabbath day's journey' and is mentioned in the Gospels.

Joshua 3:4

In spite of the absurdity of some of their standards, there can be no doubt that many Pharisees did actually keep these rules. Josephus says that 'the people of the cities hold them in the highest esteem, because they both preach and practice the very highest moral ideas'. But Jesus denounced them as hypocrites. He could see that the keeping of their own sectarian rules and regulations had become far too important.

Jewish Antiquities 18.1.3
Matthew 23:13, 15

Like many others since, they came to equate knowing God with being a member of their group – a Pharisee. To be a member of the sect was ultimately more important than knowing and understanding the will of God himself. Though they often claimed to be keeping God's Law, they were in fact only drawing attention to their own moral achievements. This is something to which all moralists are prone.

In Jesus' view what was really wrong with the Pharisees was that they believed God was only concerned with the demands of the Law. The theology of the Pharisees had no room for the kind of God whom Jesus knew as his Father – a God who was kind and loving, and more concerned for prostitutes and beggars in their need than for those who were conventionally religious. No Pharisee could ever say with Jesus: 'I came not to call the righteous but sinners.'

Mark 2:17

The Pharisees had distinctive views on other subjects, of course. They accepted the authority of the whole of the Old Testament, and not just the Law of Moses. Unlike the Sadducees they had no difficulty in believing that there was a life after death. They may well have expected a Messiah to come and right the wrongs of their people – and though they themselves never took part in a revolt against the Romans they probably admired those people who did.

● **The Zealots** were the people who became most involved in direct action against the Romans. They probably shared many of the religious beliefs of the Pharisees. But their overriding conviction was that they could have no master but God, and so the Romans must be driven out at all costs. According to the writer Josephus, their founder was a man called Judas, a Galilean who led a revolt in AD 6 at about the same time as Archelaus was removed from office by the Romans. He also tells us that 'these men agree in everything with the opinions of the Pharisees, but they have an insatiable passion for liberty; and they are convinced that God alone is to be their only master and Lord . . . no fear can compel them to give this title to anyone else . . .'

Jewish Wars 2.8.1

Jewish Antiquities 18.1.6

The Zealots continued as a guerilla movement until the siege of Jerusalem in AD 70, and perhaps even after that. At least one of Jesus' disciples, a man called Simon, was a Zealot, and it is often thought that Judas Iscariot was, too. But the more typical Zealots seem to have been men such as Barabbas, whom the crowd chose to liberate in preference to Jesus, and the trouble-maker with whom Paul was once confused.

Mark 3:18

Mark 15:6–15
Acts 21:37–39

●**The Essenes** are spoken of by several writers. Philo (a Jew from Alexandria in Egypt, who wrote in Greek), the Latin author Pliny, and Josephus all mention them. They are not explicitly mentioned by any of the people who wrote the New Testament.

Many people believe that one section of the Essenes wrote the documents known as the Dead Sea Scrolls. This group had their headquarters at Qumran near the north-west corner of the Dead Sea. The people of Qumran had withdrawn from normal life and lived in a commune in the desert, trying to preserve the traditions of religious and moral purity which they believed they could find in the Old Testament.

But not all the Essenes lived in this way, for Josephus says that the Essenes 'occupy no one city, but settle in large numbers in every town'. He also speaks of others who, unlike the monastic groups, were married – though he goes to some pains to make it clear that they looked on this only as a means of continuing the human race. We also have written evidence that another group lived in the desert near Damascus; their organization was slightly different from the group at Qumran.

Armed resistance to the Romans was the aim of the Zealots in the first century. Guerilla warfare is still a feature of the Middle East; here young Palestinian boys train with rifles.

Jewish Wars 2.8.2–13

No one really knows the relationship between these groups nor how they were related to the Essenes scattered throughout Palestine. We know most about the community at Qumran, because of the discovery of their writings, and at most points these documents support the account given by Josephus.

From the Dead Sea Scrolls we know that the people of this community regarded themselves as the minority in Israel who were faithful to God's covenant. They regarded the Jewish nation as a whole, and even the temple and the priests in Jerusalem, as unfaithful. Only their own leader, the 'Teacher of Righteousness', and his faithful followers could fathom the mysteries of the Old Testament.

Like some of the other sects, the Essenes looked forward to a day of crisis in history. At this time God would assert his sovereignty over the world by defeating the native-born heretics as well as foreign enemies such as the Romans. Then the members of the sect, and not the whole Jewish nation, would be recognized as God's chosen people. They would take over and put right the worship of God at the temple in Jerusalem. They expected three leaders to appear: the coming prophet who had been predicted by Moses; a royal Messiah who would be a descendant of King

Deuteronomy 18:18–19

A modern orthodox Jew praying on a roof-top. The phylactery on his forehead contains extracts from the Old Testament Law.

David; and a priest Messiah who would be the most important.

So that they might be in a constant state of readiness for these events, the Essenes of Qumran went through many ritual washings. Everything they did had some religious significance. Even their daily meals were an anticipation of the heavenly banquet which they believed would take place at the end of the age.

With the possible exception of the Sadducees, then, all the dominant religious groups in Palestine at the time of Jesus were hoping and praying that God would do something in the life of their people. They all had their own ideas about what he should do, and when and how he should do it. Some, for example the Zealots, were prepared to give God a helping hand when they thought it necessary. Others, such as the Pharisees and Essenes, believed that God had his predetermined plan which could be neither changed nor enforced by human intervention. But we can be sure that there were many ordinary people who were interested neither in political manoeuvering nor in theological disputes. They simply knew that they needed God to do something for them. Their only desire was to be in the right place and frame of mind when God's promised deliverer arrived.

The apocalyptists

The future expectations of the Jewish people found their fullest expression in the work of the 'apocalyptists' which literally means 'people who reveal secret things'. The books they wrote are 'revelations of secrets', 'apocalypses'. The exact significance of these people is uncertain, since we know of them only through their writings. It is not clear whether they formed any sort of sectarian group, or whether they were individuals belonging to any of the various religious sects. It is unlikely that any of the apocalyptists were Sadducees, since they claimed to receive new revelations from God (Sadducees could not accept that any revelation had been given since the time of Moses). In some ways their beliefs are similar to those of the Pharisees, for they placed great emphasis on God's predetermined plan for the history of the world.

Whatever the apocalyptists may have been, their writings have a number of unusual characteristics which make them readily recognizable.

● They have a strong emphasis on the life of heaven rather than the everyday world of human experience. Though events in this world are mentioned, they are important only in so far as they reveal something about events taking place in the spiritual world. One apocalyptic writer states that 'the Most High has made not one world but two' (2 Esdras 7:50), and this viewpoint would be shared by many apocalyptists. It was their job to reveal what was happening in God's world, and to assure their readers that they had a central position in God's activities.

● This means that the apocalyptic writings also emphasize dreams, visions and communications through angels. Since God is remote in his own world ('heaven'), he needs to use go-betweens in dealing with men and women. A typical apocalypse is an extended report of how its writer has received speculative visions and messages revealing what is happening in heaven.

● Corresponding with this is an unusual literary form. For the visions are not described in straightforward terms, but use a kind of special coded language. There are often many references to the books of the prophets in the Old Testament, and mythological beasts and symbolic numbers are used to stand for nations or individuals.

● Apocalypses were normally written under the name of a great figure of the past. Enoch, Noah, Adam, Moses, Ezra and a number of other outstanding Old Testament characters all had apocalyptic works attributed to them. This may have been necessary because it was widely thought by the Jews that the time of genuine prophecy had passed. Any contemporary seer who wanted to get a hearing for his message therefore had to attribute his work to somebody who had actually lived in the age of the Old Testament. Revelation, the only New Testament book to use extensive apocalyptic imagery, is quite different in this respect. The book of Revelation is not ascribed to some ancient figure; its author is identified as John, a contemporary and friend of his readers (Revelation 1:1-9).

Why did this kind of writing become so popular in the centuries immediately before the birth of Jesus? An attractive answer is that apocalyptic writing was a response to the difficult realities of life in Palestine at the time. The Old Testament prophets had often suggested that the course of Israel's history somehow depended on their attitude to God. If they were obedient they prospered; if not, they could expect hard times.

These hard times had culminated in the capture of Jerusalem by

Nebuchadnezzar in 586 BC, and the exile of its population to Babylon. After only a short time in exile, the Jews had been allowed to return to their homeland, and those who returned were determined that they would not make the same mistakes as their ancestors. So they went out of their way to try to keep every detail of the Old Testament laws.

Yet, as things turned out, they did not prosper either. As time went on the way to prosperity seemed to lie more in collaboration with outsiders such as the Romans than in remaining faithful to their own religion. Those who tried to keep the Old Testament faith alive found themselves more and more in a minority, and those who prospered often did so by sitting loosely to their fathers' faith, or even abandoning it altogether.

Apocalyptic writing may well have begun as an answer to this problem. Why did faithfulness not lead to prosperity? Why were the righteous suffering? Why did God not put an end to the power of evil forces? To these questions the apocalyptists answered that the present difficulties were only relative. Seen in the light of God's working throughout history, the righteous would eventually triumph and the oppressive domination of evil would soon be relaxed.

It is often asked whether Jesus had any connection with these apocalyptists and their visions of the heavenly world. Albert Schweitzer certainly thought so, as we shall see in the next section of this book. There is also a good deal of evidence to show that Jesus was familiar with the ideas that the apocalyptists put forward. A good deal of the imagery and language Jesus used in his own teaching on the future is similar to that of the apocalypses (Mark 13, Matthew 24–25, Luke 21). But there are some important differences.

● Apocalyptic literature is always the report of visions and other insights into the heavenly world given to men through some special means. But Jesus did not base his teaching on visions and revelations of this kind. He spoke on his own authority, and his main concern was not with the affairs of some other, heavenly, world, but with life in this world. He did not reveal secrets; he made disciples and reminded them of their responsibilities to God.

● The apocalyptists were always concerned to encourage and comfort their readers by demonstrating that they were in the right, and their enemies would soon be overcome. But Jesus' teaching, even in what are called the 'apocalyptic discourses', was never designed to comfort his disciples. Nor does he suggest that they will automatically triumph over their enemies. Quite the opposite is the case, for Jesus makes his teaching on the future an occasion to challenge his disciples' attitude to life; and he makes it clear that when God intervenes in human affairs it is a time of judgement for those who are his disciples as much as for everyone else.

● There is no systematic view of the future in Jesus' teaching. This is quite different from the apocalyptic outlook, in which every detail of the future has already been mapped out in advance. It is all in God's predetermined plan, and those who hold the key to the coded language can know precisely what the future holds. Some New Testament interpreters have, of course, tried to find such a system in Jesus' teaching. But the great variety of systems they have produced shows their lack of success. Nor can we expect them to be successful, for Jesus himself stated that 'No one knows . . . when that day and hour will come – neither the angels in heaven, nor the Son; the Father alone knows' (Matthew 24:36, Mark 13:32). No apocalyptist could ever have said that.

In view of the fundamental differences between Jesus and the apocalyptists, it is clear that he cannot simply be classed with them. He did not have an apocalyptic outlook on life. To be sure, he did occasionally give his teaching in the language and imagery of the Jewish apocalyptists – just as he referred to the 'Golden Rule' of the rabbis (Matthew 7:12). As a good teacher he realized that he needed to speak the language of his hearers, and it may well have been that many of the ordinary people of Palestine were most familiar with apocalyptic language. But, characteristically, Jesus took these familiar concepts and gave them a new meaning. On his lips they were not platitudes to compliment the pious, but a devastating challenge to commitment applied to disciples and sinners alike.

Chapter 2 Jesus' birth and early years

THE STORIES of how Jesus was born show that it was the ordinary people and not the religious experts who first recognized God's promised deliverer when he came. The first chapter of Luke's Gospel paints a vivid picture of the little-known priest Zechariah and his wife Elizabeth waiting for God to deliver their people, and being rewarded for their vigilance by the announcement of the birth of their own son, known as 'John the Baptist'. Mary, the mother of Jesus, belonged to the same family. From the stirring poetry of Mary's hymn of praise, the Magnificat, we can see just how eagerly these people were waiting for God to act in their lives. Mary and her friends were really excited that God was going to act in a new and fresh way.

Luke 1:5–28, 57–80

Luke 1:46–55

The same themes are emphasized throughout the familiar stories of that first Christmas. The first people to hear the good news that God's promises had been fulfilled with the birth of Jesus were some shepherds in the Judean hills, then Simeon and Anna in the temple. None of these people were of any significance to the world at large. The stories in the first chapters of Luke's Gospel emphasize that officialdom – whether political or religious – had no eyes with which to recognize Jesus. This lesson is repeated throughout the story of Jesus' life, as it becomes clear that to have a real understanding of God's actions in Christ even the most important people must become like little children.

Luke 2:8–20
Luke 2:25–38

Luke 18:17

Bethlehem, where Jesus was born, is a small town south-east of Jerusalem. Matthew's Gospel quotes the prophet Micah who emphasized the apparent unimportance of Bethlehem (Matthew 2:6).

When was Jesus born?

The Emperor Tiberius is portrayed in this statue at the Vatican museum.

Deciding exactly when the birth of Jesus took place is not as simple a matter as we might think. The obvious thing to suppose is that Jesus was born between 1 BC and AD 1. But this has been known to be untrue for a long time, because of mistakes made as long ago as the sixth century in calculating the extent of the Christian era. There are four pieces of evidence to be considered:

● According to Matthew, Jesus was born 'in Bethlehem of Judea in the reign of Herod the king' (2:1) – that is, before the death of Herod the Great in 4 BC.

● Luke was much more interested in placing his story in the wider context of affairs in the Roman Empire, and he says that Jesus was born during 'the first enrolment, when Quirinius was governor of Syria' (2:2). Josephus tells us that a man called Quirinius was indeed sent to Syria and Judea to take a census just after the beginning of the Christian era (*Jewish Antiquities* 18.1). But this census was part of the clearing-up operation after Herod the Great's son Archelaus had been deposed. It must have been in the year AD 6 or 7, and could not have been before the death of Herod the Great in 4 BC.

Because of this, some people have suggested that the man Luke calls 'Quirinius' was in fact Saturninus, the imperial legate in Syria, who took a census in 6 BC. However, we have no evidence at all to show how Luke could have confused the two men. In the rest of his Gospel, and also in his second volume, the book of Acts, he is extremely careful, and also very accurate, in his use of the names and titles of Roman officials. In any case, we have no absolutely conclusive evidence that this man Saturninus did actually take a census.

● At the same time, Luke makes other statements about the date of important events in the life of Jesus. He tells us, for example, that Jesus was about thirty years old when he was baptized, and that this was 'in the fifteenth year of the reign of Tiberius Caesar' (3:1). Tiberius became ruler of the Roman Empire in AD 14, and so the fifteenth year of his reign would be AD 28. But in fact, Tiberius had shared power with his predecessor Augustus from about AD 11, so although he only became emperor

after Augustus died in AD 14 he had been in power for the previous three years. It is likely that Luke was reckoning the fifteenth year of Tiberius from AD 11, and this means Jesus would be thirty years old in AD 25–26. This means, in turn, that he must have been born in 5 or 4 BC, and so before the death of Herod the Great.

● Some people have tried to be more specific by calculating that there was a conjunction of certain planets about 6 BC, and that this astronomical event could explain the bright star mentioned in Matthew's Gospel. But this kind of argument requires a lot of imagination to be convincing.

We can see from this that there are two pieces of evidence pointing to a date for Jesus' birth round about 4 BC, and another piece of information given by Luke about the census under Quirinius which does not seem to agree with this dating. There are three possible explanations of this problem.

● Luke has been misunderstood. A number of scholars have argued that the problem as we have presented it simply does not exist. They point out that it is possible from a grammatical point of view to translate Luke 2:2, 'This enrolment was before that made when Quirinius was governor of Syria', instead of the usual translation, 'This was the first enrolment, when Quirinius was governor of Syria'. This understanding is certainly possible, though it is by no means the most obvious meaning of the statement, and it does involve an implicit emendation of the text. Some notable New Testament scholars have supported it, and continue to do so, but this explanation of the matter is by no means universally held.

● Luke made a mistake. Most scholars are in fact inclined to dismiss the information given in Luke 2:2 as erroneous. This is an easy way out of the problem. But it also leaves some difficulties. We have already remarked that in other places in his Gospel and the book of Acts where Luke is concerned with people and events in the Roman Empire, he shows himself to be a very trustworthy historian. It is therefore rather unlikely that he would have made such a specific reference here unless he had good reasons for doing so. We have also seen that his statement about the date when Jesus was baptized by John fits in with the assumption that Jesus was born in the reign of Herod the Great, something like ten years before the rule of the Quirinius whom Josephus mentions. It is certainly unlikely that any intelligent historian would have made two contradictory statements in such a short space within his narrative. If we assume that Luke used his sources carefully and wrote with discrimination and insight there are a number of important difficulties involved in simply saying that he was wrong about the census under Quirinius.

● Luke does not tell the whole story. A rather better explanation can be found if we consider the practical realities of life in the Roman Empire. Ruling Judea from Rome in AD 7 was not the same thing as it would be today. Nowadays we have instant communications between different parts of the world. The United Nations in New York can take a decision affecting a country on the other side of the world, and its decision can be delivered there within a matter of minutes. But in ancient Rome things were different. Even in ideal conditions, it could take months for a decree signed by the emperor in Rome to be delivered to a distant province like Judea – and there was always the possibility that the messenger could be shipwrecked, and the emperor's orders delayed even further or lost altogether. At a later period, for example, the Emperor Caligula sent orders that his own statue should be erected in the temple at Jerusalem. The local governor was wiser than the emperor, and realized that this would create great resistance from the Jews. So he wrote and asked the emperor to think again. But Caligula insisted on his plan going

ahead, and wrote to the governor to tell him so. The ship carrying his message took three months to make the voyage from Rome to Judea. But in the meantime Caligula was assassinated, and another ship that left Rome much later bringing the news of his death and the end of his policies, arrived twenty-seven days earlier than the first one!

When we think of the practical details involved in taking a census in an empire with such problems of communication and government, we can see that the difficulty over the exact date of Quirinius's census is nothing like as great as we would think if we looked at it only in a modern context. It is a well-known fact that the Roman enrolments (carried out for tax purposes) were often resisted in many parts of the Empire. One such census in Gaul, for example, was so resisted by the people that it took forty years to complete! Add to that the communication problems, and it is clear that a census completed by Quirinius in AD 6 or 7 must have been based on information collected much earlier.

The Emperor Augustus was very keen on gathering statistics, and he may well have persuaded Herod the Great to carry out a census. Quirinius was sent in AD 6 to clear up the mess left by Archelaus, and it is quite possible that he would use information gathered earlier rather than beginning the tedious process all over again. If this is the case, then there is no real reason to suppose that Luke's information about the census is necessarily contradictory to the rest of the evidence suggesting that Jesus was born about 5 BC. In any case he was far more interested in telling of the birth of Jesus than explaining the complexities of Judean politics which surrounded it.

A bronze head of the Emperor Augustus, who shared power with Tiberius from AD 11 until his death in AD 14.

Jesus grows up

We know very little about Jesus' life as a child. His home was presumably the typical flat-roofed, one-roomed house of the time, built of clay. Joseph probably carried on his business, assisted by Jesus, from his house. They would make agricultural tools, furniture, and perhaps also worked on building projects. Every small village the size of Nazareth would have its joiner, who was probably a kind of odd job man as well as being a skilled craftsman in wood. The pictures we sometimes see of Jesus as a boy making smooth yokes for the backs of oxen certainly do not represent all that he would do, and we can be sure that he must have been as adept at plastering walls as he would have been at planing wood.

Yet in spite of the relative simplicity of his home life, Jesus must have had a good education. He was considered a suitable person to read the Old Testament in Hebrew in the synagogue at Nazareth, and by no means every person of his age could read Hebrew, even though they may have been able to speak in that language. Jewish boys were usually educated in the local synagogue, and Jesus must have been one of the brighter ones in his class.

Luke 4:16–20

Nazareth itself would be an especially stimulating place for a bright boy to grow up in. It is true that it was not a very important place. It is never mentioned in the rest of the Bible, or in any other contemporary literature. But that is probably because the very strictest Jews felt that the people of Galilee, of which Nazareth was a part, had too much contact with non-Jewish people. Galilee itself was often called 'Galilee of the Gentiles', because there were more non-Jews than Jewish people living there. The people in the southern province of Judea, on the other hand, were isolated from all but their own society, and so they became introverted and self-centred, as well as being self-righteous and hypocritical. But Galilee was quite different. The great roads that brought oriental traders from the East and Roman soldiers from the West passed through Galilee. In Nazareth Jesus would meet and mix with many people who were not Jewish, and he no doubt spent much of his time thinking and talking about the ideas of the Greeks and Romans as well as the religious heritage of his own people.

One of the special advantages of growing up in Galilee was that Jesus would be able to speak three languages. We have noticed already that he could speak and read Hebrew. But that was no longer the normal language of the Jewish people. For several centuries before his time the Jews had used another language similar to Hebrew, called Aramaic. This is the language Jesus would speak in his home and among his friends. Since there were so many non-Jewish people in Galilee, he probably spoke Greek as well, for this was the international language used everywhere throughout the whole of the Roman Empire.

Apart from what we can infer from our knowledge of the kind of society in which Jesus was brought up, the New Testament tells us virtually nothing about his life before he was thirty years old. Christian writers in the second century thought there was something wrong and unnatural about this, and they lost no time in compensating for what they saw as a deficiency in the New Testament. We have a number of accounts of the childhood of Jesus, stories with titles such as *The Gospel of the Nativity of Mary*, *The History of Joseph the Carpenter*, or *The Childhood Gospel of Thomas*. There is no need to take seriously any of the stories about Jesus' childhood that we find in these so-called 'gospels'. They are all just the kind of legends that often grow

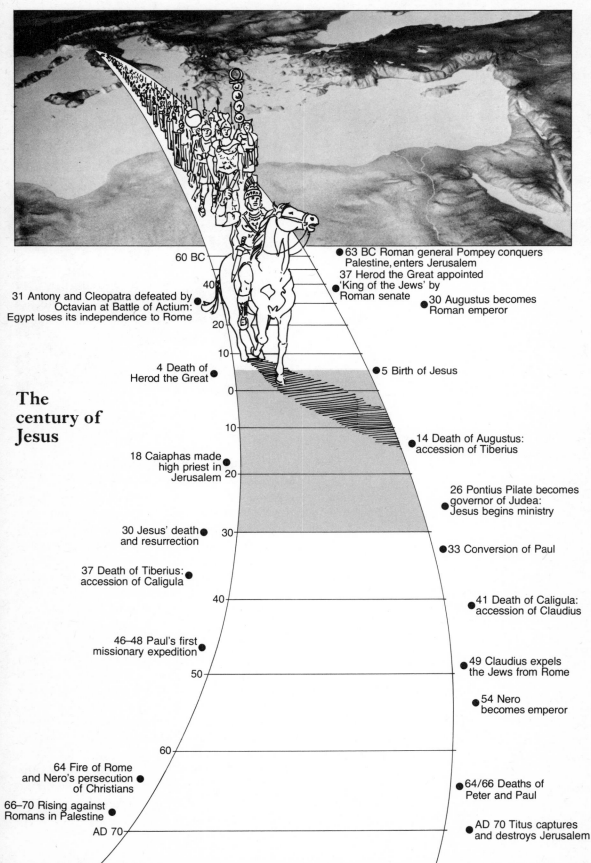

The century of Jesus

60 BC

40

● 63 BC Roman general Pompey conquers Palestine, enters Jerusalem

37 Herod the Great appointed 'King of the Jews' by Roman senate

31 Antony and Cleopatra defeated by Octavian at Battle of Actium: Egypt loses its independence to Rome ●

● 30 Augustus becomes Roman emperor

20

10

4 Death of Herod the Great ●

● 5 Birth of Jesus

0

10

● 14 Death of Augustus: accession of Tiberius

18 Caiaphas made high priest in Jerusalem ●

20

26 Pontius Pilate becomes governor of Judea: Jesus begins ministry ●

30 Jesus' death and resurrection ●

30

● 33 Conversion of Paul

37 Death of Tiberius: accession of Caligula ●

40

● 41 Death of Caligula: accession of Claudius

46–48 Paul's first missionary expedition ●

● 49 Claudius expels the Jews from Rome

50

● 54 Nero becomes emperor

60

64 Fire of Rome and Nero's persecution of Christians ●

● 64/66 Deaths of Peter and Paul

66–70 Rising against Romans in Palestine ●

AD 70

● AD 70 Titus captures and destroys Jerusalem

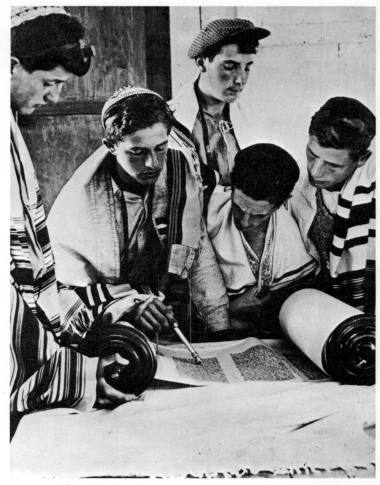

Little is known about Jesus' boyhood except that he was brought up in an orthodox Jewish home and was well educated.

up around an important person when those who actually knew him have died. But there are some second-century writings often called 'apocryphal gospels' that may contain authentic sayings of Jesus, writings such as the *Gospel of Thomas* and the *Gospel of Philip*. These are considered in more detail in section three.

Luke describes Jesus' childhood very simply by saying that he *Luke 2:40* 'grew and became strong' like any other boy. But he goes on to add that Jesus was also 'filled with wisdom; and the favour of God was upon him'. And he then tells just one story as an *Luke 2:41–52* illustration of what he meant.

The story tells how Jesus was lost in Jerusalem when he was twelve years old. He had gone there on a religious pilgrimage with Mary and Joseph to take part in one of the great Jewish festivals. When his parents eventually found him in the temple, he asked them: 'Did you not know that I must be in my Father's house?' Even at this age, Jesus was growing not just physically and mentally, but also in a spiritual dimension. He had an unusual sense of the presence of God in his life. God was his Father, and this relationship was more important to him than anything else.

The next we hear of Jesus is when he was about thirty years old. His cousin, John the Baptist, had started a religious movement and had attracted quite a following. John lived a simple kind of life in the Judean desert. His clothes were made of camel's hair, and he ate only the food of the desert, 'locusts and wild honey'.

Mark 1:6

John was by no means the only wandering prophet at that time. Many people were talking about the coming of God's promised deliverer to inaugurate some kind of new society. Further south in the same desert the people of Qumran were talking about similar things. And, even later, many rabble-rousers and prophets made a name for themselves in the same place.

But the difference about John was that he did not want to make a name for himself. Palestine had more than its share of crackpots, each claiming to be God's promised deliverer appointed to get rid of the political and social injustices of the time and with the authority to set up a new society. But John made no such claims. He claimed only to be 'a messenger', 'a voice' sent to bring the good news that the new society was about to begin.

Mark 1:2–3

Those Jews who were looking for God's new society had learned from the Old Testament to expect such a messenger, who would be like the Old Testament prophet Elijah. The Gospel writers leave us in no doubt that they saw John the Baptist as this very person. Their description of his way of life and of his message is closely modelled on the stories of Elijah in the Old Testament book of Kings.

Malachi 4:5

The New Testament and the Jewish writer Josephus both describe John's work as a call to the Jews to put their lives in order so that they would be morally fit to meet the person who was to establish the new society. The prophets whose sayings are preserved in the Old Testament had often seen that though the Jews were God's people they were in no fit state to meet their God. If God was ever to work in their lives, his coming would have to begin with judgement – and the judgement would be most severe for those who had had the greatest privilege.

John's message was exactly the same. He called on the Jewish people to be prepared to change their way of life, so that they would be fit to meet their God. Those who were ready to face up to the challenge showed their willingness to change by being 'baptized'. The Greek word from which we get the word 'baptize' simply means 'to dip'. It was often used, for example, of the dyeing of clothes as they were immersed in a bath or tub. 'Baptism' in the religious sense was just the same, except that it was people who were immersed, and they were dipped not in dye but in clean water. John presumably used the River Jordan as a handy source of water.

Most Jews would know what baptism was. It may have been used as a means of admitting non-Jews into the Jewish religion. It was certainly used in this way later. There is also ample evidence from the Dead Sea Scrolls that the Essenes used baptism regularly as a way of preserving their moral and religious purity.

Jesus came to be baptized by John the Baptist in the Jordan Valley.

A Bedouin tent in the Judean desert, the area in which John the Baptist lived.

One of the most conspicuous features of the ruins of the monastery at Qumran is the incredibly complicated system of aqueducts and water tanks that provided enough water in the desert for people of the community to undergo their baptismal rites. Of course, the rituals of people like the Essenes were not quite the same as the baptism of non-Jews into the Jewish religion. Ceremonial baptisms and washings were repeated over and over again at Qumran. But baptism of converts into Judaism was a once-for-all event.

It is difficult to decide whether the background of John's ritual is to be found in repeated washings, like those of the Essenes, or in the once-only baptism of Gentile converts. The radical nature of John's message and the opposition he provoked would certainly be easier to understand if he was calling Jews to take part in something that had been designed not for God's chosen people but for pagans. John saw that if the Jews were to have any part in the new society that was about to come they too would need to begin all over again, just as if they were Gentile pagans getting to know God for the first time.

Luke 3:7–17

Yet John did not see the full implications of that new society. He was standing in a kind of no-man's land between the promises of God in the Old Testament and the fulfilment of those promises that was about to take place. He saw the coming of the Messiah in the conventional terms of judgement and condemnation. He describes God's promised deliverer as a person who would chop down fruit trees that gave no fruit and burn the chaff away from the wheat. Admittedly, he saw much more clearly than the Pharisees or the Zealots. They thought that the objects of God's damnation would be the Romans, but John insisted instead that God would judge his own people – with the Pharisees first in line.

Mark 8:31–33

At the same time, he did not fully appreciate the true character of the society God was about to introduce. For God's new society would be based not on damnation and judgement but on love, forgiveness and a fatherly concern for all people. This was the one thing that the Jewish people found most difficult to understand. Even later, Jesus' disciples did not fully understand him when he spoke of the society coming through service and suffering. The precise nature of God's activities was not clear until after the death and resurrection of Jesus.

Jesus is baptized

Matthew 3:15

Jesus came to John and asked to be baptized. At first John did not want to allow Jesus to share in this symbol of repentance. After all, if Jesus really did have the special relationship with God which John believed he did, what could he possibly have to repent of? But Jesus assured John that he must take part in it. He told him: '. . . in this way we shall do all that God requires.'

What did Jesus mean by saying this? The simple explanation is that Jesus felt he must identify himself with those repenting sinners who would be his own first disciples. Far from separating him from other people, the special relationship he felt he had with God was a powerful reason for becoming completely involved in the lives of the most ordinary of folk. But some have suggested there is even more than that implied in these words. They suggest that Jesus regarded his baptism as the first step on the road to the cross, which he saw as the climax and goal of his whole life. It is certainly true that he later called his death a 'baptism', and that in it he really and truly fulfilled God's will.

Mark 10:38

It was probably in the experience of being baptized that Jesus first began to understand the precise nature of his special relationship with God. According to Mark, Jesus heard the words: 'You are my own dear Son. I am pleased with you.' This is a combination of statements found in two passages in the Old Testament. On the one hand there is an echo of Psalm 2:7, 'You are my son, today I have become your father.' In its original context, this statement referred to the kings of ancient Israel. But by the time of Jesus it was widely regarded as a prediction of the coming Messiah. On the other hand, there is also a clear allusion to the poem of the suffering servant in Isaiah, where the servant is described as 'the one I have chosen, with whom I am pleased'. This idea of the servant was never connected with the expectation of a Messiah before the time of Jesus.

Mark 1:11

Isaiah 42:1

It therefore seems likely that at his baptism Jesus learned two lessons: he was reassured of his own special relationship with God as the person who had been specially chosen to inaugurate God's new society; and he was also reminded that to be God's promised deliverer meant something very different from what most people expected. It meant the acceptance of suffering and service as an essential part of his life. This was very difficult, as Jesus was soon to discover. But he faced the problem with the power of God himself – something of which he was reminded when the Holy Spirit symbolically came to him in the form of a dove.

Jesus decides his priorities

The Gospels tell how, immediately after he was baptized, Jesus was challenged to get his priorities right as God's promised deliverer, the Messiah. Each of the temptations he faced was a temptation to be that deliverer in a way which would not involve the suffering and humble service that Jesus knew to be God's will.

Luke 4:1–4

● First of all came the temptation to bring in the new society by economic means, to make stones into bread. There were certainly plenty of hungry people in the world who would have welcomed bread from any source. Jesus himself was in the desert, and must have been hungry enough at the time. In addition, the Old Testament had often pictured the new society as a time of great material prosperity when the hungry would be fed and everyone's needs would be satisfied. So there were plenty of good reasons why Jesus should be concerned with such matters. But he knew that the fame and popularity of an economic miracle-worker was not the same as suffering and service.

A word of God to the people of Israel at a crucial moment in their past history helped him to overcome the temptation: 'Man shall not live by bread alone'. It was not that Jesus failed to recognize that people had economic needs. Rather, he recognized, on the one hand, that this was not their deepest need and, on the other, that this was not what God intended to be the main emphasis of his work. As a matter of fact, Jesus did later produce food for hungry people. But he knew this was not to be his main purpose in life.

● A second temptation was to throw himself down from the tower of the temple into the crowded courtyard below without injuring himself. It would have been an easy thing to show that he was the Messiah by working miracles, because the miraculous and unusual had a special kind of appeal to the people whom Jesus knew best. Paul, who knew Judaism better than most, said it was characteristic of the Jews to 'demand signs'. Even in our sophisticated scientific age, most of us are still drawn by the strange and spectacular, and anyone who claims to be able to perform wonders has no difficulty in attracting followers.

Here again, there was more to this temptation than just the logic of the situation. For there was actually a prophecy in the Old Testament about the Messiah suddenly appearing in a dramatic way in the temple. There was also a promise in Psalm 91 to the effect that God would protect those who put him to the test. Was this not the time to put God to the test? If Jesus was really God's Messiah, then surely he could expect God to honour his promises. A very attractive thought. But the answer to it came from the same crucial time in the experience of the people of Israel: 'You shall not put the Lord your God to the test.' The context of God's promise in Psalm 91 makes it clear that it was valid only to those who were living in obedient service to God's will. And for Jesus to do God's will meant service and suffering, and not the arbitrary use of God's promises for his own selfish ends.

So Jesus rejected the temptation to be known as God's promised deliverer by a display of miraculous power. He did, of course, perform miracles. But, as we shall see later, he also made it clear that the miracles were living signs of his message: they were not the message itself.

● The third temptation was to be a political Messiah. Luke places this one second, but Matthew puts it last. He probably does this to emphasize its importance. There is no doubt that this must have been the strongest of all temptations. After all, this was precisely what most Jews expected the Messiah to be. They also commonly believed that they would rule all the other nations in the new age that was coming – and Jesus was tempted to accept the authority of Satan in order to gain power over the world. The idea was made even more vivid by a vision of the splendour of the world's kingdoms. But Jesus realized again that

Deuteronomy 8:3

Mark 6:30–44

Luke 4:9–12

1 Corinthians 1:22

Malachi 3:1

Deuteronomy 6:16

Matthew 4:8–10

Jesus knew that his work would include hardship and suffering. Out in the Judean desert he faced three temptations which would avoid the suffering and make his claim to be God's special deliverer more spectacular.

Above: Jesus was tempted to use spectacular stunts to attract a large following.

Below far left: Jesus decided his priorities out in the Judean desert.

Below left: Many people were looking for someone who would use military power to deliver them from the Roman occupation.

Below: The Jews expected the Messiah to inaugurate an age of plenty when all the hungry would be fed.

this was far different from the kind of new society that he was to inaugurate. Not that Jesus was unsympathetic to the deeply felt desire of his people for freedom. After all, he had himself lived under the tyranny of Rome. He had worked with his own hands to produce enough to pay Roman taxes. He knew well enough the miserable condition of his countrymen.

But he rejected political messiahship for two reasons. First, he rejected the terms on which the devil offered it to him. According to the Gospel narratives the devil offered to share sovereignty with Jesus. If Jesus accepted that the devil had authority over the universe as a whole, then he would be given limited political authority in exchange. That was something Jesus could not accept. His own commitment, and the commitment that he later demanded of his followers, was exclusively to God as sovereign and Lord. To acknowledge the devil's power in any area of life would have been to deny God's ultimate authority.

But in addition, Jesus was offered the possibility of ruling by the 'authority' and 'glory' of an empire like that of the Romans. And he knew that this was not his job. He knew that God's rule in men's lives and in society could never be imposed from outside. If there was one lesson to be learned from the history of his people, this was it. They had all the rules, in the Old Testament, but time and again they had been quite incapable of putting them into operation. Jesus saw that what men needed was to give their will and free obedience to God, and so be given the moral freedom to create the kind of new society that God wanted them to have.

This third temptation, then, was certainly the strongest and the most pressing. And it was also rejected in the most decisive fashion: 'Begone Satan!' Jesus would not try to impose a new authoritarianism on the world to replace the old authoritarianism of Rome. His new society was not to be a rule of tyranny and cruelty such as many Jews envisaged, but something that would spring from the new, inner nature of those who were a part of it, as they served and worshipped God alone.

Matthew 4:10

The stories of Jesus' birth

The stories of how Jesus was born are certainly not the easiest parts of the Gospels to understand. We have already seen that even the date of Jesus' birth presents a number of problems. But that difficulty is overshadowed by much larger questions about the whole nature of the stories. We have assumed so far that the Gospel narratives provide sufficient reliable information for us to uncover at least the bare outline of events. But some scholars have tended to ignore altogether the stories told about Jesus' birth by Matthew and Luke.

They regard these stories as later narratives produced by the early church to portray Jesus as the kind of person they saw him to be after the events of the first Easter, rather than as the kind of person the 'historical Jesus' really was.

To the first Christians, Jesus was their risen Lord and the Son of God. He was not just the son of Mary and Joseph, a joiner from Nazareth. He was none other than God himself. The argument goes that because of their beliefs, the first Christians realized that such a person could not have had an

Jesus was born in the stables off a courtyard such as this ancient one behind an inn in Bethlehem.

ordinary birth – and so they produced the stories we now have in the Gospels. The problem about these stories centres on the statements by both Matthew and Luke that Mary and Joseph had never had a sexual relationship at the time when Jesus was conceived (Matthew 1:18; Luke 1:26–27). Since this is something we know from our own experience to be impossible, many people, both Christian and non-Christian, have denied that there is any historical truth in these stories. Instead they have often seen them as symbolic attempts to convey religious truths – a poetic, picturesque way to emphasize that Jesus had a special relationship with God right from the very beginning of his human existence, and even before that.

The answer to questions such as these will depend ultimately on our own basic attitudes and presuppositions in understanding the New Testament. Those who see these stories as religious rather than historical truth begin from the fact that we can never have children unless we have sexual intercourse with another person of the opposite sex. Therefore, they say, it can never have happened differently: things just don't work that way. If we start out from the basic position that anything contrary to our own experience of life cannot exist, then

of course we must conclude that the stories about Jesus' birth in the New Testament are legendary additions to the authentic stories of Jesus' life and teachings. It seems to me, however, that this is not the most useful way to approach the problem.

None of us finds it easy to believe in, still less to understand, miracles and the supernatural. But the sensible question to ask is surely not whether our own experience leads us to believe that miracles can happen, but whether the evidence we have leads to the conclusion that in a given case what we call a miracle has taken place. This means that the question of the birth of Jesus without human intervention (the 'virgin birth') must be approached by asking: Does the evidence of the Gospels make good sense as historical evidence? If the answer to that question turns out to be 'No', then we must regard the stories told by Matthew and Luke as later attempts to show how a miraculous birth would be appropriate for a remarkable person. If the answer turns out to be 'Yes', then similarly we must be prepared to come to terms with what the evidence suggests.

Now this is not the same as saying that we should naïvely accept as historical fact every statement made in the whole of the Gospel narratives. What I am saying is that we must be prepared to examine every piece of evidence on its own merits – and if we find that there is good historical evidence which points to something 'supernatural', then it should not be dismissed as irrelevant.

As it happens, the stories of Jesus' virgin birth give us a particularly good example of the kind of issues with which we have to deal. Several arguments are involved here:

● Except in the first few chapters of Matthew and Luke there is no explicit statement in the whole of the rest of the New Testament that Jesus was virgin born. There is no mention of it in the accounts of the preaching of the first disciples in the book of Acts. Paul never mentions it. Nor is it found in the Gospels of Mark and John – though, of course, neither of those Gospels mentions Jesus' birth at all. It therefore seems certain that it was possible for the earliest Christians to have a complete understanding of what God had done for them through Jesus Christ without any mention of the virgin birth. Later Christian writers have often tried to argue that the virgin birth is essential if Christians are to believe that Jesus was sinless, and that he was both human and divine. But Paul, amongst others, believed all these things without ever basing his arguments on the particular way that Jesus was born.

This may appear to be a very strong argument for suspecting the authenticity of the stories in Matthew and Luke. But in fact it is a double-edged argument. Since the idea of a virgin birth was not essential for a complete understanding of the precise nature of Jesus' person, why would Matthew and Luke want to invent it? This is an especially pressing question, since no theological points are explicitly made in the stories that describe Jesus' birth. Neither Matthew nor Luke ever say, for example, that Jesus was sinless because he was born in this way, or that this made him the Son of God as well as being a human person. They simply present it as a factual statement about the way Jesus was born. It is very difficult to find any

religious motive for the fabrication of such stories. It is in fact far easier to suppose that Matthew and Luke had access to historical traditions of some kind which contained these stories of Jesus' birth, and that they both incorporated their own rather different stories into their respective Gospels.

● In certain passages of the Gospels, Jesus is referred to as 'the son of Joseph' (Luke 4:22; John 1:45; 6:42), and the lists in both Matthew (1:2–16) and Luke (3:23–38) trace his ancestry through Joseph. It is therefore sometimes suggested that even within the Gospels themselves there is no consistency. For how could Joseph be Jesus' father if Mary was a virgin when Jesus was conceived? This is not as serious an objection as it appears to be. When Joseph married Mary he would be, in the eyes of both public opinion and of the Jewish law, the legal father of Jesus. Besides, there is no word for foster-father in either Hebrew or Greek, and so the Gospel writers were probably just recording the common description of Jesus as 'Jesus son of Joseph'. Luke certainly thought this was what he was doing (3:23). It is in any case unlikely that either Gospel writer would have contradicted himself in so obvious a fashion.

● It has sometimes been suggested that the idea of the virgin birth was derived from Greek or oriental stories about the gods having intercourse with human women and producing children. This is not a very serious argument, and the stories of the Gospels move in a very different atmosphere from the stories told of the Greek gods. We need only to read the account of the announcement of Jesus' birth to Mary (Luke 1:26–38) and compare it with the licentious stories of Greek mythology to realize that there can be little contact between them. In addition, the whole of Luke 1–2 has a very primitive kind of character by comparison with the rest of Luke's writing. Though some scholars believe this to be a deliberate device used by Luke in imitation of the style of the Greek Old Testament (the Septuagint), others have argued that Luke's Greek is of a sufficiently consistent character to suggest that he is here quoting or depending on an Aramaic source. If that is true, then he must have

obtained these stories of Jesus' birth from the very earliest group of Christians in Palestine itself, the only Christians ever to speak Aramaic.

● Matthew's account presents a problem of a rather different kind. In support of his story he quotes from the Old Testament: 'All this took place to fulfil what the Lord had spoken by the prophet: "Behold, a virgin shall conceive and bear a son, and his name shall be called Emmanuel" . . .' (1:22–23). What is more, this passage from the Old Testament prophet Isaiah has a very different meaning in the Greek version of the Old Testament from that which it had in the original Hebrew text. Matthew quotes from the Greek version. But in the Hebrew text of Isaiah 7:14 the mother of Emmanuel is said to be a 'young woman'; she is not called by the technical term for a 'virgin'. Some have therefore argued that the whole idea of the virgin birth was manufactured out of this unfortunate mistranslation of a passage from Isaiah in the Septuagint. Three things need to be noted here.

In the first place this argument can apply only to Matthew since Luke does not quote the Old Testament in support of his story of the virgin birth. So, even supposing this argument is correct, it can dispose only of Matthew's account, and not of Luke's.

Then it is undoubtedly true that Matthew's sole reason for accepting and using the Greek version instead of the Hebrew text was that it was appropriate to his purpose in a way that the Hebrew was not. But this is a common feature of Matthew's Gospel. Matthew often selects Old Testament texts and says they have been fulfilled in Jesus' life and ministry in a way that to us seems irrelevant and trivial. This was almost certainly because he was writing mainly for Jewish readers. The Jews believed that God's Messiah would fulfil certain promises made in the Old Testament, and so Matthew refers to the Old Testament far more than the other Gospel writers, to convince Jewish readers that Jesus was indeed their expected Messiah.

Thirdly it is quite likely that it was not the actual author of the Gospel of Matthew who selected this particular version of the text from Isaiah. There is considerable

The Gospels record that shepherds from near Bethlehem were among the first people to see the newly-born Jesus.

Facing page: One of the most exciting and extensive discoveries of ancient Bible documents was made in some caves at Qumran near the Dead Sea. A chance discovery by a shepherd boy led archaeologists to the area and excavations began in 1947. Over 400 manuscripts dating from the first century have been discovered. All the books of the Old Testament except for Esther have been found there. The manual which contained the rules and beliefs of the Essene community who lived there at the time of Jesus has also been found. The community had separated itself from other Jewish groups to form its monastery. The scrolls were hidden in jars in the caves to protect them from the Roman Army which was attacking Jews in AD 68. Background picture: The entrance to Cave 4, where most of the scrolls were found. Top left: The caves at Qumran. Bottom left: Tourists today can visit the excavated buildings where the Essenes lived. Centre: Two jars which contained scrolls. They are the only complete ones of their kind in the world. Right: Part of a scroll of the book of Deuteronomy.

evidence to suggest that at a very early stage of its existence the church began to gather together Old Testament texts which seemed to them to predict or forecast some aspect of Jesus' life. These are the collections of texts often called *testimonia* by New Testament scholars. There were probably several different collections in existence not long after Jesus' death. The concept of a virgin birth was quite unacceptable in any form to orthodox Jews, and we know that many of the members of the first churches remained good Jews as well as being Christians. Since no one but convinced Jews would be interested in proving that Jesus fulfilled the prophecies of the Old Testament, it is highly unlikely that they would have discovered such an idea there unless they knew of some historical foundation for it.

What then are we to conclude about Jesus' birth from these stories in Matthew and Luke? We can certainly see that when we apply the normal rules of historical investigation to them, the issue is not quite as straightforward as it appears to be when we look at it from a philosophical standpoint and simply ask: Is it possible that such a miracle could have taken place? It is clear that Matthew and Luke

have rather different traditions about the birth of Jesus. Yet they are both agreed that Mary was a virgin when he was conceived, and we should not forget that the other two Gospels make no mention of Jesus' birth at all. No theological claims are made in the stories, and though the idea of a virgin birth is mentioned nowhere else in the New Testament, there is nothing else-where that contradicts it.

In addition, the whole tradition of the Christian church from the second century onwards supports the belief that Jesus was virgin born, and even in the apocryphal gospels of a later age there is no other account of the birth of Jesus. It therefore seems that the majority of attempts to deny any historical character to the Gospel narratives at this point rest on presuppositions that do not allow for the super-natural, rather than on a scientific and historical examination of the evidence on its own terms.

Have we taken a long time to prove nothing? If the only outcome of our investigation is to show that Jesus was born without the benefit of a human father, then we have not said anything very profound or relevant. But the first Christians wanted to say much more than that. And Jesus himself wanted to say a great deal more, as we shall see in the next chapter.

Was John a member of the commune at Qumran?

In view of the similarities between what we know of John the Baptist and the activities of the commune at Qumran, it is inevitable that we should ask if there was any connection between them. There are two main similarities between them that we need to consider.

In the Judean desert

According to Luke, John the Baptist lived in the desert until he began his public work (1:80; 3:2). Since his baptizing took place in the River Jordan, it is natural to assume that the desert in question was the Judean desert surrounding the Dead Sea, into which the River Jordan flows. This means he was probably living in the same desert as the Qumran people, and at about the same time. Since their monastery must have been one of the few places where it was possible to live in the desert, it is suggested that John may well have known

them, even that he may have been a member of their commune.

It is certainly not difficult to believe that John would know of the existence of the monastery at Qumran. But some people have suggested that he was a member of the group, and that he was brought up by them from an early age. They base this argument on the statement in Luke 1:80 that as a child John 'grew and developed in body and spirit. He lived in the desert until the day when he appeared publicly to the people of Israel.' This statement can be put together with a piece of information given about the Essenes by Josephus. He says that they often adopted other people's children in order to indoctrinate them with the ideas of their sect (*Jewish Wars* 2.8.2). This is an attractive theory, but there are many problems about it.

●The Greek words used in Luke 1:80 and 3:2 do not

necessarily suggest that John was actually brought up as a child in the desert. It is certainly implied that he was in the desert thinking about his life's work immediately before he began baptizing people – but the natural implication of the story about his birth is that he was brought up in the normal way by his parents.

● It is also unlikely that his parents would have allowed a group like the people of Qumran to adopt their child. Not only were they longing to have this son, but John's father Zechariah was a priest – and one of the distinctive beliefs of the

Baptism was seen by John as a symbol of repentance. It is still used by Christians today to signify faith in Christ, whether of children or adult converts.

Qumran group was that the Jerusalem priests were corrupt. It is difficult to think that John's parents would have given their child to a group who were so hostile to all that they themselves stood for.

● We must also remember that the Judean desert was a big place, and by no means everyone who lived there would need to live at Qumran. The shores around the Dead Sea are full of caves that would make ideal lodgings for hermits, as they did for the Zealots who resisted Rome after the destruction of Jerusalem in AD 70. Even Josephus tells us how he once joined a man called Bannus who was living a solitary life in the desert (*Life of Josephus* 2). The appeal of this kind of life has always been strong to people of a particular disposition, and we can be quite sure there must have been plenty of individuals living like this in the desert surrounding the Dead Sea.

Baptism

If it is difficult to make any direct connection between John and the Essenes through their style of life, it is certainly no easier to do it through their religious rituals. We know that both John and the Qumran people made use of water in their religious rites, but there is little we can say beyond that. There are in fact several striking differences between John's concept of baptism and the ritual washings that went on at Qumran:

● The people who took part were different. John baptized people who wanted to change their way of life. The community at Qumran accepted only those who could prove that they had already changed their way of life. An initiate often had to wait for a year or two before being allowed to take part in the ritual washings at Qumran, whereas John was prepared to baptize immediately anyone who was willing to repent.

● The character of the ritual was different. A person baptized by John was baptized once and for all. But at Qumran the ritual washings were repeated over and over again. Indeed, Professor H. H. Rowley has pointed out that 'baptism' in the sense we usually understand it is not really the right word to describe what went on at Qumran. The Essene 'baptisms' were a means of effecting a ritual purification in the lives of those who were members, rather than being a rite of admission to the sect.

● The meaning of the ritual was different. John's baptisms were carried out as part of the preparations for the arrival of God's expected Messiah. But the Qumran washings were not connected with the expectation of a Messiah, or of anyone else. They were simply means of expressing in symbol the moral and spiritual purity which the community hoped to preserve among its members.

So, was John a member of the Dead Sea sect? The best answer seems to be that if he had at any time been a member, he had certainly changed his outlook quite radically by the time he began his public work. But arguments in favour are not very strong, and we would certainly need further evidence if they were ever to be conclusively shown to be correct.

Chapter 3 Who was Jesus?

John 1:38; 3:2; 9:2

Mark 1:21;
Luke 4:16; 6:6
Mark 1:16–20

AFTER HE had met John and been baptized, most of Jesus' life was spent as a religious teacher. It was quite normal for Jewish religious teachers, or rabbis as they were called, to live an itinerant life, wandering about from place to place, often accompanied by their disciples. Jesus plainly fitted into this pattern. He had his disciples, and he was often called 'Rabbi' or 'Teacher'. Like the other Jewish teachers he carried out much of his work in the synagogue, the place where Jews met for worship each sabbath day. He also spoke with people wherever he met them. He called his first disciples from their fishing boats, and often taught out in the open countryside where large crowds could gather round him.

It was Jesus' teaching that really caught the imagination of the people. For as they listened to him they realized that this was no ordinary rabbi. He was not just someone else's disciple passing on what he had heard from others. He was saying totally new things about men and women and their relationship with God. And he was saying them in such a way that no one could escape making a decision about him. One had to accept either the verdict of many ordinary people that 'he taught them as one who had

Matthew 7:29
Mark 2:7

authority', or the opinion of the Pharisees that he was the worst kind of religious pretender.

The teaching that caused such a sharp division among his hearers was on just two subjects. On the one hand Jesus made many bold claims about his own person and significance. He clearly believed that he himself was the promised deliverer whom the Jews were expecting to be sent from God. He alone was the Messiah who could establish the new society. On the other hand, alongside Jesus' claims about his own destiny and importance, we have statements about the exact nature and meaning of the new society Jesus believed he had come to inaugurate. We will be looking at some of Jesus' statements about the new society in section two. It is important that we look first of all at Jesus' claims about himself. For his ideas about God's new society and its place in the lives of men and women are meaningless unless we have understood what Jesus claimed about his own significance in God's plan.

The Son of man

So far we have seen how the Jewish people were looking for God to send a promised deliverer, the Messiah, who would inaugurate the new society. Of course, the term 'God's promised deliverer' is not used in the Gospels: I have used it here to try to convey in everyday language something of what the Jewish people understood by the word 'Messiah'.

But it is surprising to look at the Gospels and see how few times even the word 'Messiah' (or its Greek translation, 'Christ') is used there to describe Jesus. Take Mark's Gospel, for example. This was perhaps the first Gospel to be written, and the word for 'Messiah' or 'Christ' is used only seven times. One of these is in the title of the Gospel, and of the other six only three could be taken as a reference to Jesus being the Messiah or Christ. And in only one does Jesus himself make a direct claim to be the Messiah. It is also striking that in the only passage where Jesus does directly claim to be the Messiah, he at once goes on to speak of a different figure, and identifies the Messiah with someone he calls 'the Son of man'.

Mark 1:1

Mark 8:29; 9:41; 14:61–62

Mark 14:61–62

Mark 14:62

So who was the Son of man? It is impossible to read far through any of the stories of Jesus' life without realizing that this 'Son of man' was a very important concept for Jesus. The actual term is used fourteen times in Mark's Gospel; in the longer account of Matthew it occurs no less than thirty-one times. 'Son of man' is in fact the term that Jesus used most often to describe himself and his work. So what did it mean?

Some people would say that when Jesus spoke of himself as 'the Son of man' he was simply wanting to emphasize that one part of his nature was ordinary and human, while another side of his character could be described by the term 'Son of God'. But the phrase 'Son of man' must mean more than this. Jesus speaks, for example, of 'the Son of man coming in clouds with great power and glory', or 'seated at the right hand of the power of God'. Claims like that can hardly have been intended to emphasize Jesus' human character over against his claims to have a special significance in the plans of God!

Mark 13:26

Luke 22:69

The meaning of 'Son of man'

The *exact* meaning of the term 'Son of man' is one of the most hotly disputed subjects in modern study of the New Testament. What we can say here is only the barest summary of what some of the scholars are saying.

One point on which all scholars are agreed is that the most helpful question to ask is: What would come into the minds of those people who actually knew Jesus when they heard him use the term 'Son of man'? Since his first hearers were Jews, it would be best to look to the Jewish religion for the answer.

It is always helpful to look first at the Old Testament. Here we

find that the expression 'Son of man' is used in two ways.

More often than not, it simply means man as distinct from God. In this context, it usually emphasizes the weakness and poverty of human beings in contrast to the might and power of God himself (Numbers 23:19; Job 25:6; Psalm 8:4; 146:3; Isaiah 51:12). One or two of the Old Testament prophets were addressed by God as 'son of man', and this was a means of emphasizing the difference between them and their Master (Ezekiel 2:1; Daniel 8:17).

But the term is also used in a quite different way in Daniel

It is not possible to compile a complete calendar of the events in Jesus' life. This table lists the main events of his life as they are recorded in the Gospels.

7:13–14. Far from indicating the weakness of men and women as opposed to the greatness of God, 'one like a son of man' here 'came to the Ancient of Days and was presented before him. And to him was given dominion and glory and kingdom, that all peoples, nations and languages should serve him.' And 'his dominion is an everlasting dominion, which shall not pass away, and his kingdom one that shall not be destroyed'.

We may also look at some of the apocalyptic books that may have been current at the time of Jesus. In *2 Esdras* and the *Similitudes of Enoch* 'the Son of man' again appears as a supernatural figure sent from God as the future judge of humanity (*2 Esdras* 13, *1 Enoch* 37–71). We cannot be sure that

The life of Jesus

recorded in the synoptic Gospels

	Matthew	Mark	Luke
BIRTH AND CHILDHOOD			
Jesus' ancestors	1:1–17		3:23–28
The promise of Jesus' birth to Mary			1:26–38
The birth of Jesus	1:18–25		2:1–20
Visitors from the East	2:1–12		
Jesus' circumcision			2:21–40
Jesus' parents escape to Egypt	2:13–23		
Twelve-year-old Jesus in the temple			2:41–52
IN AND AROUND GALILEE			
Jesus' baptism	3:13–17	1:9–11	3:21–22
The temptation	4:1–11	1:12–13	4:1–13
First preaching in Galilee	4:12–17	1:14–15	4:14–15
Jesus rejected by people in Nazareth			4:16–30
The call of the first disciples	4:18–22	1:16–20	
Teaching and healing in Capernaum		1:21–38	4:31–43
Miraculous catch of fish			5:1–11
The Sermon on the Mount	5:1 – 7:29		
Jesus heals a leper	8:1–4	1:40–45	5:12–16
Healing the sick and calming the storm	8:5–34		
Healing a paralysed man	9:1–8	2:1–12	5:17–26
Matthew called to be a disciple	9:9–13	2:13–17	5:27–32
Discussion about fasting	9:14–17	2:18–22	5:33–39
Jairus' daughter and an old woman healed	9:18–26	5:21–43	8:40–56
Two blind men and a dumb man healed	9:27–34		
The twelve commissioned and instructed	9:35 – 10:42	6:6–13	9:1–6
Jesus talks about John the Baptist	11:1–19		7:18–35
Teaching about the sabbath	12:1–14		
The sermon on the plain			6:20–49
A slave healed and a boy brought back to life			7:1–17
The women who served Jesus			7:36 – 8:3
Jesus debates with the religious leaders	12:22–50	3:20–35	
Parables of the kingdom	13:1–58	4:1–41	8:4–25
The Gerasene demoniac		5:1–20	8:26–39
Jesus feeds 5,000 people	14:13–21	6:30–44	9:10–17
Jesus walks on the water	14:22–33	6:45–52	

	Matthew	Mark	Luke
Teaching on religious traditions	15:1–20	7:1–23	
Jesus heals many who are ill	15:21–31	7:24–37	
Jesus feeds 4,000 people	15:32 – 16:12	8:1–21	
He predicts his death	16:13–28	8:27–37	9:18–27
The transfiguration	17:1–27	9:2–32	9:28–45
Jesus sends out seventy helpers			10:1–24
Teaching on love, prayer and materialism			10:25 – 12:59
Healings and parables			13:1–30
Jesus leaves Galilee			13:31–35
Some well-known parables told			14:15 – 16:31
Ten lepers healed			17:11–19
JESUS GOES TO JERUSALEM			
Jesus predicts his death again	20:17–19	10:32–34	18:31–34
The sons of Zebedee seek privilege	20:20–38	10:35–45	
The healing of blind Bartimaeus	20:29–34	10:46–52	18:35–43
Zacchaeus meets Jesus			19:1–10
Jesus enters Jerusalem like a king	21:1–9	11:1–10	19:28–44
He turns out the traders from the temple	21:10–22	11:11–26	19:45–48
More parables	21:28 – 22:14		
Indictment of the Pharisees	23:1–36	12:37–40	20:45–47
Jesus predicts the destruction of the temple	24:1–3	13:1–4	21:5–7
Jesus' apocalypse	24:4–36	13:5–37	21:8–36
DEATH AND RESURRECTION			
The conspiracy against Jesus	26:1–5	14:1–2	22:1–2
Judas betrays Jesus	26:14–16	14:10–11	22:3–6
The disciples prepare for the Passover	26:17–19	14:12–16	22:7–13
The last supper	26:20–29	14:17–25	22:15–38
Jesus is captured	26:30–56	14:26–52	22:39–53
The trial of Jesus	26:57 – 27:26	14:53 – 15:15	22:54 – 23:25
The crucifixion	27:27–44	15:16–32	23:26–43
Jesus dies	27:45–56	15:33–41	23:44–49
Jesus is buried	27:57–66	15:42–47	23:50–56
The empty tomb	28:1–10	16:1–8	24:1–12
Jesus appears alive to his followers	28:11–20		24:13–53

One interpretation of Jesus' title 'Son of man' is that it emphasizes the weakness of people compared with the greatness of God. To Jesus, God was the provider of everything man enjoyed.

It is quite likely that all these facts are significant. If the term 'Son of man' had no very clearly definable meaning in the Aramaic that Jesus spoke, he may have chosen to use it simply because he was free to make it mean exactly what he wanted it to mean. If he had used the term 'Messiah' it would not have been easy for him to explain precisely what he understood his role to be, since people had so many preconceived ideas. By using the ambiguous term 'Son of man' he avoided such problems.

At the same time, for those with the perception to see it, the background of the term provided some very important clues to the things Jesus wanted to say about himself. For he wanted to claim both that he was an ordinary human being, and that he was specially sent from God himself – and both these ideas could be found in the Old Testament use of the 'Son of man'.

Jesus actually uses the name in three rather different ways which illustrate this.

● Quite often, he uses the term 'Son of man' instead of the personal pronoun 'I', simply as a means of describing his ordinary human existence. At those points where the different Gospels have the same sayings, one Gospel often uses 'Son of man' where another writer uses the pronoun 'I'. Compare, for example, Mark 10:45 and Luke 22:27; or Mark 8:27 and Matthew 16:13; or Matthew 19:28 and Luke 22:30.

● At other times, Jesus uses the title 'Son of man' with reference to his future coming on the clouds of heaven and to his exaltation at God's right hand (Matthew 24:27, 37; Luke 17:30; 18:8; 21:36; 22:69). This is the same use as in Daniel 7 and the Jewish apocalypses.

● But most often it is used in a new and different way, with some reference to the suffering and death that Jesus expected to be part of his experience. In nine out of the fourteen uses in Mark, the term 'Son of man' is used by Jesus to refer to his coming death (Mark 8:31; 9:9; 14:21; Matthew 26:2). It is at this point that he has given an entirely new meaning to what may well have been a little-known idea before his time. And it is characteristic of him that he should have talked about himself most often as a suffering Son of man.

either of these apocalyptic books were actually in writing by the time of Jesus. But they do certainly reflect opinions that were held by many of his contemporaries. At the same time, we need to remember that not all Jews were interested in such apocalyptic speculations. Nor would all Jews know their Old Testament well enough to make an automatic association between these ideas and Jesus' use of the term. Indeed, some competent Aramaic scholars have suggested that the actual words probably used by Jesus would not have had any clear-cut meaning at all.

So we have three facts to consider before we can decide what Jesus meant by calling himself the Son of man:

● The actual Aramaic words 'son of man' may well have had little meaning. They were probably just a longer (tautological) phrase for 'man'.

● In the Old Testament, the term 'son of man' had been used to describe human beings and their difference from God.

● In the book of Daniel and other Jewish apocalypses, the 'son of man' was a transcendent, heavenly figure who shared in God's own power.

The Messiah

Mark 9:41

We need not spend long thinking about Jesus' claims to be the Messiah. It was not a title Jesus used for himself. In Mark, the first Gospel to be written, there is only one instance where he may have been doing so. There are, however, four very significant occasions when other people called Jesus 'the Messiah', and he apparently accepted the title.

Jesus' 'Son of man' sayings occur most often in the context of his suffering and death. He identified most readily with the poor and needy; like these Asian refugees he had no permanent home of his own.

● When Peter finally realized the truth about who Jesus claimed to be, and told him 'You are the Christ', Jesus replied that he was 'blessed' to have received such a special insight.

Matthew 16:16–17

● Another occasion was during his trial before the Jewish authorities, when Jesus acknowledged to the high priest that he was the Messiah.

Mark 14:61–62

● There is also the story of how Jesus healed a man who was thought to be possessed by demons. Not only did he allow this man to address him as 'Son of the Most High God'; he also told him, 'Go home to your friends, and tell them how much the Lord has done for you'.

Mark 5:1–20

● On another occasion Jesus was going along a road near Jericho when a blind beggar called Bartimaeus shouted out and addressed him as 'Son of David'. Though others who were standing around evidently told the man to be silent, Jesus did not do so, and therefore seems to have accepted this title for himself.

Mark 10:46–52

From these four instances it is clear that Jesus did not have the same attitude towards the claim that he was the Messiah, 'the Son of David', on each occasion. By the time he appeared before the high priest it was obvious that he was to be condemned anyway, and so he had no qualms about claiming to be the Messiah. Though even here he at once went on to re-define the concept of 'the Messiah' in terms of his own favourite name 'the Son of man'. But at an earlier stage, when Peter confessed that he was the Messiah, Jesus told him and the other disciples not to tell anyone about it, but to keep it secret. On the other two occasions he apparently accepted a Messianic title from other people without saying anything about it – and in the case of the man possessed with demons he told him to share his experience with his friends and relatives. It is obvious that Jesus' attitude to letting people know he was the Messiah varied according to the circumstances, and was partly dependent on the question of whether or not this claim should be publicized. What are we to make of all this? Two explanations seem possible.

●Jesus never claimed to be the Messiah. One way to solve the problem is to say that Jesus never in fact claimed to be the Messiah at all, and that Mark and the other Gospel writers have written their stories of Jesus' life and teaching with an eye more to what they believed about Jesus than to what he claimed for himself. They believed he was the Messiah because they were living after the resurrection. From this new perspective they came to see that it was fitting to think of Jesus as the person who had fulfilled God's promises made in the Old Testament. When they came to write their Gospels, however, they wanted to make it perfectly clear that Jesus was actually the promised Messiah. So they bridged the gap between their own beliefs and what they knew to be the historical truth by inventing the idea of 'the messianic secret'. This is a phrase first coined by a German scholar, Wilhelm Wrede, to explain why it is that whenever Jesus is depicted talking to his disciples about his position as Messiah he always tells them to keep it a secret. Wrede thought that the whole idea of this 'messianic secret' was the invention of Mark, the writer of the earliest Gospel.

The difficulty with his suggestion is that although it fits in with some of the evidence, there are other pieces of information which do not fit. There are, for example, the incidents involving the demon-possessed man at Gerasa and Bartimaeus at Jericho. Then there is also the undeniable fact that Jesus was actually condemned to death because he claimed to be 'king of the Jews', that is, their Messiah. It is difficult to see how Mark could have left these stories in his narrative in this form if he had been so intent on making the idea of the 'messianic secret' convincing.

●Jesus believed, but never claimed, he was the Messiah. We seem to be left with the implication that Jesus thought he was the Messiah, but that he did not explicitly claim he was. But how can we explain such an odd state of affairs? Three things can be said about it.

First, we have to remember that the Gospels were written not so much to preserve the story of Jesus' life and teaching as to be helpful to Christians later in the first century. And the Christians who first read the Gospels had the same perspective as we have now. They knew of the resurrection of Jesus and the coming of God's power into their own lives. On that account they had no difficulty in recognizing that Jesus must be the Messiah, God's promised deliverer sent to inaugurate the new society. How could they have any doubt, since they themselves were members of this new society? Gradually, the word 'Messiah' or 'Christ' came to be used as a kind of second name for Jesus, and it is still used in this way today. This probably explains why the word 'Christ' is used so many times in John's Gospel, whereas it is hardly ever used in the other three. It is generally thought that John was writing later than the others, and by that time the word had become almost a surname for Jesus.

Then the Gospels themselves make it clear that Jesus and his contemporaries were at cross-purposes when they spoke of the Messiah. To the Jews, the Messiah was to be a political king. For Jesus, being the Messiah meant humble service and obedience to God's will. And for him to have spoken openly of being the Messiah would have concealed the real meaning of his coming, and brought about an early encounter with the Romans. Even the disciples, including Peter who declared that Jesus was the Messiah, did not fully understand who Jesus was until after the resurrection. Despite their close relationship with Jesus, they displayed their ignorance of his intentions on more than one

Mark 8:14–21; 9:30–32; 10:35–45

occasion. And we can be quite sure that this is an accurate historical picture, for when the Gospels were written the disciples were the church's heroes, and no one would have made up stories that portrayed them in a bad light.

There were many beggars in the streets of Israel during Jesus' lifetime; one of them, Bartimaeus, addressed him as the Messiah, the 'Son of David'.

Thirdly, it seems certain that Jesus' attitude did in fact vary, and that his whole life and work was a mixture of revelation and secrecy. This comes out in the way he liked to call himself 'the Son of man', which had no ready-made meaning. To those who were not prepared to think very deeply about it, it was a name that could only confuse them and conceal Jesus' claims rather than reveal them. At the same time, many incidents in Jesus'

Mark 1:9–11
Luke 4:1–13
Mark 11:1–11

life – including the miracles, but also occasions such as his baptism, his temptations and his entry into Jerusalem – would lose their meaning if Jesus was not claiming to be the Messiah.

Facing page: The crowds that
thronged the narrow streets of
Jerusalem nearly two thousand
years ago were expecting a
political leader to deliver them
from the Romans. Even some of
Jesus' closest followers
thought he would be this kind
of Messiah.

Many of the things he did and said were exactly the things that
the Messiah was expected to do and say when he came.

The best conclusion seems to be that Jesus did not use the
word 'Messiah' of himself because he knew that it would suggest
to his hearers an earthly king and a new political state. Jesus
certainly had no intention of being that kind of 'Messiah'. He
had already decisively rejected the idea in the temptations. So he
cast his whole ministry in a mould that would conceal his claim
to be Messiah from those who did not want to understand it in
the same way as he did, but that would reveal his true identity
to those who really wanted to know.

The Son of God

The belief of the Christian church from the very earliest times
has always included the statement that Jesus was 'the Son of
God'. This too was an expression that would be familiar to the
people of Jesus' day. Greek-speaking people often used the
phrase to indicate some heroic human figure. When the Roman
centurion at the cross said of Jesus, 'Truly this was the son of
God', all he probably meant was that Jesus was a great man.
Indeed, Luke's account clearly suggests this, for there the
centurion says, 'Certainly this man was innocent'.

Matthew 27:54

Luke 23:47

Like the terms 'Son of man' and 'Messiah', the term 'Son of
God' had also been used in the Old Testament. The nation of
Israel was often called 'God's son'. The kings of Israel, especially
those who were descendants of David, also had this title. Many
of the psalms refer to the king as God's son – though the Jews
soon came to regard such passages as references to the coming
Messiah.

Hosea 11:1

But there can be no question that in the Gospels the phrase
'Son of God' was used to indicate that Jesus claimed a special
relationship with God himself. Jesus was very conscious of a
close spiritual relationship with God as his Father. Even at the
early age of twelve he regarded the temple at Jerusalem as 'my
Father's house'. And in the story about the wicked tenants of
the vineyard he made it clear that he himself was the son whom
the owner had sent to put things in order.

Luke 2:49

Mark 12:1–11

The claims that are implied in these stories were also made
very explicitly by Jesus. Take, for example, this statement
recorded by both Matthew and Luke: 'All things have been
delivered to me by my Father; and no one knows the Son except
the Father, and no one knows the Father except the Son and
any one to whom the Son chooses to reveal him.' It is clear that
Jesus was claiming a unique relationship with God, and his
claim is of such a character that it leaves very little room for
misunderstanding.

Matthew 11:27; Luke 10:22

There is certainly no place for saying, as many non-Christians
do, that Jesus was a good man who did not in fact claim to be
divine. If Jesus' claims were not true, he was either a deliberate
impostor or a deluded imbecile – and neither the evidence of

the Gospels, nor common historical opinion, pictures him in either of these roles.

So what did Jesus mean when he claimed to be 'the Son of God'? This is, of course, one of the great questions that theologians have thought and talked about for centuries. So nothing we can say here is likely to be the full and final answer to the question! But there are at least three essential facts to note if we are ever to have any intelligent understanding of what Jesus and the first Christians were saying when they used this term.

● We must never forget that when we describe Jesus as 'the Son of God' we are using pictorial language to describe something that is in principle indescribable. Jesus was using an analogy. He took the human relationship of child to parent, and said: 'My relationship with God is rather like that.' He did not mean us to take the analogy literally. Nor was he suggesting that every aspect of our own relationship to our parents fits exactly the relationship between Jesus and God. Not everyone has a happy relationship with their parents. And although many people may be able to say truthfully, 'He who hates me hates my Father also', no human could ever say 'I and my Father are one'. Indeed, the whole of Jesus' teaching, especially in John's Gospel, makes it clear that this relationship between Father and Son was unique. It existed long before Jesus was born in Bethlehem: Jesus was 'in the beginning with God'.

John 15:23
John 10:30

John 1:2

● Like all the other titles we have looked at here, this one had also been used in the Old Testament. The term 'son of . . .' was a common idiom of the Hebrew language. For example, in the Old Testament the Israelites are often called 'sons' or 'children' of Israel, though modern translations have disguised the wording. Wicked people are often called 'sons of wickedness' or 'sons of Belial'. And the Hebrew for our word 'human beings' is 'sons of men'.

Deuteronomy 1:1;
Judges 1:1

Deuteronomy 13:13;
1 Samuel 2:12

Now if we described ourselves as 'sons of men' we would be saying that we share precisely the same characteristics and nature as the whole of the human race before us. So when the New Testament says that Jesus is 'the Son of God' it is stating that Jesus shared the characteristics and nature of God himself. He was claiming to be really and truly divine. Some people, the Jehovah's Witnesses for example, have been unable to see this because they have forgotten that Jesus was using an analogy when he described himself as 'Son of God'. And they have also ignored the real meaning of the term 'the son of . . .' in the language that Jesus was speaking.

● In the first chapter of John's Gospel, and in Revelation, this relationship between Jesus and God is expressed in another way. There Jesus is called the 'word' or *logos* of God. God's word is, of course, the way that God communicates. But when the New Testament calls Jesus 'the word' it says something more than that. For John says that 'the Word was God' – that is, God's message to mankind was not just written in a book, it was

John 1:1–18;
Revelation 19:13

John 1:1

displayed in the person of God himself. He also says that 'the Word became flesh' – that is, God himself was embodied in 'the Word', in Jesus.

John 1:14

So when Jesus claimed to be the 'Son of God', and when the New Testament writers described this in terms of 'the Word of God', they were all saying that because of Jesus we can truly know what God is like. Jesus himself said: 'He who has seen me has seen the Father.' We all have our ideas of what God is like, ideas formed according to our own prejudices and preconceptions. But if Jesus' claims are correct, we can now substitute God as he really is for our imaginary pictures of him. That is why it is so important for us to get back to what Jesus was actually saying and doing, for in his life and teaching we can see and hear what God is really like.

John 14:9

Jesus told his followers, 'I am among you as one who serves'. The idea was familiar to them; there were many servants and slaves in contemporary Palestine.

The servant

Perhaps we discover what God is really like most adequately in this final title – 'the servant' – that Jesus seems to have applied to himself and his work. It is true that nowhere in the Gospels do we find Jesus using of himself the title 'the servant of God'. Yet we have seen already that it was just because he lived and died in the way predicted of the suffering servant in Isaiah that his concept of what it meant to be Messiah was so very different from the kind of Messiah expected by the Jews of his time. We also have many references to Jesus' conviction that it was to be his lot to suffer and, as we have noticed, the most distinctive use of the term 'Son of man' was in connection with Jesus' statements about his own suffering and death.

Isaiah 52:13–53:12

From the time he was baptized, and perhaps before that, Jesus saw that the course of his life was to be one of suffering. The voice he heard at his baptism, echoing words from one of the passages in Isaiah about the suffering servant, made it clear to him that his life's work was to consist of humble self-denial, and this conviction was vigorously reiterated in his reactions to the

Mark 1:11
Isaiah 42:1

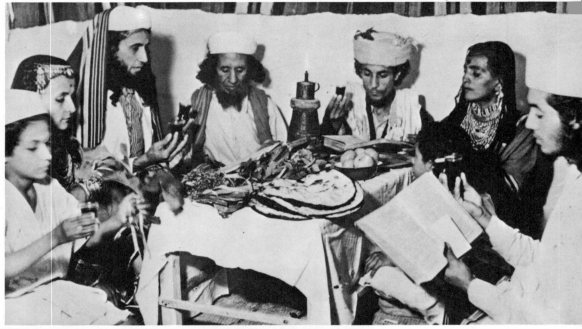

Many Jewish religious customs have continued almost unchanged since Old Testament times. A series of festivals throughout the year, celebrated by whole families, remind them of the great events in their past history. The Passover is the most important of the festivals. It is held each spring as a reminder of the 'exodus' or escape of the Israelites from Egypt. For the family above, the Passover they are celebrating is their first one since they settled in modern Israel.

The Passover plate (centre left) contains foods symbolizing different aspects of the event: a boiled egg; a shankbone of lamb; parsley dipped in salt water; horse-radish and bitter herbs; a mixture of chopped fruit and nuts.

Centre right: A Jewish rabbi wearing traditional costume. Over his head and shoulders is a tallith, or prayer shawl, and attached to his forehead and left arm are phylacteries containing short portions of the Jewish scriptures.

The wailing wall (bottom) in Jerusalem is a place where Jews frequently go to pray. It is part of the original wall which protected the temple court in the first century.

temptation experience. According to Mark, Jesus warned his disciples at a very early stage in his ministry that the day was near when he, the bridegroom, would be taken away from his friends. Immediately after Peter declared his belief that Jesus was the Messiah, Jesus again repeated that 'the Son of Man must suffer many things'. A great purpose was to be accomplished by his service and suffering: 'the Son of Man also came . . . to give his life as a ransom for many.'

Mark 2:20

Mark 8:31

Mark 10:45

We have spent a lot of time looking at the various titles that Jesus used to describe himself. Most of them are difficult to understand in detail. But all have one very clear implication. There is no doubt that by using them Jesus was claiming a unique relationship with God, and a unique authority. We find this authority expressed in his claim to forgive the sins of other people. The Jewish religious experts saw quite correctly that this was a claim to exercise power that belongs only to God. He also demanded from his followers a loyalty and devotion that no ordinary human being could ever have the right to claim. He told would-be followers: 'Whoever does not bear his own cross and come after me, cannot be my disciple.'

Mark 2:1–12

Luke 14:27

This claim to a unique relationship with God is expressed in John's Gospel in terms of a complete identification between Jesus and God: 'I and the Father are one . . . He who has seen me has seen the Father.' And we find exactly the same claims in the Gospels of Matthew and Luke.

John 10:30, 14:9
Matthew 11:27;
Luke 10:22

Despite this we are often told by secular historians that Jesus lived as a wandering Jewish teacher, that he may not even have claimed to be a prophet, and that it was the early church, especially Paul, who first made him divine. But the claims Jesus made for himself are clearly expressed in the very earliest records about him, and we must not forget that by comparison with other historical writings of that age, the Gospels were written down a very short time after the events that they describe. What is more, the work of scholars who have investigated the way the Gospels actually came to be written, the Form Critics, has shown that there is no trace anywhere in the New Testament of a Jesus who did not make supernatural claims for himself. It really is quite impossible to separate the purely human figure, the 'Jesus of history', from the Christ and risen Lord who is equal with God in early Christian theology.

If Jesus' claims were false, we are left not with a pious Jewish rabbi, as some historians like to imagine, but with either a man suffering from delusions, or a self-conscious fraud. In either case, Jesus could only be classified with the other 'Messiahs' who appeared sporadically in the first century, whose influence was short-lived, and who are now mostly forgotten. But Jesus was not forgotten and, if his followers later made any new claims about his importance, these claims were firmly grounded in his own teaching about himself and his place in the plans of God.

Chapter 4   Why did Jesus die?

WHY DID Jesus die? Of all the questions we can ask about Jesus, perhaps no other can be answered in so many different ways. To a certain extent, the answer we give depends on the way we approach the question. We can see this quite clearly, even in books written as long ago as the first century AD.

Take Josephus, for example. He says very little about Jesus. But he does say that 'he was the Messiah; and when Pilate heard him accused by the most highly respected men amongst us, he condemned him to be crucified'. He was obviously convinced that Jesus died as a result of political intrigue and collaboration between Pilate, the Roman prefect of Judea, and the leaders of the Jewish people. This is also clearly stated in the stories of Jesus' death in the Gospels.

Jewish Antiquities 18.3.3

But if we look at some other parts of the New Testament and ask, 'Why did Jesus die?', we find a slightly different emphasis in some of the answers. According to the book of Acts, Peter said on the day of Pentecost that though Jesus was 'crucified and killed by the hands of lawless men', he was also 'delivered up according to the definite plan and foreknowledge of God'. Paul expresses the same point. In explaining his most deeply held convictions to the Christians in the Greek city of Corinth, he said that 'Christ died for our sins in accordance with the scriptures'.

Acts 2:23

1 Corinthians 15:3

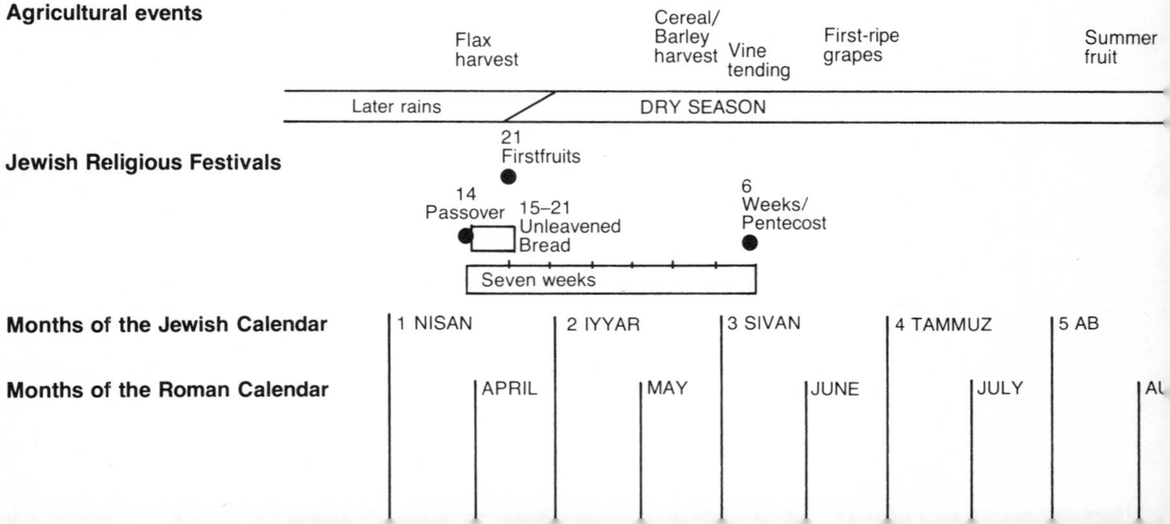

Agricultural events		Flax harvest		Cereal/ Barley harvest	Vine tending	First-ripe grapes		Summer fruit
		Later rains			DRY SEASON			
Jewish Religious Festivals			21 Firstfruits ●			6 Weeks/ Pentecost		
		14 Passover ●	15–21 Unleavened Bread			●		
			Seven weeks					
Months of the Jewish Calendar		1 NISAN	2 IYYAR	3 SIVAN		4 TAMMUZ	5 AB	
Months of the Roman Calendar		APRIL	MAY	JUNE		JULY	AU	

So in the New Testament itself the question, 'Why did Jesus die?' is given two kinds of answer. One is based on the historical facts that brought about Jesus' death. The other is based on the claims Jesus made about himself, and on the beliefs of the early church about his significance in God's plan for humanity. We are, then, dealing with a subject that can be understood in two ways. Jesus' death can be understood as a simple matter of history. But at the same time, we can never forget that in the last analysis Jesus' death can only be fully understood as part of God's plan. In the light of what Jesus himself claimed, we must give some sort of explanation of his execution as a common criminal.

Luke 19:10

History and the death of Jesus

A question that is often asked about the Gospels today is whether they intended to give any sort of chronological outline of Jesus' life, or whether the individual stories and sayings were strung together by the Gospel writers in the way that would best suit their own purposes in writing. We shall look at this question in some greater detail in section three, when we consider the way the Gospels were written.

The course of Jesus' life

The Jewish and Roman calendars
There are a number of references to special days and festivals in the Gospels. John, for instance, records how Jesus went to the feast of Tabernacles, and his death took place at Passover time. Some of the festivals, such as the Passover itself, were memorials of great events in the history of Israel. Others, such as the feast of Firstfruits, were associated with events in the agricultural calendar.

Regardless of our detailed answer to the question, it is obvious that we must be able to make certain assumptions about Jesus' career. We can, for example, assume that his baptism by John did take place near the beginning of his ministry. We can assume too, that his ministry took place not only in Galilee, his own home territory, but also in Judea, the area surrounding Jerusalem. Then there is also the indisputable fact that Jesus was crucified in Jerusalem; so we can assume that at some stage immediately before his death he had spent some time teaching in and around Jerusalem itself.

Stories telling of Jesus' work in all these areas show that from the start Jesus' presence created divisions among those who met him. John explains this in a theological way by saying that when Jesus came, God's light had come into the world. Faced with this revelation of God, men and women must make a decision. They

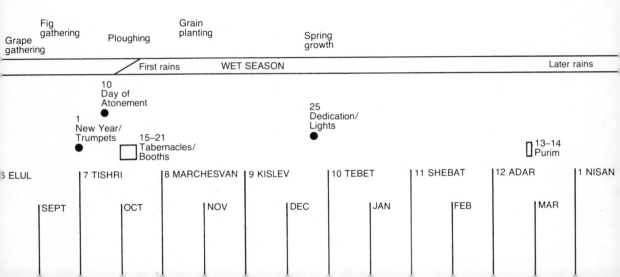

John 3:16–21

must be on one side or the other: on God's side, or against him. Jesus put it like this: 'No one can serve two masters; for either he will hate the one and love the other, or he will be devoted to the one and despise the other. You cannot serve God and

Matthew 6:24

mammon.' And there are many stories about Jesus which show how he enjoyed great popularity as a teacher and healer, but was also opposed by the religious and civil authorities of the day.

The Roman rulers of Palestine were always suspicious of anyone who made a following for himself, just as we are often suspicious of bureaucrats who have too much power in their own hands. According to Josephus, Herod Antipas got rid of John the Baptist because he was afraid of political revolts. It must have been difficult for the authorities not to think of Jesus in the same way. After all, he attracted very large crowds of people, and on at least one occasion a crowd of 5,000 wanted him

John 6:15

to become their king and lead a revolt against the Romans.

The Gospels show Jesus resisting such political power time and again. But they also show that he had no such qualms about getting on the wrong side of the Jewish religious authorities. Right from the very start, the crowds declared that his teaching

Mark 1:22

was different from that of their own religious experts. And Jesus accepted this. What is more, he had no hesitation in condemning the Pharisees and Sadducees outright. They were 'blind leaders

Matthew 23:16–24

of the blind', men who had perverted and denied the word of God. Though they appeared to be very religious and holy, he said that deep down inside they were as rotten and worthless as a

Matthew 23:27

grave full of old bones!

What is more, Jesus' criticism of these people appears to have been a deliberately planned policy. Though Jesus is portrayed spending a short time in more remote areas teaching his disciples, all the Gospels suggest that there was a specific moment at which

Mark 10:32–34;
Matthew 20:17–19;
Luke 18:31–34;
John 11:55–57

he decided the time had come to confront the Jewish authorities in Jerusalem itself. Different explanations have been given of this step.

●The oldest view is that Jesus realized the time for his death had come, and so he set himself to go to Jerusalem to fulfil God's will. This is clearly implied in what Jesus said to his disciples according to Luke's account: 'Behold, we are going up to Jerusalem, and everything that is written of the Son of man by

Luke 18:31

the prophets will be accomplished.'

●Albert Schweitzer argued that Jesus made a deliberate gamble that did not pay off. According to Schweitzer, Jesus expected God to intervene in history in a dramatic and more or less immediate way, and his visit to Jerusalem was an attempt to force God's hand. But God did not act, and Jesus found himself unexpectedly dying on the cross.

●Others have suggested that Jesus went to Jerusalem simply because he had been to most other parts of Palestine and he wanted to continue his teaching in the religious capital. The fact that he became involved with the political authorities there was just an unexpected and unfortunate miscarriage of justice.

Albert Schweitzer's theory is considered separately later, in chapter six. The other two explanations of Jesus' visit to Jerusalem probably both have some truth in them. No doubt Jesus did want to share his teaching with the people of Judea as well as those in other parts of Palestine – though according to John's Gospel, he may well have done so on more than one occasion before his final visit there. But if we admit that Jesus was aware of his unique relationship with God, we must recognize that he cannot have been ignorant of the growing opposition he was arousing among the religious leaders of his people. A visit to Jerusalem was bound to bring him into direct confrontation with them.

Shortly before his trial and death, Jesus' disciples borrowed a donkey for him to ride into Jerusalem. The cheering crowds who lined the route spread palm leaves on the path and hailed Jesus as king.

If there had previously been any doubt as to who Jesus was claiming to be, his entry into the holy city made it plain. For Jesus entered Jerusalem in a way that amounted to an open declaration that he was the Messiah. He came on an ass, in accordance with a prophecy in the Old Testament book of Zechariah, and the crowd accepted him as their king entering his capital city. Immediately after this he went to the temple. The Messiah was popularly expected to drive the Gentiles out of Jerusalem. Instead Jesus made a symbolic attempt to restore to the Gentiles the only court of the temple in which they were allowed to worship, by throwing out the Jewish bankers who used it as a place of business.

Mark 11:10;
John 12:12–19

Mark 11:15–17

Jesus obviously knew what he was doing, and he can hardly have been surprised to discover that the Jewish leaders soon put a price on his head. He does not even appear to have been surprised when one of his own followers, Judas Iscariot, picked up the money offered by the high priests. He was betrayed by one of his own disciples, arrested, and put on trial for his life.

Jesus on trial

The Gospels appear to report two different trials of Jesus. One was before the Jewish authorities, when he was charged with a religious offence. The other was before the Roman prefect Pontius Pilate, where he was charged with a political offence. Probably the Jews had no authority to carry out a death sentence themselves, and this was why they needed the support of the Roman prefect. But scholars disagree about this, and also about the precise relationship of the different trials to one another. It certainly makes good sense to suppose that Jesus' enemies would make much of the charge of blasphemy before a Jewish court, and then change to a charge of political revolt as the one most likely to secure the death sentence from a Roman official.

John 18:12–14

According to John's Gospel the trial began in the house of Annas, father-in-law of Caiaphas, the high priest. Annas had no official position, but he was a former high priest and a leading Sadducee. He was obviously a man of great influence. Perhaps this trial was an informal investigation held to formulate proper charges. The supreme Jewish court of seventy members, the Sanhedrin, could not officially meet until daylight, but as soon as it was morning the members were summoned to Caiaphas's house.

Mark 14:53–15:1;
John 18:15–27

After Jesus had refused to answer questions about his teaching, and the witnesses had failed to agree in their evidence, Caiaphas asked Jesus a direct question under oath: 'Are you the Christ, the Son of the Blessed?' To this Jesus not only replied 'I am', but added 'and you will see the Son of man sitting at the right hand of Power, and coming with the clouds of heaven'. This confession convinced the whole Sanhedrin that Jesus was guilty. But it can hardly have been the actual claim to be Messiah that condemned him in their eyes, for many of them would certainly have welcomed a political leader who would strike a blow against

Mark 14:61

Mark 14:62

the Romans. What they found shocking and blasphemous was the kind of Messiah Jesus claimed to be: the Son of God coming on the clouds of heaven.

The next step was to bring Jesus before Pilate. Here the charge of blasphemy was dropped. A charge based on Jewish religious scruples would never have appealed to a Roman official. It appears that Jesus' accusers first tried to get Pilate to confirm the Jewish sentence without stating a charge at all. But when Pilate insisted on a charge, three accusations were made:

John 18:28–30
Luke 23:1–2

● Jesus was perverting the Jewish nation. The Jewish leaders, of course, thought of this in terms of perverting the nation from their own brand of Judaism. But they wanted Pilate to think of it in terms of perverting the nation from their loyalty to the emperor.

● Jesus had forbidden the payment of taxes. This was the usual charge made against Zealots.

● Jesus had claimed the title 'king' – something that only the Roman senate could give.

After Pilate had interviewed Jesus, he realized that though Jesus may have upset the sensitivities of the Jews he was not really guilty of any crime under Roman law. If he had claimed to be a king, he was certainly not the kind who could rob Caesar

Luke 23:13–16

of his power. But Pilate also realized that to upset the Jews was a very serious thing. Pilate was caught in a cleverly contrived trap. On the one hand he could acquit Jesus and risk a riot – which would be looked upon very seriously by his own superiors. On the other hand, he could condemn Jesus – and have to live with a guilty conscience for the rest of his life. It was the fear of Jewish riots that eventually forced his hand, as the crowd told him:

John 19:12

'If you let this man go you are no friend of Caesar's.' That was the last thing Pilate could face. He did not want any bad reports of his conduct going to Rome.

John 19:19

So Jesus was crucified. As usual in such cases, a placard was nailed to the cross to show his offence. It said: 'Jesus of Nazareth, the King of the Jews.' The Jews were satisfied that the claim to be king meant a claim to be the Messiah. The Romans were satisfied that Jesus was worthy of death as a revolutionary opposed to their own power. To both crucifixion was a daily occurrence. The only difference between Jesus and the thousands of others who had died that way was that his death took perhaps a little less time, only six hours. It was just as well, for the Jews needed to get rid of his body as fast as they could in order to be ritually pure for the sabbath day, which began at sunset. As soon as he was sealed in a grave they could get on with their own brand of conventional religiosity, giving thanks to God that yet another disturbing influence had been removed from their lives.

Or had he? We have gone as far as we can in understanding the crucifixion in purely historical terms. But for the earliest Christians it was an event of tremendous religious significance as well.

A model of Fort Antonia, which was adjacent to the temple in Jerusalem. It was here that Jesus appeared before Pilate.

Understanding the death of Jesus

The first generation of Christians, like all Christians ever since, were convinced that Jesus' death on the cross had a profound effect on their own lives. They claimed that their own lives had become meaningful in a new and fresh way because of what Jesus did on the cross. They expressed it in many different ways. Some said their sins had been forgiven. Others that they had found peace of mind, or that they had been reconciled to God. But all of them were convinced that what had happened to them as a result of Jesus' death was real – as real as the fact that Jesus had died. Indeed, in one way they knew it better. For whereas they knew about Jesus' death from hearing the reports of other people, each one of them had personally experienced this dynamic change in his or her own life.

But how could such a thing be explained in terms that other people would understand? For if Jesus really was the Son of God, as he claimed to be, there must be something profound and mysterious about such a person dying at all – let alone dying on a cross between two common criminals. This was not something that could be analysed scientifically. It was an event that needed to be described and talked about in pictorial language, using the familiar and ordinary to describe something that was quite extraordinary. So the New Testament uses many different figures of speech to describe what Jesus was actually doing when he died on the cross. He was sacrificed for us. He took the punishment for our sins. He ransomed us. He justified us. Each of these statements, and many others, brings out some of the things the early Christians understood about Jesus' death. But in talking about them we must remember two things.

1 Corinthians 5:7
1 Corinthians 15:3
1 Timothy 2:6
Galatians 2:16

●We must remember that they are pictures, or analogies. Just as it was important not to press too literally the metaphors and images that Jesus used in talking about his own person, so it is important that we recognize the essentially illustrative nature of the New Testament language of his death. Otherwise we can end up in absurdity.

●We must also remember that the theology of the New Testament is more like a landscape than a portrait. Just as a landscape is made up of any number of different items, so the New Testament's explanation of Jesus' death is made up of many different images. We can, if we wish, consider certain parts of the landscape separately and in greater detail than others. But it is always important that we view each detail in its context, in the total picture. Every one of the metaphors used in the New Testament to describe Jesus' death contains an indispensable element of truth. But not one of them by itself contains the whole truth. For that we need to look at the New Testament as a whole, and consider the entire experience and theological understanding of the early church.

It is particularly important for us to try to understand at least five things that the New Testament says about Jesus' death on the cross.

Jesus' death was a battle

The Gospels show the whole of Jesus' life and ministry as a battle against the forces of evil. In his temptations Jesus faced God's enemy, the devil. His miracles were often concerned with releasing men and women from the power of evil. And Jesus saw his whole life as an effort to win a victory over the evil powers that dominate the world, over suffering, sin and death. Paul also regarded the cross as the final and decisive struggle against the powers of evil. In spite of Jesus' apparent defeat, this struggle resulted in a complete victory over sin and death in the resurrection.

Luke 11:21ff.

Colossians 2:8–15

Jesus himself certainly shared this view, for he said of his death: 'Now shall the ruler of this world be cast out.' The picture of the cross as a battle with the forces of evil is one that often appears in Easter hymns. But to understand Jesus' death only in these terms leaves unanswered a very important question. If Jesus triumphed over sin in his cross and resurrection, why is there still so much evil in the world today?

John 12:31

The French theologian Oscar Cullmann has to some extent given an answer to this question by using yet another military picture. He points out that in a war there is usually a decisive moment that settles the outcome (D-Day), but that the final day of victory (V-Day) can often be much later. He describes the day of Jesus' crucifixion as the D-Day of God's warfare against sin. But the V-Day is still to come, at a future date when all things will be subject to Jesus and evil will finally be conquered. This is not the full answer to the problem of evil, as we shall see. But it is a partial answer to it when we think of Jesus' death in terms of a battle.

Jesus' death was an example

Many of the best-known Christian hymns look at Jesus' death as an example. It is based on the fact that on the cross Jesus revealed God's love for the world. Jesus himself never spoke of the cross as a revelation of God's love, but both Paul and John do. They also suggest that as we consider Jesus' sufferings, we ought to be challenged to share such sufferings ourselves. The writer of 1 Peter used this as a powerful motive to encourage Christians who were being persecuted for their beliefs: '. . . to this you have been called, because Christ also suffered for you, leaving you an example, that you should follow his steps.'

Romans 5:8; 1 John 4:10

1 Peter 2:21

This is a concept we find quite easy to understand and accept. We can think of many people who have selflessly given their lives for a good cause. We admire and respect them, and we may even be moved to take up their cause ourselves. But this is obviously not the whole truth about Jesus' death. For the New Testament makes it plain that he was not simply an innocent man dying for a good cause. And if it was in some sense God who was there on the cross, then there is only a very limited sense in which we can take up and share that experience. It is this that makes the death of Jesus quite different from that of all other martyrs.

Jerusalem

Herod the Great transformed
Jerusalem from a well-
populated but unspectacular
centre of religion to an
important provincial city. He
built many public amenities,
including an amphitheatre, and
reconstructed the temple. This
is a reconstruction of the city in
the first century, based on
archaeological excavations.

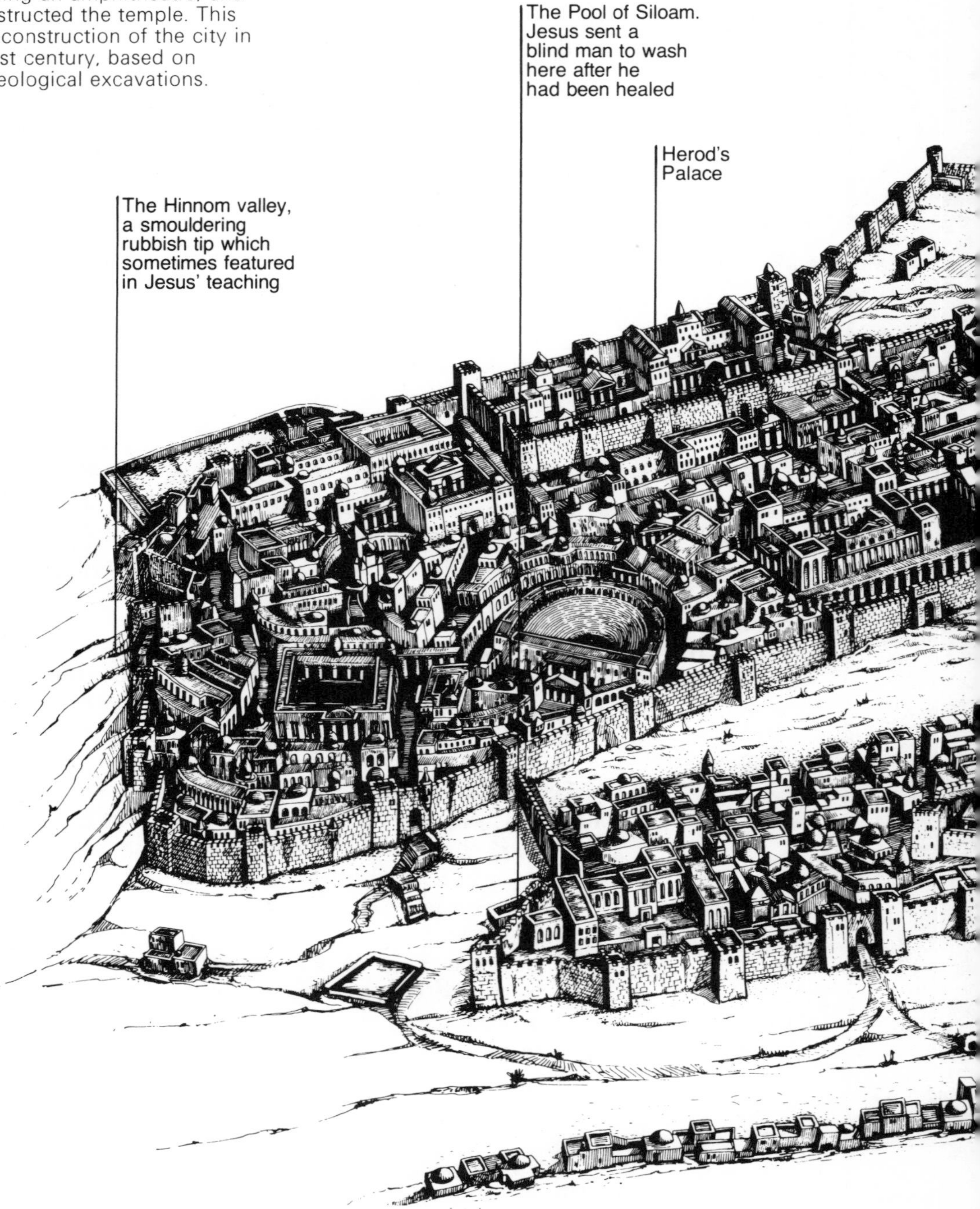

The Pool of Siloam.
Jesus sent a
blind man to wash
here after he
had been healed

Herod's
Palace

The Hinnom valley,
a smouldering
rubbish tip which
sometimes featured
in Jesus' teaching

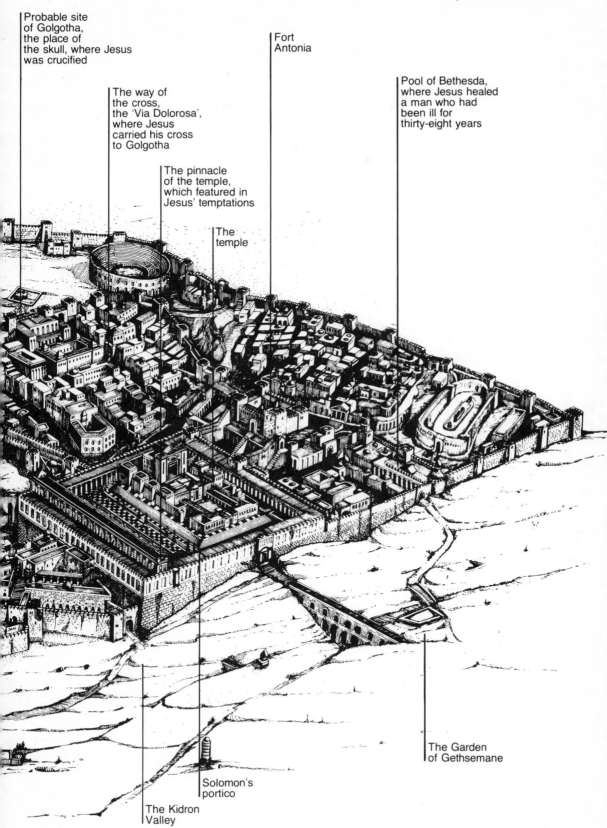

Probable site
of Golgotha,
the place of
the skull, where Jesus
was crucified

Fort
Antonia

Pool of Bethesda,
where Jesus healed
a man who had
been ill for
thirty-eight years

The way of
the cross,
the 'Via Dolorosa',
where Jesus
carried his cross
to Golgotha

The pinnacle
of the temple,
which featured in
Jesus' temptations

The
temple

The Garden
of Gethsemane

Solomon's
portico

The Kidron
Valley

J. PAARTSVELD '74

Jesus' death was a sacrifice

John 1:29
1 Corinthians 5:7
1 Peter 1:19

Leviticus 5:17–19

Exodus 12

It was natural for Jewish people to use the picture of sacrifice. Animals were sacrificed as part of their own religious ritual. Sacrificial language is used in connection with the death of Jesus throughout the New Testament. John the Baptist exclaimed when he saw Jesus: 'Behold the lamb of God . . .' Paul speaks of 'Christ our Passover lamb'. Peter describes Jesus as 'like a lamb without blemish or spot' – and the writer of Hebrews goes to great pains to show that Jesus' death was the fulfilment of the whole sacrificial ritual of Judaism.

Two questions about this picture naturally arise in our minds today: First of all, what was 'the lamb' Jesus was compared with?

Since the New Testament writers were conscious that their sins had been removed through Jesus' death, it is natural to see the background to this language in the 'sin offerings' of the Old Testament. We read about this in the book of Leviticus. But there was also the well-known event of the first Passover, at which the people of Israel were delivered from slavery in Egypt, and in which the sacrifice of a lamb played a large part. Jesus himself seems to have made a deliberate connection between his own death and the annual death of the Passover lambs (see the note on the Last Supper). He reminded his disciples that what he was to do on the cross was to be as great a turning-point in their own lives as the Passover had been in the experience of their nation. So when the New Testament describes Jesus' death in terms of a lamb being sacrificed, there were probably these two images in view: the lamb of the sin offering, and the lamb of the Passover.

The second question is even more important: What did the act of sacrifice mean?

Most of us will never have seen an animal sacrifice. It is something that plays no part in our lives today, and we tend to think of it as a rather barbarous ritual from an uncivilized past. But, however crude it may have been, the important thing to notice is that for people who practise sacrifice its real importance lies in what it represents or symbolizes rather than in what takes place.

The worshipper who made a sacrifice in ancient Israel did so out of a consciousness of being alienated from God because of his sin and disobedience. He knew that he needed to be reconciled to God before life could be full and free. The first step in this process of reconciliation was for the sinner to approach the altar of God with the sacrifice. He then laid his hand on the animal's head, to indicate that he wished to be identified with the animal. So what happened physically and outwardly to the animal was to happen to the sinner inwardly and spiritually. Four things then took place:

● The animal was killed. In this action the sinner was reminded of the consequence of his sin: evil results in death, which is to be separated from fellowship with God who can know no evil. He was declaring that he was fit only for death himself.

John the Baptist described Jesus as 'the Lamb of God that takes away the sin of the world'. The sacrificial lamb, in Old Testament thought, was a means of removing people's guilt and restoring their relationships with God but the New Testament writers believed that Jesus' death rendered such sacrifices unnecessary. Animal sacrifices are still a feature of some religions; this is a sheep killed for a Moslem festival in Pakistan.

● The priest then took the blood of the sacrifice (which now represented the sinner's life given up to God) to the altar. This was the act of reconciliation, or 'atonement' as it is sometimes called. The sin had been dealt with, and God and the sinner had been reunited in fellowship.

● After this, the animal's body was placed on the altar in the temple, as a sign that the forgiven sinner was offering his whole being to God.

● Then, finally, some of the meat still left was eaten in a meal. This indicated that the sinner had been reconciled not only to God but also to his fellow human beings. Fellowship – with man and God – had been restored.

So in the Old Testament the ritual of sacrifice was a symbolic means through which a sinner could be reconciled to God. And this is what the New Testament means by describing Jesus' death as a 'sacrifice'. Indeed, the writer of Hebrews went so far as to say that there was some logical connection between the Old Testament concept and the death of Jesus. The death of Jesus was, he said, the true fulfilment of the Old Testament symbol. His death was the reality, the sacrifices the picture. In Jesus,

Christians can know that they are reconciled to God. He has suffered the ultimate alienation from God that sin brings. Now, too, as people 'made new', Christians must offer themselves to God. This is what Paul meant when he urged Christians 'to *Romans 12:1* present your bodies as a living sacrifice, holy and acceptable to God'.

Jesus' death was a ransom

Mark 10:45

Jesus himself explicitly said that his intention was to be 'a ransom'. This is a figure of speech that we find much easier to understand. We all know of cases where one group of people has been kidnapped by others, and a third party has been forced to pay a ransom to have them released.

The background to this picture in the New Testament was not, of course, the hijacking of aeroplanes or the kidnapping of rich businessmen. The 'ransom' was the price paid to set a slave free. This ransom was often paid by a third party. In the Roman world, the slave and the person who was to pay his ransom went along to the shrine of their local god, and in a religious ceremony the ransom was paid to the slave's owner. Legally, this ceremony was meant to indicate that the slave had been bought by the god, and so he could no longer be owned by men.

This is certainly a very appropriate picture of Jesus' death, for a person set free by Jesus is set free so that he can really and truly belong to God. Throughout the New Testament, it is emphasized that Christians are the property of God. They have *1 Peter 1:18* been 'ransomed from . . . futile ways'. And Paul often reminds his readers: 'you are not your own; you were bought with a price, *1 Corinthians 6:19–20* so glorify God in your body.' This then is perhaps the most comprehensive of all the pictures used in the New Testament to describe what Jesus did on the cross: he paid the price of sin.

Jesus died in our place

1 Peter 2:24

Mark 10:45

To say that Jesus died as a sacrifice, or to pay our ransom, is basically to say that he died in our place. On the cross he did something for us that we are unable to do for ourselves. In 1 Peter, for instance, we are told that Jesus 'bore our sins in his body . . . that we might die to sin and live to righteousness'. And Jesus' statement that he came 'to give his life as a ransom for many' can hardly have any other meaning. But it is important to clarify what we mean by saying that Jesus suffered in our place, for it is so easy to interpret the pictorial language of the New Testament in such a way that it simply does not make sense.

Opponents of the Christian faith have often taken this picture of Jesus' death to imply that we are talking about a kind of celestial law court. In the chair is God the Father, a harsh, authoritarian figure, like Shylock in Shakespeare's *Merchant of Venice*, demanding his pound of flesh. We ought to be in the dock, and because we are alienated from God through our disobedience we deserve the ultimate penalty. But instead Jesus is in the dock, and despite his own perfect obedience he is to become the unfortunate victim of God's harsh and unbending

The cross was used by the Romans to execute criminals. It has become the central symbol of Christianity because Jesus was put to death on a cross. This is a reconstruction of the scene from the film *Jesus Christ Superstar.*

demand that justice must be done.

If we think of the picture in this way, then it is very difficult to accept it as an adequate account of what Jesus did on the cross. Can we, for example, accept that God is less just than a human judge – and how many of us would consider justice to be satisfied if an innocent person were punished in place of a guilty one? How many of us would even say that it is always good for a repenting sinner to escape all punishment? And how can we reconcile this with the fact that God does sometimes allow us to suffer the consequences of our misdeeds – indeed, that we sometimes suffer for no apparent reason at all?

The fact is that if we think about Jesus' death in our place in the context of a law court we have missed the point of much of what Jesus was trying to say. The Jews often regarded God as a terrible and awesome figure, certainly remote from their own lives, and generally more interested in punishment than in forgiveness. But Jesus described God on more than one occasion as a loving Father who cares for every member of the human race. So, when we talk about Jesus suffering instead of us, we should be talking not in the context of a law court but in the context of a family. Jesus' suffering for our sins was not something imposed by a stern judge to fulfil the demands of justice. It was suffering in the way that a person suffers for the wrongdoing of a member of his family. God's justice in dealing with sin is not so much the justice of a judge imposing a sentence in court: it is the justice of a father who is brokenhearted and eager to restore his children to their proper place.

Even so, this picture leaves much unexplained, and the analogy is ultimately inadequate. When one person suffers for another's wrong, his suffering does not blot out or cancel that wrong. But the New Testament is insistent that Jesus' death does in a very real way cancel our sin, so that by it we can be forgiven.

Each of these five ways of talking about Jesus' death has its inadequacies, for they are all only pictures, and to most of us the cross still remains a great mystery. But, despite that, the mystery of Jesus' death and its exact significance does tell us two very important things about God and his relationship with men and women.

●For many people, one of the most pressing problems in life is the problem of evil. If God is really loving and forgiving, why is there so much evil in the world? If God is a forgiving God, we say, then surely he would arrange the universe differently so that the misdeeds of his silly creatures would not cause so much suffering to themselves and to other people. There is no easy answer to such questions. Indeed, I doubt if there is any answer at all. They are part of the frustration of a world that has been so spoiled by sin that Paul could speak of 'the whole creation . . .

Romans 8:18–25 groaning in travail' as it waits to be released from its suffering. But the cross shows us that, even if God does not remove the suffering that followed man's sin and is now so inherent in life, he certainly shares it with us. God was not a harsh judge passing an unreasonable sentence on the innocent Jesus. God himself was actually sharing in the cross the final and extreme consequence of human sinfulness.

●The cross shows us what God's forgiveness costs. It often costs a lot for us to forgive another person, even someone in our own family. Yet many people forget that when they talk about God's forgiveness. The nineteenth-century German poet Heinrich Heine said as he was dying: 'God will forgive me. It's his trade.' And that absurd statement seems to sum up the attitude of many people, who take it for granted that God must automatically forgive them in the end. But forgiveness is not God's trade: it was his crucifixion. God cannot forgive arbitrarily. If he were simply to overlook evil that would deny his very nature. It costs him a lot to forgive even one sinner, and the cost of our forgiveness is seen in the cross: 'He . . . did not spare his own Son, but gave him up for us all.'

Romans 8:32

All these statements are figures of speech, pictures, metaphors, analogies. From our twentieth-century perspective they may seem remote, even irrelevant. We naturally ask ourselves: Why did the first Christians come to think of Jesus' death in these terms? Why couldn't they be content to regard him as a good man dying a bad death? Why did they have to 'theologize' the whole thing, and make it so complicated?

The answer to questions like that is to be found in what they believed to have happened three days after the cross. For they were convinced that Jesus came to life again. If they had not believed that, then the cross would have meant nothing to them. But because of their belief in the resurrection and their experience of the risen Christ at work in their own lives the earliest Christians were totally convinced that Jesus really was who he had claimed to be. On the cross he had fought and won the decisive battle against evil. He had made it possible for God to pardon sinful men and women and receive them into his family. And he was offering them the possibility of a life filled with the reality of God's own presence.

But were they right? This is the crucial question for us today, and one that we must now look at in some detail.

Did the Jews condemn Jesus?

Some people have doubted whether what we have called Jesus' Jewish trial was really a trial at all. The problem is that we have no contemporary evidence about Jewish customs and practice at this time. Our only knowledge of the subject comes from the Jewish law book, the *Mishnah*, which dates in its present form from about AD 200.

The *Mishnah* contains traditions that are much earlier than the time when it was written down, but it is impossible to know how far these regulations were in force at the time of Jesus.

Judged according to these later standards, we would certainly have to conclude that a trial such as that which the Gospels describe was very irregular. The leading members of the Sanhedrin were the prosecution as well as the judges, and they had already been involved in the plot to have Jesus arrested. The trial appears to have begun with no definite charges, and no evidence was called for the defence even though the prosecution witnesses contradicted each other. Moreover, two very important rules of later Jewish law were ignored completely. These laid down that twenty-four hours had to elapse between a death sentence and its execution; and that a trial should not be held on the day before the Jewish holy day, the sabbath.

Because of these irregularities most Jewish writers have insisted that there is no historical truth in the Gospel narratives at this point. But there is no convincing reason why we should regard this trial as fiction. Though the Jews had very little real influence over their political society, we know that they were always keen to apply their own law whenever they could. This was not only a kind of psychological prop to the Jewish leaders: it was also a useful means of gaining the support of the mass of the Jewish people for their policies. A death sentence passed on Jesus under Jewish law by a religious court would certainly have influenced the ordinary people against him, and it might even have been expected to exert a certain moral pressure on the Roman judge who was to have the final word.

It is, however, not very likely that this Jewish trial was as illegal as it can be made to appear if compared with the rules of the

This slave chain dates from Roman times. One of the images used in the Gospels to explain Jesus' death is that he 'redeemed' those who were 'enslaved' to their wrong ways of living.

Mishnah. We have already seen that we cannot be sure that these rules were in operation at the time. But it is also significant that, of all the charges made by the first Christians against the Jews, they never accused them of breaking the law in order to have Jesus executed. There is also the fact that the members of the Sanhedrin were not, by and large, rogues and scoundrels. Most of them would be men of high moral ideals – people such as Paul before his conversion. Perhaps they met with their minds already made up, and to that extent were unable to give Jesus a fair trial. But they were genuinely convinced that their view of things was right, and that Jesus was nothing but a messianic pretender and a trouble-maker.

The Last Supper

All four Gospels give an account of what is generally called the 'Last Supper' of Jesus. They relate how Jesus acted as host to his disciples in a room loaned by a friend in Jerusalem, on the evening before he was crucified (Matthew 26:20–30; Mark 14:12–26; Luke 22:7–39; John 13:1–30). The first written account of this meal is contained not in the Gospels but in the writings of Paul in 1 Corinthians 11:23–26. But his account of the Last Supper agrees in its main details with the stories told in the synoptic Gospels – Matthew, Mark and Luke. John's Gospel gives a fuller account of some aspects of the meal, and includes the story – not mentioned by the other Gospel writers – of how Jesus washed his disciples' feet. At the same time, John omits to mention the central feature of the other accounts, the institution of the Lord's Supper.

At this last meal with his disciples, Jesus followed the normal Jewish custom and gave thanks to God for the meal. He then proceeded to break the bread that was on the table, and handed it to his disciples, saying, 'This is my body which is for you. Do this in remembrance of me' (1 Corinthians 11:24; compare Matthew 26:26; Mark 14:22; Luke 22:19). Then he handed them a cup of wine, telling them: 'This cup is the new covenant in my blood. Do this, as often as you drink it, in remembrance of me' (1 Corinthians 11:25; compare Matthew 26:27–28; Mark 14:24; Luke 22:20).

The new covenant

The disciples, like all other Jews, would be quite familiar with the idea of a 'covenant'. The Last Supper took place at about the same time as the Jewish people were preparing to celebrate one of their most important religious festivals, the Passover. In the Passover festival, the Jews celebrated and recalled the inauguration of God's 'covenant' with their ancestors. They remembered how, long ago, God had delivered Israel from slavery in Egypt, and in gratitude for his deliverance Israel had given her obedience and devotion to God (Exodus 12–23). Ever since that time they had regarded themselves as 'the people of the covenant'. And the 'covenant' was simply the fact that God had done something for his people, and they had responded in love and obedience.

When Jesus compared his own death to the inauguration of a 'new covenant', he was saying to his disciples that through him God was performing a new act of deliverance, and that a similar promise of loyalty and devotion would be required of those who share in its benefits. The new society makes demands of those who enjoy it, and Paul says that Christians ought to repeat this meal regularly as a constant reminder of the fact that their new life of freedom was won by Jesus on the cross. Because of that, they owe him their unfailing loyalty and obedience.

Paul, of course, was not intending to give a historical account of the Last Supper; he mentions it more or less incidentally. His main intention was to emphasize that the Lord's Supper (as it came to be called) was a continuing reminder to Christians of how much they owe to God. But in the case of the Gospel accounts of the Last Supper, the matter is much more complex. They were intending to give some sort of historical explanation of the Last Supper, and we are therefore justified in asking historical questions of them. The most important of these is the question of whether the Last Supper was a celebration of the Jewish Passover, or whether Jesus was observing some other kind of feast with his disciples.

Two main questions are involved. First: *Do Jesus' actions at the Last Supper suggest that he was observing the Passover with his disciples?*

Here we shall restrict our discussion to what Jesus and his disciples actually did. The question of what the Gospel writers *thought* he was doing is dealt with separately.

Within the Gospel stories it is possible to find arguments both for and against the idea that Jesus was observing the Jewish Passover. The following facts seem to be in favour.

● The meal of the Last Supper was eaten in Jerusalem, and not at Bethany where Jesus was staying (Mark 14:13; Luke 22:10). With growing opposition from the Jewish religious leaders, this can hardly have been a sensible time for Jesus to make unnecessary excursions into Jerusalem. But if Jesus was intending to share in the Passover Festival, he would have to do so, since the Passover feast could only be eaten within the walls of the city. This could explain the emphasis on the disciples' concern to find a room in a suitably located house (Matthew 26:17–19; Mark 14:12–16; Luke 22:7–13).

● According to John 13:23–25, Jesus and the disciples took their meal reclining on couches. This was not the invariable Jewish custom, but it was obligatory at the celebration of the Passover. The instructions for the Passover (the Passover *Haggadah*) say: 'On all other nights we eat and drink either sitting or reclining, but on this night we all recline.' The *Mishnah* adds that even the poorest person in Israel must not eat the Passover feast except while reclining (*Pes.* 10:1).

● The meal took place at night. This was also a distinctive custom associated with the Passover. The usual custom was to eat the main meal of the day in the late afternoon. But the Passover was always at night, the time when the events it commemorated had taken place.

● The dipping of pieces of food into a sauce (Mark 14:20; John 13:26) was definitely a custom used only at the Passover. The Passover *Haggadah* does not refer to bread being served in this way. But it does say: 'all other nights we do not dip . . . even once, but on this night twice.'

● The disciples sang a hymn before they left the room (Mark 14:26). And the singing of the so-called 'Hallel' psalms (Psalms 113–18) was a special feature that marked the end of the Passover meal.

Despite all these similarities between the Last Supper and the Passover, however, there are other parts of the Gospel stories that suggest the Last Supper was not a Passover feast:

● It is most unlikely that Jesus would have been judged, condemned and crucified in the middle of such an important feast as the Passover. In particular, it is unlikely that a Roman governor would have been so foolish as to take the great risk involved in the public execution of a popular figure at a time when Jerusalem was crowded with pilgrims. To have done so would have defiled the day of the great festival, and could easily have sparked off a riot among the Jews.

● It would have been against Jewish Passover laws for Jesus to be tried in the middle of a festival. All forms of work were prohibited on the Passover, and this included the work of the Sanhedrin. In addition, the Jewish leaders would have risked ritual defilement by having anything to do with Pilate at this time (John 18:28). The whole business of the trials, and especially the element of urgency about them, is better explained if the Passover was about to begin than if it was already taking place.

● A number of circumstantial details do not seem to fit in with the assumption that Jesus was keeping the Passover. There is, for example, no mention of a lamb or of unleavened bread, though these were the most important items of the Passover meal. It would also be surprising to find Simon of Cyrene coming in from the fields at the height of such an important festival when work was strictly forbidden (Mark 15:21). It is also surely significant that the earliest Christians observed the Lord's Supper once a week and not annually, as we may have expected them to do had it originally been a Passover celebration. Taken by themselves small details like this would not prove very much. But when considered along with the other evidence they can be given some weight in the argument.

Faced with these apparently conflicting pieces of evidence, equally reputable scholars have made different judgements. The German theologian Joachim Jeremias, for example, has argued strongly in favour of the view that Jesus was actually keeping the Jewish Passover. Others have argued just as strongly that Jesus was not keeping the Passover. They suggest it was a *Kiddush*, a type of feast with which pious Jews often approached the beginning of the weekly sabbath. It has also been understood as a feast of a more general nature known as a *Haburah*. Such feasts are well-known in later Judaism, and still form a part of modern Jewish observances. But we have very little evidence to show that such feasts existed at the time of Jesus, and even less to show what may have taken place at them.

So the problem remains. If we were to make a judgement solely on the basis of the evidence we have reviewed so far, the balance of the argument seems to be slightly in favour of the view that the Last Supper was not a Passover meal.

This stepped road in Jerusalem dates from the century before Jesus, and leads to the garden of Gethsemane.

But before we claim this as the final answer to the problem, we need to ask another crucial question: *Did the Gospel writers think Jesus was observing the Passover with his disciples?*

This is the really awkward question, for the three synoptic Gospels say quite definitely that the Last Supper was a Passover meal – though, as we have seen, not every detail of their description of the meal fits in with this assumption (Matthew 26:18; Mark 14:12; Luke 22:15). On the other hand, John says equally clearly that the Last Supper was not the Passover, but took place on the day before the Jewish festival – yet here, again, not every part of his description of the supper fits in with this statement (John 13:1, 18:28).

This is one of the most difficult questions that New Testament scholars have had to try to resolve, and it is not possible to give any simple answer. There is no possibility of explaining it from the text of the Gospels themselves, for Matthew, Mark and Luke all say quite categorically that Jesus was keeping the Passover, and John says quite clearly that he was not.

Twenty years ago it would have been easy for scholars to solve the problem simply by saying that John made a mistake – and there are some scholars who still take that approach today. But they are now very much in the minority. For it is increasingly recognized that even if John's Gospel was one of the latest books of the New Testament to be written, it is by no means a later fabrication of the life and teachings of Jesus. Indeed, as we shall see in section three, the accounts preserved by John are now generally believed to contain authentic, reliable and early traditions.

What, then, can we say about a problem like this? First of all it will be helpful for us to understand the precise nature of the difficulty. Jewish chronology is notoriously difficult to understand, and in this case the matter is made more complex for us by the fact that the Jewish day begins at sunset, whereas the Roman day (like our own) began at midnight. So, for example, the weekly Jewish sabbath begins at sunset on Friday evening and ends at sunset on Saturday evening. But for the sake of convenience we would normally say that Saturday is the Jewish sabbath.

Now the Gospels all agree that Jesus was crucified on a Friday afternoon, and his resurrection from the grave was discovered on the Sunday morning. In between this was the sabbath, which was always a holy day for the Jews. But on the particular week that Jesus was crucified, the Passover was also being celebrated, and this in itself was a specially holy day. Putting together this information with what we learn from the Gospels, it seems that the synoptic writers thought that the Friday was the Passover Festival, whereas John believed that the Passover fell on the sabbath in that particular year.

sectarian movements within first-century Judaism.

One of the most striking differences between the Essenes of Qumran and the Pharisees in Jerusalem, for example, was on the question of their religious calendar. The normal Jewish calendar was based on calculations related to the movements of the moon, whereas the commune at Qumran appears to have used another calendar as well, based on calculations about the movements of the sun.

The same calendar features in the Jewish *Book of Jubilees*, and according to it the Passover meal was *always* on the day that began in the Tuesday evening. If Jesus used this same calendar, then he could

	Synoptics	John
Thursday		
evening	Passover Last Supper Arrest	Last Supper Arrest
Friday		
morning	Trials and	Trials and
afternoon	crucifixion	crucifixion
evening	Beginning of sabbath	Beginning of sabbath and Passover
Saturday	Sabbath	Sabbath and Passover
Sunday	Resurrection	Resurrection

So there is no problem with the statements made about Jesus himself. The difficulty is concerned with the chronology of the Jewish religious festivals.

We must beware of giving too easy an answer to this question. There is no answer that could claim to be the generally accepted consensus of opinion. But a number of scholars have recently tried to explain the awkward distinction between John and the synoptics by supposing that the two traditions were using different calendars, and that what was in one calendar the day of the Passover would be another day in a different calendar.

Nowadays we would find it impossible to believe that there could be different opinions about something as basic as the date. But in the context of first-century Judaism this is not such a far-fetched explanation as it sounds. The Jews were constantly speculating on calendrical calculations, and their differing outlooks on the matter are to a large extent reflected in the existence of the various

have celebrated a real Passover with his disciples on the *Tuesday* evening, but still have been crucified as the official Passover was about to begin on the Friday evening. This is the ingenious solution proposed by the French scholar Annie Jaubert. But it still leaves unanswered a number of vital questions:

● We have no reason to suppose that Jesus did in fact use anything other than the official calendar. He appears to have moved in the mainstream of Judaism rather than in any sectarian movements, and is often depicted taking part in the worship of the synagogue. If, as John suggests, he had often attended the great Jewish religious festivals in Jerusalem, it would be more natural to suppose that he kept the same calendar as the Jerusalem authorities – otherwise he would not have attended the festivals at the right times (John 7: 1–39). What is more, Jesus often appears to have been in conflict with the Pharisees about the observance of religious festivals like the sabbath. He was often accused of doing things that were not allowed on the sabbath. Yet he never claimed that he did them because he used a different calendar. He explained his actions by reference to the fact that he believed himself to be 'lord even of the sabbath' (Mark 2:28).

● The Passover lambs had to be ritually slaughtered in the temple, and this would obviously be done according to the official calendar. It is therefore difficult to see how the disciples could have had a lamb available in Jerusalem on the Tuesday evening – yet without the lamb, there could be no Passover meal.

● This alternative calendar would mean that Jesus was held in custody for two days before his crucifixion. It is difficult to reconcile this with the unanimous testimony of all four Gospels that the trials took place in a hurry so that Jesus could be condemned and executed before the beginning of the Jewish sabbath.

It therefore seems to me that this theory rests on rather shaky foundations. It may well be, of course, that new evidence to strengthen it could be discovered in the Qumran texts or elsewhere. But in the present state of our knowledge it is difficult to accept this explanation of the difference between the synoptic Gospels and John.

A more likely explanation has been put forward by the American scholar Massey H. Shepherd Jr. He has suggested that John's Gospel was written from the perspective of the Jews of Palestine, and that they celebrated the Passover on the sabbath in the year in question. Mark, however, followed by Matthew and Luke, was following the customs of the Jews of the Dispersion, and on their reckoning the Passover was held on the Friday in the year that Jesus died.

Many more speculative theories have been advanced on the matter, and it could be that the wisest answer to the problem is that given by the Australian scholar Dr Leon Morris, who writes: 'I do not see how with our present knowledge we can be dogmatic. But on the whole it seems most probable that the explanation is to be found in calendrical confusion.'

Of course, we must not allow this one detail to hide the fact that all four Gospels are in complete agreement on everything else. Nor must we conclude that because we know of no answer at present, that means there is no answer. But if an explanation lies in the speculations of the Jewish leaders about their calendar, it will be a long and tedious process before a widely acceptable answer is found.

In any case, we will never find a full explanation of the Last Supper if we only ask what sort of Jewish feast Jesus was keeping. What Jesus was doing at the Last Supper fits in with many Jewish customs. We would expect that anyway, since he and his disciples were Jews. But the precise nature of what he was doing cannot be fitted exactly into any specific occasion in the Jewish religious calendar. It seems unlikely, for the reasons already given, that the disciples were celebrating the Jewish Passover. But at the same time it seems obvious that their Last Supper with Jesus followed fairly closely the formal setting of the Passover meal.

Perhaps we ought to leave a little more room for the creative originality of Jesus himself than most scholars are prepared to do. In the nature of the case the Passover lamb was absent, but in this supper that was of little importance. Jesus knew that God was already providing a lamb, and he was here offering himself in symbol to his disciples as 'the Lamb of God who takes away the sin of the world' (John 1:29). The lamb of God was Jesus himself, and he knew that he was to be crucified for the sin of the world. It was no coincidence that he was crucified at the very same time as the symbols of God's past deliverance were being sacrificed in the temple courts.

But what Jesus did on the cross was not merely a re-interpretation of an ancient ritual. God was about to do something quite different and revolutionary, that would both sum up and supersede the events associated with the first Passover. The new society was being inaugurated and in the Last Supper, surrounded by the nucleus of this society, Jesus was symbolically offering himself for their freedom in the bread and the wine. And so these things became within the church the external symbols of that deliverance from sin and its consequences which Jesus' death as God's chosen Son was to accomplish.

Chapter 5 The resurrection

Jesus prayed in the garden of Gethsemane shortly before his arrest.

ALL THE New Testament writers agree that Jesus was raised to life on the third day after his death. Our reaction to this claim will of course depend to a large extent on our basic presuppositions about the supernatural. If we believe that such things as the renewal of a dead person are impossible, we will have to find some other explanation for what the first Christians thought was the resurrection of Jesus. If we are willing to accept the possibility of supernatural occurrences, we will think it worthwhile to examine critically some of the claims of the New Testament.

In this book we have taken the statements made in the documents as they stand; we have taken belief in the supernatural as a viable option. This does not of course mean that we necessarily assume that everything claimed about Jesus can simply be accepted by reference to our presuppositions. But it does mean that we can examine the evidence without any fear of being embarrassed by the results of our investigation – whatever those results may turn out to be.

In the case of the resurrection, the most striking thing about it is that the earliest Christians were completely convinced that the resurrection event, or complex of events, was a real, historical happening that had taken place in their own world, and which had made a profound influence on their own lives. We have already seen that it is not easy to know just how widespread was belief in the virgin birth of Jesus. We do not know, for instance, what Paul knew about it. We certainly do know that neither he nor anyone else ever claimed that belief in the virgin birth was an indispensable part of being a Christian.

But the resurrection was a different matter altogether. Paul spoke for the whole of the early church when he declared that if the reality of Jesus' resurrection was denied the Christian faith would be emptied of its meaning: 'If Christ has not been raised, **1 Corinthians 15:17** your faith is futile and you are still in your sins.' Because of this conviction, Paul goes on in the same passage to give a list of witnesses who could verify that Jesus had come to life again. He obviously thought of the resurrection event as something that could be attested by witnesses – an outward, public happening rather than a private religious experience. Yet it is very striking that the New Testament nowhere provides witnesses to the actual act of rising again, only to the results of that act in the appearances of the risen Jesus, and the fact that his tomb was found empty.

The evidence itself can be arranged in four parts.

The belief of the early church

The earliest evidence we have for the resurrection almost certainly goes back to the time immediately after the resurrection event is alleged to have taken place. This is the evidence contained in the early sermons in the Acts of the Apostles. Of course, these are now contained in a document that was compiled in its present form at least thirty years after the death of Jesus, and perhaps as much as fifty years later. But there can be no doubt that in the first few chapters of Acts its author has preserved material from very early sources.

Scholars have discovered that the language used in speaking about Jesus in these early speeches in Acts is quite different from that used at the time when the book was compiled in its final form. It is also quite different from even the letters of Paul, which were certainly written long before the book of Acts. So we may be reasonably certain that here we have very early sources.

The early speeches show a largely Jewish type of Christianity, holding a set of simply expressed beliefs about Jesus, and providing a generally accurate picture of what really happened in the first days of the church. According to this picture, the central feature of the message of the early Christian church was the story of Jesus himself – how he had come to fulfil God's promises, how he had died on the cross, and how he had come back to life again. The message of the first Christians was so consistent that Professor C. H. Dodd was able to find a regular pattern of statements that were made about Jesus from the very earliest times. He called this pattern of statements the *kerygma*, a Greek word meaning 'the declaration'. Every authentic account of the Christian message contained these statements:

- Jesus has fulfilled the Old Testament promises.
- God was at work in his life, death and resurrection.
- Jesus has now been exalted to heaven.
- The Holy Spirit has been given to the church.
- Jesus will soon return in glory.
- Men and women who hear the message must respond to its challenge.

If we removed the resurrection from this *kerygma*, most of it would no longer make sense. The whole existence of the early church was based on the belief that Jesus was no longer dead, but was alive.

It also seems likely from the evidence in Paul's letters as well as from Acts, that the recognized qualification for an apostolic preacher was that he had seen the risen Jesus. This was explicitly

Acts 1 : 21–22

Galatians 1 : 11–17

made a condition when the apostles came to appoint a successor to Judas Iscariot, and Paul also claimed that his own vision of Jesus on the road to Damascus gave him the same status as that of the older apostles.

The evidence of Paul

1 Corinthians 15

The second main piece of evidence for the resurrection of Jesus is given to us by Paul himself. If there is room for differing opinions on the importance of the evidence of Acts, there is no such room in the case of Paul's evidence. He was certainly writing this letter no more than twenty-five years after Jesus was crucified, and his statements may well form the earliest piece of evidence for belief that Jesus had risen again. If we read 1 Corinthians 15, and look at its context, we see that Paul's main intention there was not to give a reasoned argument for believing in the resurrection of Jesus. He was in fact trying to help his Christian readers to overcome a specific set of problems that had arisen in their local church. The information he gives us about how Jesus rose from the dead is more or less accidental. This makes it all the more impressive, for he reminds the Corinthians that what he says is something they have always known. And even though he does so in just a few sentences, he shows that at a very early date Christians, even in Greece, were quite familiar with the full story of how Jesus had died and come back to life again.

1 Corinthians 15 : 6

1 Corinthians 15 : 7–8

In this account Paul refers to an occasion when the risen Jesus was seen by more than 500 disciples at one time, most of whom were still alive when he wrote and could confirm what he said. He also mentions an appearance to James, the brother of Jesus, and includes his own conversion encounter with the risen Lord among these resurrection appearances. The Gospels say nothing about any of these appearances of the risen Jesus. Yet they were probably written later than Paul's letter to Corinth! The fact of Jesus' resurrection must have been considered to be so widely believed that the people who wrote the Gospel stories did not

Paul wrote to the Christians at Corinth about twenty-five years after Jesus' death, explaining the significance of the resurrection.

even think it important to marshal *all* the evidence for it. As with the rest of their narratives, they used only a small selection of the material that was at their disposal.

The Gospel traditions

When we think of the resurrection, we naturally think first of the stories found at the end of each of the four Gospels. There are certain distinctive features about these stories.

● They all emphasize two main facts: that the grave of Jesus was found empty, and that the risen Jesus was seen by different people on several different occasions. Both these pieces of evidence are important. By itself, the fact of the empty grave would prove nothing except that Jesus' body was not there. Without the empty grave, the visions would prove nothing objective, though they might tell us something about the psychology of the disciples. But the combination of the two facts, if they are indeed correct, would be strong evidence in support of the claim that Jesus was alive.

● If we read right through the Gospels, we notice that by comparison with many of the other stories about Jesus, the stories about his resurrection are told very simply. They contain no symbolism requiring special insight to understand. There are no allusions to the Old Testament. Nor do they make any attempt to bring out the theological significance of the events they describe. If we compare them in this respect with, say, the accounts of how Jesus was baptized, the contrast is very marked indeed.

Why do the accounts differ?

Despite the fact that the information given in the Gospels is told in a simple way, the Gospel accounts are not easy to reconcile with one another. Though many people have tried, no one has really been successful in producing an 'agreed version' of how it all happened. It is unlikely that anyone ever will. Throughout their work, the Gospel writers were selective. They used only those stories and teachings of Jesus that would be helpful to their first readers. That is one of the reasons why we have four different Gospels. This process of selection was clearly applied to the resurrection stories, as we can see from the fact that Paul had some pieces of information not mentioned by any of the Gospels.

At first sight, this may appear to be an argument against the resurrection having happened at all. But in fact it is a strong argument on the other side. Eye witnesses often give very different accounts of what they have seen, especially when they see things that do not fit in with their concept of life. The disciples themselves no more expected a dead person to come to life again than you or I would. According to Mark 9:9-10 they had no idea what 'resurrection' could possibly mean: it was something quite alien to their way of thinking. So we need not be surprised that the disciples did not tell a logical and coherent story. The story of someone rising from the dead would be much more difficult to believe if all four Gospels had given exactly the same account. Yet despite minor discrepancies in detail, all our accounts are agreed on the main parts of the story. In all of them the tomb is empty and Jesus appears to the disciples.

In Mark, the earliest Gospel, the account ends at 16:8, and what follows in some English versions as 16:9-20 is generally considered to be a later addition to an originally mutilated or unfinished book. In this account, we are told that some women who came to the grave on the Sunday morning to finish the process of embalming Jesus' body found that the stone slab used as a door to the rock tomb had been rolled back. They were terrified by the sight of a young man in white sitting inside. This 'young man' said, 'Do not be amazed; you seek Jesus of Nazareth, who was crucified. He has risen, he is not here; see the place where they laid him. But go, tell his disciples and Peter that he is going before you to Galilee; there you will see him, as

After his crucifixion, Jesus was placed in a tomb carved from the solid rock. Tombs of this kind often had a heavy stone which could be rolled across the entrance.

he told you' (Mark 16:6–7). The women ran terrified from the graveyard, and because of their fear they told no one of what they had seen and heard.

In Luke, two disciples walking home to the village of Emmaus met the risen Jesus without recognizing him. They spoke of women visiting the grave and seeing a vision of angels who assured them that Jesus was alive (Luke 24:22–24). No reference is made there to the message about Galilee. Perhaps the women did not deliver the message about Galilee for the simple reason stated by Mark: they were afraid to go back there, for

they thought that the king of that area, Herod Antipas, would now be ready to get rid of any of Jesus' followers who were found there.

Matthew repeats Mark's account with some additional details, such as the great earthquake on the Sunday morning, and the terror of the guards at the graveyard (Matthew 28:1–4). The women left the grave in a mixed mood of fear and joy, and they were met by Jesus himself, who repeated the message about going to Galilee (Matthew 28:5–10). According to Matthew, the disciples appear to have obeyed this instruction at once, and on a mountain in Galilee Jesus gave them the commission to preach the gospel to all nations and to make them his disciples (Matthew 28:16–20). This appearance of Jesus does not seem to be the same as the ascension story told by Luke. Though Jesus made some similar statements, the ascension took place not in Galilee but in or near Jerusalem (Luke 24:44–53, Acts 1:6–11). Matthew brings the story begun by Mark to its logical conclusion: Jesus' appearance in Galilee and commission to the disciples to proclaim the good news about him.

Luke's story has certain differences from Mark's: there were two angels in the tomb, and Galilee is mentioned, not as the place where Jesus would meet the disciples later, but as the place where he had originally foretold his death and resurrection (Luke 24:1–11). When the women told the disciples their story, it was not believed. In some old manuscripts of Luke, there is at this point a story of how Peter and John visited the tomb to confirm what the women reported. But this is probably only a later effort to harmonize Luke's story with the incident recorded in John 20:1–10. After telling of how Jesus met the two disciples on the road to Emmaus, and then all the disciples in a room in Jerusalem (Luke 24:13–43), Luke goes on to record the ascension on the road to Bethany, as if it followed immediately after the resurrection (Luke 24:44–53). But in Acts he makes it clear that the ascension took place after an interval of forty days (Acts 1:3). He does not mention an appearance in Galilee.

John's Gospel, on the other hand, describes appearances of Jesus both in Jerusalem and in Galilee. Of the women described in the other Gospels as having discovered the empty grave, only Mary Magdalene is mentioned in John (20:1). But the fact that she uses the plural pronoun 'we' in describing the event to Peter suggests that others may have been with her (John 20:2). They found the tomb empty and returned to tell the disciples. Peter and John then went to the tomb and found the grave clothes lying undisturbed – proof that the tomb had not been robbed (John 20:3–10). At this point Mary saw two angels in the tomb and was greeted by Jesus, whom she mistook for the gardener (John 20:11–18). An account follows of two appearances to the disciples in Jerusalem. During the first of these appearances Jesus breathed on them and gave them the Holy Spirit (John 20:19–29). The last chapter of John, which many scholars regard as a later addition, though by the same author, describes Jesus' appearance to the disciples on the shore of Lake Galilee and how he had breakfast with them before re-commissioning Peter.

The disciples

The fourth, and final piece of evidence for the resurrection event is the indisputable fact that a thoroughly disheartened band of disciples, who should by all the rules of historical probability have been depressed and disillusioned by their master's crucifixion, were in the space of seven weeks transformed into a strong band of courageous witnesses, and the nucleus of a constantly growing church. The central fact of their witness was that Jesus was alive and active, and they had no hesitation in attributing the change in themselves to what had happened as a result of his rising from the dead. They themselves were obviously convinced that this was what had actually happened. For the resurrection was not just something they talked about: it was something they were willing to die for. And men and women are not prepared to die for something unless they are totally convinced of its truth.

Facts and faith about the resurrection

So much, then, for the evidence. What are we to make of it? To understand its importance, we must remember three things.

● There is no evidence that the risen Jesus appeared to anyone apart from his own followers, though it is possible that he may have done so. Those who wrote the Gospels were writing for a specific readership – in every case a Christian readership. Their first interest was in what happened when Christians met their risen Lord.

● Evidence about somebody who appeared and disappeared in a room with closed doors is obviously not the kind of evidence that historians are used to dealing with, and it does not fit into the ordinary rules of evidence.

● The fact that Mary Magdalene, the two disciples on the road to Emmaus, and the disciples in the boat on Lake Galilee failed to recognize Jesus, though they knew him well and had seen him only a few days before, suggests that his physical appearance must have changed in a way that would certainly be confusing to any ordinary witness in giving evidence.

What, then, has our examination of the evidence established? We can say with absolute certainty that the earliest church believed that Jesus had come back to life again. The disciples and their followers knew that something had happened to change their lives after the crucifixion of their master, and they explained this change by the fact that he had risen from the dead. Every reader of the New Testament must accept this, for the fact of the change in the disciples' lives is established beyond all reasonable doubt. But to speak of the 'resurrection faith' is one thing; to speak of a 'resurrection fact' is quite another. The relationship of facts to faith is discussed more fully in the last chapter of section three. Here we need only note that there must have been *something* we can call 'the resurrection fact' that created the disciples' 'resurrection faith'. But what was this? Several possible explanations spring to mind.

The Mount of Olives overlooked the city of Jerusalem. It was the site of Jesus' last resurrection appearance, his ascension.

The 'resurrection fact' was a subjective experience

Our natural reaction to the evidence about the resurrection is to suppose that the so-called 'resurrection appearances' were purely subjective. The pious might call them visions; psychologists

Disheartened and upset by Jesus' sudden trial and execution, some of his closest followers went back to Galilee, and returned to their old job of fishing. They used nets cast from a boat; here a modern Galilean fisherman draws in the nets he has thrown from the shore.

would be more inclined to call them hallucinations. If we could assume that this is what happened, it would solve the problem. But there are many facts against such an explanation.

●The fact that the tomb was empty, and that neither friend nor enemy produced the body of Jesus is so strongly emphasized in the Gospels that it must be accounted for. The Jews and Romans obviously had a vested interest in producing a body, for that would have squashed the Christian message once and for all. So presumably they had not taken it. The disciples, on the other hand, were prepared to stake their lives on the fact that Jesus was alive – and it would have been psychologically impossible for them to do that if they had themselves taken the body away and buried it somewhere else.

●Although an individual experience like that of Peter or James might reasonably be regarded as subjective, and an appearance to a crowd of 500 might sound like a mass hallucination, an encounter such as that on the road to Emmaus, with the absence of excitement and the gradual recognition of the stranger by two people, has all the marks of an authentic account. The statements that the risen body could be touched, that the risen Jesus ate food with his disciples, and that he breathed on them, show that the disciples were convinced that they were in contact with a real physical body and not a vision.

●Unlike the other disciples, Paul was what we might call psychically experienced. He writes of having had visions and revelations of an ecstatic nature on several occasions. But he placed his Damascus road experience in a different category altogether. It was quite distinctive, to be compared only with the appearances of the risen Jesus to the other disciples. Encounters with the risen Jesus were apparently a unique kind of experience – neither purely subjective like dreams, nor purely objective like the facts observed by scientists, but with some of the characteristics of both.

1 Corinthians 14:18;
2 Corinthians 12:1—4

The 'resurrection fact' was a theological invention

It has been argued that the 'resurrection faith' arose because the disciples saw some theological reason that required it. Because they believed Jesus to be God's Messiah it would be natural for someone who claimed this position to rise from the dead. But this explanation cannot be accepted either.

●For one thing, we have no evidence from any source at all to suggest that the Messiah was expected to rise from the dead. The Jews expected the Messiah to kill other people! If he suffered and died himself, then he was not the kind of Messiah most Jews wanted to know about.

●The Old Testament expresses a very negative attitude to the idea of resurrection, and many Jews simply did not believe it was possible. The disciples themselves appear not to have known what it was earlier in the ministry of Jesus.

Mark 9:9–10

●It is also difficult to see how the idea of the resurrection can have come from an interpretation of Old Testament expectations, since the resurrection stories are completely lacking in Old Testament quotations. In this respect there is a sharp contrast with the stories of the crucifixion, which are full of such quotations.

Many other more fanciful suggestions have been made from time to time to account for the 'resurrection fact'. But the overwhelming weight of all the evidence suggests that, however it might be described in scientific language, the 'resurrection fact' was a real, historical event. No other hypothesis gives an adequate account of *all* the evidence.

What does the resurrection mean?

To talk of describing the 'resurrection fact' in scientific language takes us beyond the categories of thought of the first disciples. One of the most striking things about the evidence of the New Testament is that the disciples had no interest at all in probing the whys and wherefores of the 'resurrection fact'. They knew that it was a real fact, because of their own experience of Jesus Christ and the evidence of the empty tomb – and that was all they needed to know. So we have no description in any of our records of *how* the resurrection actually took place. Some Christians in the second century regarded this as a deficiency in the New Testament, and produced their own vivid descriptions of what the body of Jesus looked like, how it came out of the grave, and how those who saw it were affected.

But for the first witnesses such details were not the main focus of interest. For them, the resurrection was not just a happy ending to the story of Jesus. It was the natural climax of the whole of his life, and the vindication of the high claims he had made for himself during his ministry. It was also a guarantee that the life and teaching of Jesus was not just an interesting chapter in the history of human thought, but was the way through which men and women could come to know God. This is why the fact that Jesus was alive became the central part of the message the disciples declared throughout the known world.

But why was it so very important? Why did Paul claim that without the resurrection of Jesus the whole of the Christian message would be meaningless?

The best way to answer this question is to put it the other way round. Rather than asking negatively what would be lost if the resurrection could be disproved, we should ask what positive place the resurrection held in the beliefs of the first Christians. When we ask this, we find that three things are said about the meaning of the resurrection in the New Testament.

● By the resurrection, Jesus' claims to be the Son of God were shown to be true. Peter said on the Day of Pentecost that the resurrection was a clear proof that 'God has made this Jesus, whom you crucified, both Lord and Messiah'. Paul wrote to the Christians of Rome that Jesus was 'declared Son of God by a mighty act in that he rose from the dead'. In spite of Jesus' sinlessness, in spite of the authority he displayed in his teaching and actions, and in spite of his miracles and clearly expressed claims about his central role in God's plan, if it had not been for the resurrection he might have been thought of simply as a great and good man. But after he had risen from the grave, his followers knew for certain that he was who he had claimed to be. They could now see and appreciate his whole life on earth in a new and fuller way, as the life of God himself living among men and women.

● But the resurrection was more than just a new light on the crucified Jesus. It is emphasized throughout the New Testament, and especially by Paul, that the resurrection, as well as the cross, was an indispensable part of God's action in bringing in the new society.

The first Christians were practical people before they were theologians. What they wanted was something that would work in real life. They were longing for a relationship with God in which their whole existence would be revolutionized. They wanted to be reconciled with God, and delivered from their self-centredness so that they could be better people. And they realized that they could not achieve this either by religious observance or by their own efforts at self-improvement. The only thing that can truly transform the human personality is a new centre and a new life-force.

Paul found this new life-force in Jesus – the Jesus who had risen from the dead, was alive in the real world and living dynamically in Paul's own life. This was such a striking reality in his everyday life that Paul could even say, 'it is no longer I who live, but Christ who lives in me'. This was not just pious religiosity. Paul really meant what he said: Jesus was now living in him in the most literal sense. So much so that even the details of Paul's life were directed not by him but by his living Lord.

In trying to express what he meant, Paul used a picture in which he compared the baptism of Christians with the death and resurrection of Jesus. He said that when Christians are

Acts 2:36

Romans 1:4

Galatians 2:20

Romans 6:1–11

John's Gospel records that when the fishermen came ashore, Jesus had a fire burning over which they cooked some fish for breakfast.

covered with water at their baptism, and subsequently emerge from the water, this is a physical picture of something that should happen to them inwardly and spiritually. Being drenched with water is like being buried (as Jesus was). Coming out of the water is like being raised again (as Jesus was). And the essence of Paul's understanding of these events was that to become a Christian a person must first be willing to 'die', to get rid of their old self-centred existence. Then they can be 'raised' again and receive a new existence, the life of Jesus Christ himself living within them.

So the resurrection of Jesus was crucial. If Jesus had only died on the cross, he might well have done all the things the theologians claimed. He might well have died as a punishment for sin, or to pay the ransom for our freedom. But in that case his suffering would have no power to affect our lives. Paul was quite sure that without the resurrection, the cross would have been nothing more than an interesting theological talking-point. It would have been powerless to have any lasting effect on the lives of ordinary people. But because of the resurrection, Paul *Philippians 1:21* had discovered a new life: 'For to me, life is Christ.' And he was confident that this was to be the normal experience of everyone who was a Christian: Jesus Christ actually living in those who commit themselves to him.

●But the resurrection of Jesus has a further implication for those who already have Christ's life within them. An important part of Jesus' teaching was that his followers would share in *John 3:15, 4:14, 17:3* 'eternal life'. This 'eternal life' includes two things. On the one hand, the phrase indicates that Christians are to enjoy a new quality of life. 'Eternal life' is God's life. And when Paul wrote of his own Christian experience as an experience of Christ living within him, he was faithfully interpreting the teaching of Jesus himself.

But to have the kind of life that God has does not just mean that Christians have a new dynamic for life in this world. It also means that Christians have a life that will never end. This is another part of Jesus' teaching that is reinforced and empha- *1 Corinthians 15:20* sized by Paul when he says that the resurrected Jesus is 'the first fruits of those who have fallen asleep'. By this he means that the rising again of Jesus is a pledge and a promise that his followers, too, will survive death. Those people who share in Christ's sufferings and resurrection in a spiritual sense have the assurance of a life beyond the grave which, like their present life, will be dominated by the presence of God. But it will also be distinctive and new, for Christians can expect to share the full reality of the kind of life that Jesus now has – a life in which death and sin are for ever destroyed, and replaced by the victory *1 Corinthians 15:57* which God has given them 'through our Lord Jesus Christ'.

And in order to understand the full implications of that, we must now consider Jesus' teaching about the nature of God's new society, 'the kingdom of God'.

Section Two
God's new society

Chapter 6 The nature of the new society

SO FAR we have talked of Jesus' coming in terms of a new society that the people of his day were expecting to arrive. They anticipated it as a time when the promises of the Old Testament concerning the place of Israel in God's plans would be fulfilled in a dramatic way, and the hated Romans would once and for all be driven out of their land.

It is no wonder, then, that when Jesus emerged as a travelling prophet after his baptism and the temptations, and declared that *Mark 1:15* 'the time is fulfilled and the kingdom of God is at hand', people of all kinds showed great interest in what he had to say. This was what they were waiting for. A new kingdom of God that would finally crush the old kingdom of Rome. And they fully expected that they, the Jewish people, would have a prominent part in this coming kingdom under the leadership of their Messiah.

The kingdom of God

But what did Jesus mean when he spoke about 'the kingdom of God'? What would we mean by such a phrase? My dictionary defines a 'kingdom' as 'the state or territory ruled by a king'. Perhaps then Jesus' contemporaries weren't so far wrong after all: God was going to set up a new state and rule it himself.

Or was he? Is that what Jesus really meant? Did he talk about a new state – or a new society? The difference is quite obvious. If Jesus was talking about a new state he must have seen himself as the agent of a new political dynasty, a Zealot. If he was talking about a new society, then he must have regarded his work as being concerned chiefly with the quality of life that his people enjoyed. A new state would simply replace the old authoritarianism with a new one. A new society would give to people a new and fresh reality of freedom, justice and the presence of God in their lives.

So what was Jesus really talking about? Many Christians have thought that he was mainly concerned with starting a society that was to be ruled by God, as distinct from political states that are ruled by men and women. Many of the churchmen of the Middle Ages, for example, followed St Augustine in thinking that the kingdom of God Jesus was talking about was the

Jesus taught that the kingdom of God was radically different to other ways of life. This girl, tattooed as a child in a cruel ceremony, has since become a follower of Jesus.

organized society we call the church. Even in our own day, Christian preachers often speak as if 'the kingdom' is just another word for 'the church', and others talk of the kingdom of God as if it is a new kind of political manifesto. But it is now widely recognized by those who study the New Testament that, whatever Jesus meant by his term 'the kingdom of God', it was not any of these things.

Kingdom and new society

One clue to what Jesus really meant can be found in the language that he spoke. Although Jesus may well have been able to speak two or three languages, it is likely that most of his teaching was given in Aramaic, the language that most people in Palestine knew best. The Gospels were written in Greek, of course, like the rest of the New Testament, and we therefore have no direct record of the actual Aramaic words used by Jesus. But even the Greek word that is translated into English as 'kingdom' (*basileia*), more often means the activity of a king rather than the territory he rules. And the Aramaic word which most scholars think Jesus himself used (*malkutha*) certainly has that meaning. So we are justified in supposing that Jesus was talking about what we might call 'the kingship of God', rather than his 'kingdom'.

That is why we have thought of his message here in terms of 'the new society'. For Jesus was concerned more than anything else about the quality of human life, and the relationship of men and women with God and with each other.

This helps to explain some of the more difficult things that Jesus said. For example, he told the Pharisees, 'the kingdom of God is not coming with signs to be observed; . . . for behold, the kingdom of God is in the midst of you'. On another occasion he told his disciples, 'whoever does not receive the kingdom of God like a child shall not enter it'. It is obvious that a political territory could hardly exist in the lives of individual people. They could not, 'receive' a state, nor could it be 'in the midst of them'. But Jesus was saying that from the moment God is in charge of someone's life, the new society has really arrived. He could say that God's society was 'among' his hearers, because he himself was there – and God was in complete control of his life.

Professor W. G. Kümmel helpfully draws attention to the way Jesus says that 'entering the kingdom' means 'entering into life'. Those people who 'inherit the kingdom' also 'inherit eternal life', and the gate leading to the kingdom is 'the way that leads to life'. The well-known story of the son who ran away from home also emphasizes the fact that to be a member of the kingdom is to share in God's life, and to know him as Father. In the same way, Paul reminded his Christian readers in Corinth that 'the kingdom of God does not consist in talk but in power' – the power of God at work in the lives of men and women whose only allegiance is to him. God's new society is already present in the life of every person who has committed himself to God's direction.

At the same time, we would be wrong to place all the emphasis on the new society as part of an individual relationship between ourselves and God. There are many statements in the Gospels which show that Jesus regarded the kingdom of God as a tangible, real society as well as the inward rule of God in the lives of his followers. For example, he said that people will 'come from east and west, and from north and south, and sit at table in the kingdom of God'. At the Last Supper Jesus told his disciples: 'from now on I shall not drink of the fruit of the vine until the kingdom of God comes'. And Matth. records him saying that his followers will 'inherit the kingdom prepared . . . from the foundation of the world'.

It therefore seems that Jesus understood the new society in two ways. On the one hand it is God's rule over the lives of men and women who commit themselves to him. On the other hand God's rule is something that can and will be demonstrated to the world at large.

Both of these concepts were a true reflection of the expectations of the Old Testament. It is important to remember that not all the Old Testament writers had seen God's future intervention in human affairs in the self-centred, nationalistic terms that some of Jesus' contemporaries did. It is true that in parts of the

Luke 17:20–21

Mark 10:15

Mark 9:43–47
Matthew 25:34–46;
Mark 10:17–23
Matthew 7:14

Luke 15:11–32

1 Corinthians 4:20

Luke 13:29

Luke 22:18

Matthew 25:34

Old Testament we find an overwhelming consciousness that God's sovereignty over men and women would be displayed in the form of an organized kingdom that would replace the empires of the world.

This is, especially, the outlook of the apocalyptic sections of the Old Testament. In Daniel, for example, 'the saints of the most high', represented by 'a figure like the Son of Man', receive the kingdom of God and possess it for ever. This kind of expectation was heightened and magnified a thousand times by other, later apocalyptic writers, some of them contemporaries of Jesus. It was an outlook expressed by some of Jesus' followers when they wanted to make him their king after the miraculous feeding of the 5,000. And it was an attitude that was found even among the disciples. When James and John tried to claim the chief places on either side of Jesus' throne they were obviously thinking in crude political terms.

Though Jesus rebuked them on that occasion, he never denied that God's kingdom would in some way affect society in a political sense. He sometimes suggested that it would do so in relatively undramatic ways – as yeast makes bread rise, or as a mustard seed quietly grows into a large tree. But he was also quite convinced that God would act decisively and directly, not just in the lives of individuals, but also in the political and economic life of nations.

This tension, or paradox, between the rule of God's new society in the lives of individuals and the outward expression of it in tangible political forces had existed in Old Testament days. God had been regarded as Israel's 'king' right from the time of the Judges, and perhaps even before that. The psalms are full of expressions that emphasize God's sovereignty over the course of history.

Daniel 7:13–18

John 6:15

Mark 10:35–45

Matthew 13:33
Matthew 13:31–32

Mark 13

Judges 8:22–23

Psalms 96:10, 99:1, 146:10

Many people believed that the kingdom of God would consist of a specific territory and political organization. But Jesus taught that it would transcend geographical and cultural boundaries.

At the time of Jesus, many of the rabbis were emphasizing that God's kingship over Israel was already in existence, even under the Roman rule, and that it operated through the Torah or Law. The rabbis sometimes referred to people 'taking upon themselves the kingdom of God', and by this they meant accepting and obeying the Torah as the instrument of God's rule over his people.

If we look carefully at other parts of the New Testament we can see that this tension between what God can do now in those who accept his rule over their lives, and what he will ultimately do through them in society at large, is always present. Paul, for example, says that 'the kingdom of God is not concerned with material things like food and drink, but with goodness and peace and joy in the Holy Spirit.' And since these are things that Christians already have, to be a part of God's kingdom must mean allowing God to exercise his ultimate sovereignty over our lives.

Romans 14:17

Yet, at the same time, Paul elsewhere connects the arrival of God's kingdom with the events surrounding the end of the world: 'The end comes when Jesus delivers the kingdom to God the Father after destroying every other rule and authority and power.' He clearly expected that God would break into history and alter its course – and this was to be in some way connected with the coming of God's new society, 'the kingdom'. This is made quite explicit in the book of Revelation, where, 'The kingdom of the world has become the kingdom of our Lord and of his Christ, and he shall reign for ever and ever'. It is also an important element of the teaching of Jesus himself.

1 Corinthians 15:24

Revelation 11:15

'Eschatology' and the new society

This whole question of the different things we mean when we speak of God's new society is called 'eschatology'. The actual word 'eschatology' comes from some Greek words which mean 'ideas about the end'. But eschatology is not just concerned with what may happen at the end of the world. It is essentially concerned with God's kingship, and with all the different ways that God's new society makes itself felt, whether in the lives of individual people, or in society, or in the final winding up of things.

In the last seventy years or so, three main suggestions have been made about the real meaning of Jesus' teaching about the new society, or 'kingdom of God'.

'Futurist eschatology'

The first of these views Jesus' teaching as part of a 'futurist eschatology'. When we use the word 'futurist' here, we mean in the future from Jesus' point of view, and not from the standpoint of the present day. There are many Christians today who have a 'futurist eschatology' in the sense that they expect God's kingdom to come in a tangible form at a time that is still in the future. They usually identify the coming of God's kingdom in this way with the second coming (or *parousia*) of Jesus himself. But when scholars talk of the Gospel traditions, they reserve the term 'futurist' for Jesus' own expectations about the new society, and not the expectations of modern Christians.

It was Albert Schweitzer, the German theologian who became a medical missionary in Africa, who first popularized the idea that Jesus had a futurist eschatology. He meant that Jesus held the same expectations as many Jewish apocalyptic writers of his day. He suggested that Jesus believed

Albert Schweitzer was a doctor in Africa. His ideas about the kingdom have been widely influential.

God was about to intervene immediately and dramatically in the affairs of humanity, and that his own life's work was to be the decisive climax of history – a climax that would therefore come within Jesus' own lifetime. This, said Schweitzer, is what Jesus meant when he declared that 'the kingdom of God is at hand'.

Jesus pictured himself as 'the Messiah designate', who would assume a position of full authority once the kingdom had actually arrived. But, like many other visionaries both before and after him, Jesus found the reality of life rather different from these idealistic dreams. Gradually, as life went on very much as before, it began to seem as if the dream had been only an illusion.

Early in the course of his work, said Schweitzer, Jesus was sufficiently confident to tell his disciples that the Son of man was about to appear in glory – so soon that they could expect his arrival in the course of a few days (Matthew 10:23). But it never happened, and so Jesus decided to

try to force God's hand by going to Jerusalem and pressing the issue with the authorities there. The result was that Jesus was arrested, tried and tragically sentenced to death. Even this astonishing act of faith did not bring about the desired result. Instead it ended with defeat and a cry of despair from the cross, as Jesus realized that the God he served had abandoned him. As Schweitzer put it: 'The wheel of fate would not turn, so Jesus flung himself upon it and is left there hanging still.'

Yet, though Jesus' hopes ended in apparent failure, Schweitzer claimed that an even greater power resulted from this incredible act of misplaced confidence than would have been the case if the expected apocalyptic kingdom had actually arrived. For the example of Jesus is something that can still exert a dynamic moral and spiritual influence over those who are willing to be obedient. And Schweitzer himself certainly put into practice the lessons he saw there. Not that he took Jesus' actual teaching very seriously, for he regarded even the Sermon on the Mount as an 'interim ethic', intended to apply only to a very short time during the ministry of Jesus. Instead, he attached the greatest importance to Jesus' faithfulness to his convictions. This, he said, is something that must have its effect on everyone who thinks seriously about it.

Schweitzer's views were published in a remarkable book that first appeared in English in 1909, under the title *The Quest of the Historical Jesus*. It is still regarded as one of the great theological classics. Many aspects of Schweitzer's argument are still widely regarded as valid even today. Hardly anyone would disagree with his view that Jesus' teaching about the new society must have seemed very similar to the apocalyptic expectations of the people of his time. It certainly had more in common with their expectations than with the ideas medieval churchmen developed about the kingdom and the church, or with the manifestos of the modern theologians of liberation. Schweitzer was also undoubtedly correct in seeing that Jesus' life's work, and especially his death, were an absolutely essential part of God's intervention in the lives of ordinary people.

There are, however, many difficulties involved in accepting this as an explanation of the whole of Jesus' life and teaching. For one thing, Schweitzer consistently ignored the claims that Jesus undoubtedly made about his own significance, and he confined his attention almost exclusively to Jesus' statements about the kingdom of God. We have already seen that these two parts of Jesus' teaching must be understood together. It is impossible to understand what he meant about God's new society without taking full account of his claim to have a special relationship with God himself.

Unless we are prepared to deny all historical credibility to the Gospel narratives, it is hard to believe that Jesus realized the importance of dying at Jerusalem only after the failure of all his previous efforts to bring about the new society. Nor do we need to believe with Schweitzer that Jesus' death also failed in its intended purpose, and left only a vague spiritual influence to affect the lives of those who take time to think about it.

Schweitzer made much of statements such as Jesus' words to his disciples just before his transfiguration: 'There are some standing here who will not taste death before they see the kingdom of God come with power' (Mark 9:1). According to Schweitzer's theory, this never happened. But he reached this conclusion only because of his sceptical attitude to the evidence of the New Testament. For the whole conviction of the early church was that God *did* truly intervene in human affairs in a powerful and dramatic way with the resurrection of Jesus and the gift of the Holy Spirit to his followers, and that both of these were the direct outcome of Jesus' death on the cross. And when we recall that much of the New Testament was written less than a generation after these events took place, it is clear that its evidence cannot be brushed aside quite as easily as Schweitzer thought.

'Realized eschatology'

The exact opposite of Schweitzer's theory is Professor C. H. Dodd's idea that Jesus had what he calls a 'realized eschatology'. According to Dodd, what Jesus was really saying was that the new society had already arrived in his own person. So we could say that the coming of Jesus was itself the coming of God's reign. Though the new society may need to grow and develop, the ultimate and decisive act had already taken place.

This is an attractive view, especially to people of a modern scientific age. The thought patterns familiar to first-century Jewish apocalyptists are strange to us. Most of us find it easier to think that Jesus' coming was the arrival of the new age, rather than to become involved in

the bizarre and fruitless speculations about the future that even today still occupy the attention of some fringe Christian groups.

The idea that Jesus saw his own life and work as the coming of God's new society also helps us to understand more clearly the exact nature of some of the incidents recorded in the Gospels. The miracles, for example, are much easier to understand if we regard them as signs and demonstrations that God was really at work in creating a new society than they would be if we regarded them in the traditional way as 'proofs' of Jesus' divine nature.

Dodd recognizes, of course, that not all the Gospel materials can be easily understood in the context of a realized eschatology. What are we to make, for instance, of the pictures and parables that appear to be concerned with the last judgement and some kind of future winding-up

C. H. Dodd, the British theologian who developed the idea of 'realized eschatology'.

of things – parables like the story of the ten bridesmaids or the sheep and the goats (Matthew 25:1–13, 31–46)? Dodd interprets these as pictures, not of a final judgement to come at the end of the world, but of the kind of challenge that comes to all people whenever they are confronted with the message about Jesus and God's new society.

There is certainly plenty of evidence that Jesus regarded the declaration of his message as in some sense a judgement on those who heard it and did not respond. The terms in which Jesus condemned the Pharisees often seem to imply that they were beyond being saved (Mark 3:28–30; Matthew 23); and the author of the fourth Gospel is surely giving an accurate representation of at least part of Jesus' message when he comments that 'He who believes in him is not condemned; he who does not believe is condemned already, because he has not believed in the name of the only Son of God. And this is the judgement, that the light has come into the world, and men loved darkness rather than light, because their deeds were evil' (John 3:18–19).

So it is not difficult to find passages in Jesus' teaching that can give some support to Dodd's theory. But the theory cannot explain every detailed bit of the evidence. There are two major stumbling-blocks:

● Although there are many passages in Jesus' teaching which support the theory, there are a good many more which do not. In many cases Jesus refers to the Son of man coming 'with the clouds of heaven', and his whole outlook was undoubtedly coloured by the kind of apocalyptic imagery to which Schweitzer so strikingly drew attention.

● We also have to consider what the rest of the New Testament tells us about the beliefs of the first Christians. And we find there a mixture of a 'futuristic' type of eschatology and a 'realized' type.

In the letters that Paul wrote to the church in the Greek city of Thessalonica in the early fifties of the first century we find great emphasis on the expectation of the early Christians that Jesus would again return in glory. Paul himself obviously shared this expectation, though not in the same extreme fashion as the Thessalonians

The kingdom of God, in Jesus' view, would consist of people from every generation and of every nationality.

(1 Thessalonians 4:13–5:11; 2 Thessalonians 2:1–12). In Corinth, on the other hand, Paul met some people who believed that the conventional descriptions of the end of things were to be taken as symbols of their own spiritual experience – and to them Paul again emphasized his own belief that Jesus would come again in the future (1 Corinthians 15:3–57).

But Paul himself was not totally one-sided in the matter, for in Galatians, probably his earliest letter, he suggests that in a very real sense the fullness of God's new society has come and is already at work in those who are Christians.

Now, if Dodd's theory was completely correct and Jesus did actually think that the new society had already arrived in its final form, it is hard to see how and why the first Christians should have forgotten this emphasis so soon and turned instead to speculations about the future. This is an especially important question, since so many of these Christians were not Jews, and they would not naturally think of the future in terms of Jewish apocalyptic. We must also bear in mind that the Gospel traditions themselves were preserved in the churches, and for the churches' use, and it is surely unlikely that such a glaring inconsistency between the teaching of Jesus and the actual beliefs of the church would have gone unnoticed.

'Inaugurated eschatology'

Because of the difficulties involved in both the futuristic and the realized views of Jesus' eschatology, there is considerable support today for a view that tries to take the best from both of them. This view recognizes that in a sense God's new society did actually come in the person of Jesus, but its complete fulfilment was still seen in the future. Thus Jesus' teaching is what we might call an 'inaugurated eschatology'.

This seems to me to be the best explanation of the matter. It is essential that we recognize with Schweitzer that Jesus' background was that of first-century Judaism, and his teaching included a complete view of the future course of events, including last judgement and final resurrection, as part of the consummation of God's new society. It is also important to recognize that Jesus claimed that the new society had arrived already in his own person, and so men and women must make their own response to God's demands upon them here and now.

We can perhaps summarize this

rather complex subject by saying that there are four points which seem to be basic to understanding what Jesus has to say about the coming of the new society.

● Jesus certainly used the language and perhaps to some extent shared the views of those who expected the imminent arrival of the new society through a direct intervention of God in human affairs.

● Jesus believed that the fundamental nature of the new society was being revealed in his own life and work. It is clear from the Gospels that this proved to be very different from what most Jews had expected. The society was revealed not as a tyrannical political force that would take over from Rome, but as a loving community of those whose only allegiance was to God himself.

● God's direct intervention is to be seen not only in the life and teaching of Jesus, but also in his death, in the resurrection and the gift of the Holy Spirit to his church. It may well be that it was in these events that some of Jesus' own predictions about the last things were fulfilled – for example, the statement that some of his disciples would see the new society coming with power before they died (Mark 9:1).

● There is so much variety in the

Jesus said that the demands of his kingdom were very great. 'Anyone who starts to plough and then keeps looking back is of no use for the kingdom of God' he told a would-be follower.

language used by Jesus to describe the new society that it is likely to be almost impossible to understand it by any but the most comprehensive outlook. It can arrive secretly, like the yeast working in the dough (Matthew 13:33); or it can come by the sudden appearance of Christ in glory as at the expected second coming (Mark 13).

The kingdom of God and the kingdom of heaven

One of the striking facts about the Gospel of Matthew is that it consistently uses the term 'kingdom of heaven' to describe the subject of Jesus' teaching. The only exceptions to this are in Matthew 12:28, 19:24, 21:31 and 21:43, where we find the term 'kingdom of God', which is used throughout Mark and Luke.

On the basis of this distinction, some people have thought they can distinguish two quite separate phases in Jesus' teaching. But in fact there can be no doubt that the two terms refer to the same thing. This can be demonstrated quite easily by comparing the same statements in Matthew and in the other two synoptic Gospels. For example, when Mark summarizes Jesus' message as 'the kingdom of God is at hand; repent . . .' (Mark 1:15), Matthew has, 'Repent, for the kingdom of heaven is at hand' (Matthew 4:17). The two statements appear in exactly the same context (the beginning of Jesus' teaching ministry), and it is obvious that they are different versions of the same saying. There are many other examples of the same process throughout the rest of the Gospels.

The explanation of this variety of expression is the fact that Matthew was writing for Jewish readers, whereas Mark and Luke were both writing for a predominantly non-Jewish readership. The Jews had never liked to use the name of God, in case they should unwittingly find themselves breaking the commandment, 'You shall not take the name of the Lord your God in vain . . .' (Exodus 20:7). So they often used other terms instead, and 'heaven' was a favourite alternative. Matthew therefore speaks of 'the kingdom of heaven' in order to avoid offence to his readers. But non-Jews had no such reservations, and to them a term like 'kingdom of heaven' would have been unnecessarily complicated, if not altogether meaningless. So Mark and Luke use the term 'kingdom of God' instead.

It might be thought that since 'kingdom of heaven' was the Jewish term, this must have been the one originally used by Jesus himself, later adapted for non-Jews by Mark and Luke. But the likelihood is that Jesus actually spoke of the 'kingdom of God', and it is Matthew who has adapted this to 'kingdom of heaven' for his own purposes. There are two reasons for thinking this.

● Jesus never showed any reticence in speaking about God. Not only did he claim to know God in a close and personal way – he even dared to call God his 'Father'.

● There are, as we have seen, four instances in Matthew where the term 'kingdom of God' is used. This can readily be understood if we suppose that Matthew overlooked these four occurrences of the word, but it is really impossible to think that in just these four cases he changed an original 'kingdom of heaven' into 'kingdom of God' for the benefit of his Jewish readers.

Perhaps the bewildering variety of ways in which the new society is described was designed to teach us one very important lesson about it: that what God can do among men and women through Jesus Christ is something far greater than any of us can fully understand. When God works he does it in a big way. He also does it in a simple way, so that everyone can understand enough about it to be able to respond to the challenge. That is why Jesus gave so much of his teaching in parables or simple pictures. And before we can get much further in understanding God's new society we shall have to look at some of these.

Chapter 7 Pictures of the new society

Luke 10:25–37
Matthew 18:12–14;
Luke 15:1–7
Matthew 13:1–9;
Mark 4:1–9; Luke 8:4–8

SOME OF the stories of Jesus which are best-known are the 'parables': stories such as the good Samaritan, or the lost sheep, or the sower spreading seed in his field. But if we go through the Gospels and list the different parts of Jesus' teaching that are described as parables, we discover that they include not only these story parables but also other sayings that we would more naturally classify as metaphors, similes, proverbs, allegories, or even riddles.

The pictures and their meaning

Luke 4:23
Mark 7:15–16
Matthew 5–7

John 10:1–18
John 15:1–11
John 4:31–38
John 6:35
John 7:37–39

A popular proverb such as 'Physician, heal yourself' is called a 'parable'. So is the more or less factual statement, 'there is nothing outside a man which by going into him can defile him; but the things that come out of a man are what defile him'. Some of the statements in the Sermon on the Mount are also of the same type, drawing a vivid picture of something familiar – salt, light, or a city – by means of which Jesus explains his message. Many of Jesus' pictures in John's Gospel also use the same kind of imagery to drive home their message. There, Jesus describes himself as 'the good shepherd', or 'the true vine'. He compares the disciples' task with the reaping of a harvest, and himself with bread and life-giving water.

Jesus' teaching is full of 'parable' sayings like this. But in discussing Jesus' teaching it is usual and convenient to reserve the word 'parable' for actual stories that Jesus told.

Parable or allegory?

The traditional way of understanding these story parables has been to regard them as 'allegories'. An allegory is a detailed account of a subject, written in such a way that it appears to be about something altogether different. John Bunyan's *Pilgrim's Progress* is a well-known example of this kind of writing. In this book Bunyan *seems* to be telling the story of a man on a journey. But the journey is so extraordinary, and the characters so much larger than life, that it soon becomes obvious he is not really writing about a journey at all. He is describing the things that happen in the life of a Christian, from the time when he first becomes a Christian through to the end of his life.

John 15:1–11

We find this kind of teaching in some parts of the New Testament. In John's Gospel, for example, there is the allegory of the vine and its branches. In this story Jesus is ostensibly explaining the means by which a vine bears grapes on its branches. But when he begins to talk about the branch of a vine deciding to cut itself off from the main stem of the plant, it becomes obvious that he is not really giving a lesson on how to grow grapes, but talking about what it means to be one of his disciples.

Luke 10:25–37

Though there are a few examples of allegories in the Gospels, in most cases this method of understanding the parables is neither faithful to the original intention of Jesus' teaching, nor is it very helpful. Take, for example, the parable of the good Samaritan. According to Luke, this story was told by Jesus in answer to the question, 'Who is my neighbour?' At the end, Jesus told his questioner to behave as the Samaritan had done in the story. Yet within a very short time Christians were applying an allegorical interpretation to the story, losing sight of the fact that it was an answer to a practical question.

Many of Jesus' pictures were drawn from agricultural life. One parable describes a vineyard owner whose tenants refused to share the crop with him.

Where to find Jesus' parables

	Matthew	Mark	Luke
The sower	13:1–23	4:1–20	8:4–15
The weeds in the field	13:24–43		
The mustard seed	13:31–32	4:30–32	13:18–19
The hidden treasure	13:44–46		
The unforgiving servant	18:23–35		
The good Samaritan			10:25–37
The friend at midnight			11:5–8
The rich fool			12:13–21
The great feast			14:15–24
The lost sheep	18:12–14		15:1–10
The prodigal son			15:11–32
The unjust servant			16:1–13
The rich man and Lazarus			16:19–31
The unjust judge			18:1–8
The Pharisee and the tax collector			18:9–14

	Matthew	Mark	Luke
The workers in the vineyard	20:1–16		
The pounds			19:11–27
The wicked tenants	21:33–46	12:1–12	20:9–19
The wedding feast	22:1–14		
The faithful servant	24:45–51		
The ten maidens	25:1–13		
The talents	25:14–30		

The seven 'I am' sayings of John's Gospel are similar to parables:

	John
The bread of life	6:35–40
The light of the world	8:12–13
The door	10:7–10
The good shepherd	10:11–18
The resurrection and the life	11:17–27
The way, truth and life	14:1–7
The true vine	15:1–11

According to the fourth-century thinker Augustine, the man who went down from Jerusalem to Jericho was Adam. Jerusalem represented the heavenly city of peace from which he fell, and Jericho was the human mortality that he inherited as a result of his fall. The robbers were the devil and his angels, who stripped him of his immortality. The priest and the Levite who passed by on the other side were the priesthood and ministry of the Old Testament, which could not save him. The good Samaritan was Christ himself, and his binding of the traveller's wounds was the restraint of sin. The oil and wine that he poured in was the comfort of hope and encouragement to work hard. The beast was the flesh in which Christ came to earth; the inn was the church, and the innkeeper the apostle Paul. The two pence he was paid are the commandments to love God and love our neighbour.

Augustine, Quaestiones Evangeliorum 2.19

Now this is undoubtedly an ingenious account of the whole story of salvation – and, to be fair, we should remember that Augustine tells us that he thoroughly enjoyed thinking up this kind of thing. But in the final analysis we must admit that such an interpretation is quite unrelated to the story of the good Samaritan. These 'spiritual meanings' are read into the story rather than coming out of it. In Augustine's version, the original question of Jesus' hearer is not answered at all!

The point of the parables

We may find it somewhat surprising to discover that it was not until the end of the nineteenth century that the futility of this method of interpretation was finally realized. When scholars began to read the New Testament as a historical document, they realized that Jesus probably used parables in much the same way as other teachers in the ancient world. After comparing Jesus' methods of teaching with the way parables are used in Greek literature, a German scholar, Adolf Jülicher, suggested that Jesus used parables in the same way as a modern preacher uses illustrations. They were not intended to convey a hidden meaning in every detail, but simply to illustrate and drive home a particular point.

So in the parable of the good Samaritan, the main point is that the person who proved to be a real neighbour was not a religious Jew, but one of the despised and hated Samaritans. All the other details in the story, about the ass and the inn, the oil and wine, were simply an imaginative description of the scene to make the story realistic and interesting. They had no connection with the main point of what Jesus was trying to say.

Once this fact was realized, it soon disposed of some real problems of interpretation. For in some parables the main characters are not really the kind of people whose actions Christians have ever felt they ought to copy. There is the unjust steward, for example, who gained his master's approval by manipulating the accounts to his own advantage. Was Jesus really commending this sort of behaviour? Of course not. And when

Luke 16:1–8

Today, as in Jesus' time, sheep and goats often graze together. He used the picture of a shepherd dividing the sheep from the goats to illustrate the last judgement.

we appreciate that the main point of the parable is that we should copy his far-sighted determination to be ready for a crisis in life, we can see that the rest of the story is simply a realistic portrayal of an imaginary situation.

Following on from the important insights of Jülicher, other scholars set out to discover the real meaning of Jesus' parables, notably Professor C. H. Dodd in England and Professor Joachim Jeremias in Germany. Both agreed with Jülicher that a parable generally has only one lesson to teach – though they also saw that the subject of the parables is not generalized moral truth (as Jülicher had thought) but the coming of God's new society. However, Dodd and Jeremias took over from Jülicher certain assumptions that have recently been questioned by other students of the New Testament:

● Though it is true, in general, that each of the parables of Jesus has only one main point, it can be misleading to insist that no parable can ever have more than one main point. Some of them quite obviously do have more than one lesson to teach.

Matthew 25:14–30;
Luke 19:11–27

In the parable of the talents, for example, at least two simple points seem to be made. The story tells of a man who is going away and divides his money among his servants for safe keeping. When he returns he rewards the servants in different ways, according to the different uses to which they have put his money. Now the main point of this story must be to emphasize the connection between individual responsibility and ultimate judgement. But there is another emphasis that may be just as important, for the master went far beyond either his legal or his moral obligation by generously entrusting his property to his servants. The parable of the wedding feast seems to make exactly the same two points, and of course both were important parts of Jesus' teaching about the nature of his Father.

Matthew 22:1–14;
Luke 14:15–24

Matthew 13:1–9;
Mark 4:1–9; Luke 8:4–8

Matthew 13:18–23;
Mark 4:13–20;
Luke 8:11–15

Matthew 21:33–45;
Mark 12:1–12;
Luke 20:9–19

In the parable of the sower
Jesus compared the response
of his hearers to the growth of
seed, some of which was sown
on stony ground.

● Though most of the parables are not to be given an allegorical interpretation, many scholars now recognize that this does not apply to all of them. The parable of the sower incorporates an allegorical meaning: the different kinds of ground are said to correspond to different types of people hearing Jesus' message. It is often argued that this explanation does not go back to Jesus himself, but originated in the early church, at a time when Christians were trying to explain why only a few people responded to their preaching. There is no doubt that this parable would help to answer a question like that. But if we omit this interpretation of the parable as being only a secondary meaning, perhaps added later, we are still left with the problem of explaining the main point as Jesus first told it. And the fact is that it is very difficult to see what other meaning it could possibly have.

There is an even more striking example of this in the case of the parable of the wicked tenants. The story concerns a man who let out his vineyard to some tenants for a rent that included part of the annual crop of grapes. Yet, when he sent his servants to collect his share of the crop, they were beaten and killed. After this had happened several times the man sent his son, thinking that he would command greater respect. But exactly the same thing happened to him. So when the owner himself finally comes to the vineyard it is inevitable that the tenants will be put out and destroyed. In this story, an allegorical interpretation seems to be the only meaning possible. If Israel was not the vineyard, and the prophets were not the servants sent by the master (God), and Jesus himself was not the Son, then the whole parable loses its point.

So it seems wise to adopt a more flexible approach, and to recognize that although the parables do not normally need an allegorical interpretation, some of them may.

● Dodd and Jeremias emphasized the importance of understanding the parables in their original historical context. Because they insisted on this point they made a great effort to try to discover the original meaning of the parables for Jesus' hearers, and later for the Christians who first wrote them down. But other scholars are now beginning to realize that there is a hidden dimension in the parables which gives them a distinctive appeal not found in the rest of the New Testament.

It is generally true to say that before we can be sure what the New Testament means for us today, we need to know what it meant to those who first read it. But this is not really the case with the parables. They are more like the work of a great artist than a self-conscious theologian, and their characters and situations have a correspondingly universal quality that can be understood by anyone, for they deal with the basic needs of human beings. We do not need any special insights to understand the parable of the lost son, or the talents, or the workers in the vineyard. Their meaning and their challenge is self-evident as we read them.

The pictures and their message

Matthew 13:24, 31, 33, 44

But what is the message and the challenge of the parables? In the widest sense, the subject of the parables is the coming of God's new society, or 'kingdom'. This is clearly indicated by the many parables which start with the words, 'The kingdom of God is like . . .' Because of this, the exact meaning that we see in the parables will to some extent depend on what we believe the new society to be. If, with Albert Schweitzer, we think that the spectacular and immediate intervention of God in the affairs of human society is the most important thing about it, then we will naturally want to understand the teaching of the parables in that context. If, on the other hand, we follow C. H. Dodd, we will have no difficulty in finding traces of a realized eschatology in the parables.

But the real message of the parables is rather more complex than either of these alternatives suggests. When we consider them all as a group, their message seems to be concerned with four main subjects, each of them explaining some important facts about God's society and the effect it has in the lives of those who are a part of it.

The society and its Sovereign

Most communities are strongly influenced by the character of their leader or leaders. A harsh, authoritarian ruler will not have too much difficulty in persuading his people to adopt the same attitudes. And the example of a liberal, humane ruler will usually encourage his people to share a similar viewpoint. The new society that God has founded is no exception to this. It takes its character and form from the God who is its Sovereign.

Luke 15:1–7;
Matthew 18:12–14

So we are not surprised to find that several of the parables tell us important things about the nature of God himself. The story of the lost sheep explains the fundamental fact that he is a God of grace: he takes the initiative in finding and restoring those who because of sin are out of harmony with his will. He is concerned when even one of his creatures has lost his way in life, and must go

Luke 15:8–10
Luke 15:11–32

after that lost one to restore him. The other parables in Luke 15 – the lost coin and the lost son – also emphasize God's love for sinful men and women. His undeserved love is so great that God will do everything he can to find us and he will not be satisfied until, like the lost son, we have been fully restored.

Matthew 20:1–16

The precise extent of God's generosity is illustrated in the story about the workers in the vineyard. Here Jesus tells of a master who hired men to work in his vineyard. They started work at different times of the day, so that when the time came for them to receive their wages some of them had only worked for an hour, while others had worked the whole day. But the master gave them all the same wages! He was not cheating anyone, because those who started early in the day had agreed in advance what their pay should be. But the master was generous to those who began late in the day. He gave them as much as if they had been there from the start. This, said Jesus, is what the kingdom of heaven is like. God, of course, is the Sovereign of the kingdom,

The story of the good Samaritan referred to the notorious Jericho road. It passes through desolate country making an ideal hideout for robbers.

and he is overwhelmingly generous. Those who join his society at the last minute are given as big a welcome as those who are first in at the door.

This may seem to suggest that God is a little unfair, for surely those who arrived early *did* deserve more than those who came to work late in the day. This is the kind of question Jülicher was trying to answer when he suggested that a parable normally has only one point – and in the case of this parable he was undoubtedly correct. For there are many other sayings of Jesus which show that God is overwhelmingly responsive to the needs of all his people. There is, for example, the story of the friend **Luke 11:5–8** who requested food at midnight, which is used by Luke to emphasize that God is only too willing to answer our prayers: 'Ask, and you will receive; seek, and you will find; knock, and **Luke 11:9** the door will be opened to you.' Another example is the story of **Luke 18:1–8** the unjust judge, which emphasizes a similar point.

Then there are the statements in the Sermon on the Mount which, though not story parables, are certainly parables in the wider meaning of the word. 'Look at the birds of the air; they neither sow nor reap nor gather into barns, and yet your heavenly Father feeds them. Are you not of more value than they? . . . And why are you anxious about clothing? Consider the lilies . . . how they grow; they neither toil nor spin; . . . if God so clothes the grass of the field . . . will he not much more clothe you, **Matthew 6:26–30** O men of little faith?' God cares about his people, and he cares about even the smallest details. He is their 'Father'.

This emphasis on the close personal relationship that exists between God and those who acknowledge his sovereignty over their lives is one of the most strikingly original parts of Jesus' **Mark 14:32–36** teaching. Jesus himself addressed God as his Father. In John's Gospel, God's relationship to Jesus as Father to Son is often **John 1:14, 18; 5:43; 8:19** used to emphasize Jesus' divine nature. But in the other three Gospels it is the character of the relationship that is more often emphasized. As Jesus' Father God can be addressed and known in the same intimate way as a human father is addressed by his child. Jesus spoke like that to God. He called him 'Abba', the

Aramaic word for father used in the home, and he allowed his disciples to do the same when speaking to God in prayer.

Matthew 6:9; Luke 11:2

This way of addressing God was quite new. Though the Jews did occasionally address God as 'Father', they did not use the familiar language Jesus used, and they normally qualified it by some reference to God's holiness and majesty.

But the God of Jesus' parables is not remote and out of contact with the real world. To be sure, he is 'holy': he is completely different in character from men and women. But he is a God whom we can know in a personal relationship as our Father. What is more, he is a loving Father. He watches over all those who belong to him, and cares about the very smallest detail of their lives.

The society and the individual

To be a part of the new society that Jesus talks about not only gives us the privilege of knowing God in an intimate and personal way, it also imposes certain responsibilities on us. A number of the stories Jesus told emphasize the kind of response that is required if we are to 'enter the kingdom'.

Mark 1:15

At the beginning of Mark, the main thrust of Jesus' teaching is summed up in the slogan, 'Repent and believe in the Gospel', and many of the stories told by Jesus emphasize the importance of turning away from sin ('repenting') in order to become a

Luke 15:11–32

member of God's society. The story of the lost son, for instance, not only emphasizes the goodness and generosity of the father: it also underlines the importance of the son realizing his foolishness and being willing to change his way of life.

Repentance has never been a popular idea, for it involves us in recognizing that we have done wrong. It means a certain loss of face and loss of moral credibility. But Jesus made it quite plain that those who are not prepared to accept this loss of face can never have a living relationship with God. There is the story of the Pharisee and the tax collector, who went to pray in the

Luke 18:9–14

temple at the same time. The Pharisee prided himself on his moral and religious attainments – and told God so. The tax collector, on the other hand, was so conscious of his own unworthiness to speak to God at all that he could only cry out, 'God, have pity on me, a sinner.' But, said Jesus, 'the tax collector, and not the Pharisee, was in the right with God when he went home', because he recognized his own sinfulness and came to God with no spiritual pretensions.

Jesus makes a similar point in the story of the rich fool, who thought that his wealth would place him in good standing with

Luke 12:13–21

God. And he made the teaching of these parables quite explicit in his statement that God's rule over our lives is to be accepted in an attitude of childlike trust: 'Whoever does not receive the

Luke 18:17; Mark 10:15

kingdom of God like a child will never enter it.'

But repentance and forgiveness are not the end of the matter. Indeed, they are only the beginning of a life lived under the rule of God himself. For in God's new society we enjoy a new kind of life – 'eternal life' or 'abundant life' as Jesus calls it in some of the sayings recorded in John's Gospel. Life in God's society means a life which is directed and controlled by God. Those who have entered the kingdom by repentance and forgiveness of their sins must love God with all their energy. They must serve him as their only true master, even to the point of giving him absolute control of their lives. For those who do this, there are important practical consequences in the way they live day by day.

John 3:15; 6:54; 10:28; 17:3

Matthew 22:37–38; Mark 12:29–30 Matthew 6:24; Luke 16:13 Matthew 16:24–26; Luke 9:23–25

● For one thing, they are far more concerned with what God thinks about them than what other people may think. This comes out especially in their attitudes to religious matters. Though some may accept God's rule over their lives rather reluctantly, their devotion is preferable to that of someone who makes a great show of serving God but who in reality does nothing about it. God's people must serve him in the spirit of the widow who secretly put her last penny into the offering-box at the temple. They will not behave ostentatiously so that others will see them and know of their goodness. They will pray and fast in secret and 'your Father who sees what you do in private, will reward you'.

Matthew 21:28–32

Mark 12:41–44; Luke 21:1–4

Matthew 6:5–6, 16–18

Matthew 6:4

● But this is not an excuse for doing nothing. Those who accept God's rule in their lives must make good use of God's provision for them. They must act responsibly, using the resources God has given them, and, like the unjust steward, they should always be ready to face their master.

Matthew 25:14–30; Luke 19:11–27 Luke 16:1–8

● Indeed, their main ambition in life must be to learn more of God and his ways. Two of the shortest parables illustrate this – the stories about the hidden treasure and the pearl. A man who finds a field full of treasure will have no hesitation in selling all his goods to buy that field. Or, similarly, if he is looking for fine pearls and comes across an especially good specimen, he will sacrifice everything to own it. God's kingdom is like that. It is worth sacrificing all we have to be able to enjoy the reality of God working in our lives.

Matthew 13:44

Matthew 13:45

This is what Jesus meant when he said to his disciples, 'the kingdom of God is within you'. God is already exercising his sovereign rule in the lives of those who know him as Father. The new society can be present in the experience of just one person who recognizes God's claims on his life.

Luke 17:21

The society and the community

At the same time, we would be wrong to think that Jesus' message was restricted to the purely personal, individual aspects of religious life and belief. A large part of his teaching concerns the relationship of God's people to the world at large, and to one another. Indeed in the parable of the unforgiving servant, Jesus seems to suggest that the way God deals with us will in some way depend on the way we deal with other people. Then there is also the statement of Jesus that loving our neighbour comes second in importance to loving God.

Matthew 18:21–35

Matthew 22:39; Mark 12:31

Shepherds in Israel's rough hill-country protected their flocks from wild animals and thieves. Jesus called himself the good shepherd who cared so much for his sheep that he was willing to die for them.

What this means is that those people who accept God's rule over their lives must behave in the same way as their Father in heaven. God's generosity extends even to the outcasts of society, and his followers should be no different. They are to behave like the good Samaritan in the parable. Jesus put this into practice himself, by taking God's message to the outcasts of society. That was what made the disciples realize that the kingdom of God was actually present in his person, and that they could share in its blessings here and now.

Luke 10:25–37

For those who were willing to accept God's claims over their lives, this new experience was in store. Not only did they share a new relationship with God himself; they were also bound to one another in a new community of caring service and mutual love.

The society and the future

Finally, a number of parables refer to the coming of God's kingdom in the future. They refer to Jesus coming as the heavenly, supernatural Son of man, and speak of the final judgement of men and women.

Some have thought that this was just a picturesque way of presenting the challenge of Jesus' message as it came to his hearers when they first heard it. But, in view of the strongly apocalyptic tone of much of the language that is used, it is hard to escape the conclusion that Jesus was thinking of some future time when God would assert his authority and kingship in a visible way.

At this time there will be a great day of reckoning. Those who merely profess to serve God but do not actually do so will be sorted out from those who really carry out God's will. This is the main lesson of the parables about the fishing-net, the corn

Matthew 13:47–50
Matthew 13:24–30

Matthew 25:31–33

and the weeds, and the sheep and the goats.

In other parables the future climax of the kingdom is depicted as a feast. This kind of imagery was often used by the Jews to describe the coming blessings of the messianic age. But Jesus' pictures of it make it clear that not everyone will gain admission. Indeed, the parable of the great supper suggests that the conventionally religious will have no place in it at all. Those who Matthew 22:1–14;
Luke 14:15–24 share in its blessings will come in from the streets rather than from the sanctuaries.

In Matthew's Gospel great emphasis is laid on the responsibility that all this places on those who profess to be God's people. Since no one knows the day or the hour when this will Matthew 24:36–44, cf.
Mark 13:32–37 take place, we must be in a state of constant readiness – like the bridesmaids who waited for the bridegroom to arrive at a Matthew 25:1–13 wedding.

This element in Jesus' teaching transcends the sharp distinctions we like to draw between what will happen in the future and what is already present. Because Jesus has come, God's new society has already arrived. Those who are willing to accept God's authority are even now a part of his kingdom. Whatever else may be revealed in the future will be, not so much a new beginning, as the final working out of all the implications of something that, in its essence, is already here. Though God's new society had had small and insignificant beginnings, it is the kind of beginning that must inevitably produce spectacular growth. Its development is like that of the mustard seed, 'the Matthew 13:31–32;
Mark 4:30–34;
Luke 13:18–19 smallest seed in the world' which grows up into one of the biggest plants of all.

The pictures and their hearers

Some scholars have spent a lot of time trying to discover the exact 'life situation' (*Sitz im Leben*) of the various parables, thinking that if they do so their immediate meaning will be easier to grasp. But in most cases it is not possible to discover the precise situations in which Jesus told particular stories. For, like the other parts of the Gospels, the parables have been recorded not as part of a biography of Jesus, arranged chronologically, but as a message explaining Jesus' teaching and its continuing relevance to the needs of the world and the church.

Very occasionally the parables have a story attached to them, and this perhaps gives some indication of their original life setting in the ministry of Jesus. Probably no one would doubt that the parable of the good Samaritan was given in answer to the question 'Who is my neighbour?' addressed to Jesus by a Jewish religious leader. Similarly, the parable about the unforgiving servant was told in reply to Peter's question about how Matthew 18:21–35 often he should forgive someone who was offending him. Or again, Jesus told the story of the rich fool in answer to a question Luke 12:13–21 about the best way of dividing a legacy.

Some of the parables are told in different contexts in different

Luke 15:1—7

Matthew 18:12—14

Gospels. The parable of the lost sheep appears in Luke along with the parables of the lost coin and lost son as an answer to the Pharisees' complaints about the bad company Jesus was keeping. In Matthew the same parable is told as an encouragement to the disciples to be faithful 'shepherds' of the church. It is of course not inconceivable that Jesus may have told the same story more than once, and drawn different lessons on each occasion. Many preachers re-use a good illustration.

But the fact is that these parables are exceptional in having any background information at all attached to them. We know nothing about the circumstances in which Jesus first told most of the parables. This is emphasized by the way they are collected together in blocks in the various Gospels. Matthew has a complete

Matthew 13
Mark 4

Luke 13:18 — 16:31

section of his Gospel devoted entirely to parables. Mark contains a similar (though not identical) collection, while Luke also has a long section predominantly composed of parables.

Nor is it really profitable to try to discover the use to which the parables were put in the early church. Students of what is called 'redaction criticism', the study of why the Gospels were written, have examined the ways in which different parables are used in different Gospels. For example, we can see that Matthew has a number of parables that refer to the coming of God's kingdom in the future – and we may surmise that this subject was of some importance in the churches for which Matthew was writing. Luke, on the other hand, preserves a number of parables, not found in the other Gospels, concerned with the place of non-Jewish people (Gentiles) in God's new society. Observations of this kind can tell us valuable things about Matthew and Luke and their respective readerships. But ultimately they tell us very little about either the origins or the meaning of the parables themselves.

To make his message clear to people who came to listen to him, Jesus used many illustrations from everyday life.

The real meaning of the parables must be inextricably bound up with the challenge they bring to those who read or hear them. They give us a picture of God and of his new society, and they challenge us to commit ourselves unconditionally to accept his will. It is only as we identify ourselves with the lost sheep, the wicked tenants, or the man who discovers a field of hidden treasure, that their full impact is felt. In the last analysis, the parables are nothing less than God's claim on the lives of men and women. They require both the disposition to understand and the will to obey.

Why did Jesus teach in parables?

There is a statement in Mark 4:11—12 which seems to suggest that Jesus told parables with the deliberate intention of making his teaching obscure to those who were not already his disciples, so that, echoing the words of Isaiah, 'they may indeed see but not perceive, and may indeed hear but not

understand; lest they should turn again, and be forgiven'. Such an idea is so contrary to all we know of Jesus that some explanation seems to be required. Many suggestions have been put forward, of which we mention two:
● According to C. H. Dodd (and a number of others who follow his

views), this is not a genuine saying of Jesus. It was inserted by the early church to explain why the Jewish people had rejected Jesus. It was, they said, a part of the providential wisdom of God himself, who had always intended this to happen. There are, however, two arguments against this view.

First, it was probably only the first generation of Christians who were deeply concerned that the Jews had rejected Jesus. The church was Jewish only at a very early stage of its development, and after the destruction of Jerusalem by the Romans in AD 70 Jewish Christianity almost ceased to exist. It certainly had little influence on the church at large. This means that the problem was most acute not long after the events of Jesus' own lifetime – and the nearer we are in time to Jesus himself, the less room there must be for the church making additions and alterations to his teaching.

Secondly, Matthew's Gospel has a similar saying, quoting the same passage from Isaiah. Since we know Matthew was specially interested in the relative status of Jews and Christians, we would expect him to have preserved exactly the same words as Mark, if this statement was indeed concerned with the Jewish rejection of Jesus. But in fact the statement in Matthew's Gospel has a slightly different implication. Here Jesus says: 'This is why I speak to them in parables, because seeing they do not see, and hearing they do not hear, nor do they understand' (Matthew 13:13).

● A second suggested explanation

fits in with this statement in Matthew. On this understanding we need to suppose that the word translated '*so that* . . . they may see' in Mark is actually meant to be the beginning of a factual statement, much as it is in Matthew. Evidence for this view can be drawn from a comparison of the Greek that Mark wrote with the Aramaic statements that probably lay at the back of it. Thus the statement describes, not the *purpose* of teaching in parables, but the inevitable *consequences* of doing so. Jesus was pointing out that the parables will inevitably separate those who listen to them with spiritual insight from those who are spiritually blind.

This explanation is the more likely. It fits in with what we saw in a previous chapter about Jesus' attitude to keeping his messiahship secret. It also fits well with the nature of the parables themselves. Though they do not require great mental effort, a certain degree of commitment is called for in order to understand what Jesus is saying. The parables are not a philosophical statement of the truths about God. There *is* a sense in which the truth is 'hidden', for the parables challenge Jesus' hearers to think out for themselves what the implications of his message must be. Those who were not specially interested could no doubt listen to a parable and see nothing in it but a story. But with a little careful thought, the same story can become a picture of God and his dealings with men and women in the new society that Jesus had come to inaugurate.

Did Jesus intend to found the church?

People have often asked whether Jesus intended to found a church. We do have in Matthew's Gospel two statements that seem to suggest that he did (Matthew 16:18–20; 18:17). But some scholars believe these statements come from Matthew himself, and not directly from the teaching of Jesus. Albert Schweitzer, for example, found it impossible to think that Jesus intended to found a church, for he believed that Jesus expected the immediate end of the world. But even those who do not share this opinion have often rejected the notion that Jesus was intent on starting a church. Adolf von

Harnack and the theological liberals viewed Jesus as a simple ethical teacher. Because they regarded the concept of a church as inconsistent with this, they concluded that it was a later, alien intrusion into the originally simple Gospel.

Though very few people today would agree with this point of view, it does draw our attention to two important facts that need to be borne in mind whenever we talk about Jesus and the church:

● 'The church' need not imply the kind of religious hierarchy that evolved in the second century and that is familiar to us in institutionalized Christianity today. Jesus spoke of two or three people gathered in his name (Matthew 18:20).

● In the strict sense it is probably anachronistic to speak of the existence of 'the church' in the lifetime of Jesus. The church in the New Testament is not simply a collection of like-minded people organized as a religious society. It is a living fellowship of those who share in the salvation that God has provided through the life, death and resurrection of Jesus himself. There is a sense therefore in which the church came into existence only *after* Jesus' death and resurrection.

The early followers of Jesus were not organized into any church structures, but the gathering of Christians together for worship and instruction has been called a 'church' from New Testament times.

The New Testament depicts the pouring out of the Holy Spirit on the day of Pentecost as the real 'founding' of the church (Acts 1:8; 2:1–4).

We therefore need to qualify any statement that we make about Jesus 'founding' the church. But at the same time, there are strong indications in the Gospels that he certainly intended to form a community of those who followed him.

● All the Gospels depict Jesus as the person in whom the messianic promises of the Old Testament have been fulfilled. The Messiah of whom the Old Testament speaks had come in Jesus. A significant element in the Old Testament expectation was the belief that when the Messiah came he would set up a new community, and in this community God's people would enjoy a new and close relationship with their master and with one another. As we have seen, there is good reason to believe that at least the core of Jesus' claims

to be Messiah can be traced back to the teaching of Jesus himself – and if he viewed himself as Messiah, it would be only natural for him to envisage the foundation of some kind of community among his followers. The name that Jesus regularly used for himself, Son of man, also contains this implication. It is probably incorrect to say, as some do, that every time Jesus used this name he meant to include his disciples along with himself. But there is no doubt that in the Old Testament book of Daniel the Son of man was not simply an individual; he was a representative member of 'the saints of the most high' (Daniel 7:13–18).

● When we consider the ways in which Jesus describes his own work and the work of God's kingdom, his words often suggest that he is talking about a group of people linked not only to God, but to one another. For example, he talks of himself as a shepherd, implying that he must have a flock (John 10:1–18; Luke 12:32). When he compares himself to a vine and his disciples to its branches, it is obvious that he is meaning to suggest that the branches have some kind of connection with each other as well as with the main stem (John 15:1–11). Many of the things Jesus says about the kingdom would be difficult to understand without assuming that he had some kind of visible society in mind (Matthew 23:13; Luke 16:16). And his ethical teaching is invariably concerned with life among his followers within a community (Matthew 5:22; 7:3–5).

● More striking is the fact that some of the parables suggest that the kingdom of God is to be not only a new society but also a visible society. Parables like the mustard seed (Mark 4:30–32), the corn and the weeds (Matthew 13:24–30), the fishing-net (Matthew 13:47–50), the workers in the vineyard (Matthew 20:1–16) and the wedding feast (Matthew 22:1–14) clearly suggest an organized society.

So it seems reasonable to conclude that Jesus did have in mind a continuing community of his followers, and that the kind of churches spoken of in the rest of the New Testament gave form to the community Jesus intended to found.

Chapter 8

The power of the new society

Mark 1:29–34
Mark 4:35–41
Mark 5:21–43;
Luke 7:11–17;
John 11:1–44

SOME OF the most striking parts of the Gospels are the stories about Jesus performing what we call miracles. He healed the sick, he exercised authority over the forces of nature, and on occasion he even raised the dead. Of all the subjects mentioned in the Gospels, this is the one that presents most problems for us today.

We usually have no real difficulty in understanding Jesus' teaching about God and his new society. Even people who are unable to accept Jesus' teaching as the full and final truth about God and the world can still respect his ideals, and many people who are not Christians make a genuine effort to put some of them into practice. But when it comes to the miracles, things are very different. Most people, including a number of Christians, find it hard to believe that the miracles recorded in the Gospels actually took place. They may be old superstitions, or even fairy tales, but there is a widespread feeling that it is quite impossible for modern people to accept them as literal facts.

We have already noticed in dealing with subjects such as the birth of Jesus that it is all too easy to make presuppositions of this kind an excuse for failing to take serious account of the nature of the actual evidence for remarkable events. A great many people find it difficult to conceive of the possibility of super-natural intervention in the natural world. But the question posed

Some of Jesus' miracles reported in the Gospels

	Matthew	Mark	Luke	John		Matthew	Mark	Luke	John
Healing of Peter's mother-in law	8:14–15	1:29–31	4:38–39		Feeding the 5,000	14:13–21	6:30–44	9:10–17	6:1–14
Turning water into wine				2:1–11	Walking on the water	14:22–33	6:45–52		
Miraculous catch of fish			5:1–11		Feeding the 4,000	15:32–39	8:1–10		
Healing the centurion's servant	8:5–13		7:1–10		Healing a blind man at Bethsaida		8:22–26		
Calming the storm	8:22–37	4:35–41	8:22–25		Healing the man blind from birth				9:1–12
The Gadarene demoniac healed	8:28–34	5:1–20	8:26–39		The epileptic boy healed	17:14–21	9:14–29	9:37–43	
Healing the paralysed man	9:1–8	2:1–12	5:17–26		Healing ten lepers			17:11–19	
Jairus' daughter healed	9:18–26	5:21–43	8:40–56		Lazarus raised from the dead				11:1–44
Widow's son raised from the dead			7:11–17		Blind Bartimaeus healed	20:29–34	10:46–52	18:35–43	

by the miracles of Jesus can hardly be answered simply by reference to our own disposition not to believe in miracles. Two other considerations are also important.

First of all we must ask ourselves whether the miracle stories are consistent with the teaching of Jesus himself, especially the teaching he gave about his own person. There can be no doubt that if the claims we examined in section one are in fact correct, we will not find it so difficult to accept the trustworthiness of the miracle stories. Not that this will solve the whole problem, of course. The believer can no more prove the truth of the miracles simply by reference to *his* presuppositions, than the unbeliever can disprove them by reference to his own rather different preconceptions. It is essential to take full acount of the evidence itself.

The miracles and the evidence

It is obviously important to look critically at all our sources of information before we even begin to consider the more general problems involved in understanding what we call 'miracles'. For if it can be shown that there is no good evidence for the belief that Jesus did in fact perform these deeds, we can forget all our other questions about the miracles.

When we look into ancient history it is striking to find that its evidence unambiguously supports the belief that Jesus was widely thought to have performed remarkable deeds of the kind mentioned in the Gospels. This evidence comes not only from the Gospels themselves, but also from non-Christian historical sources.

Jewish history

Josephus makes the following statement about Jesus: 'About this time arose Jesus, a wise man, if indeed it be lawful to call him a man. For he was a doer of wonderful deeds, and a teacher of men who gladly receive the truth. He drew to himself many both of the Jews and of the Gentiles. He was the Christ; and when Pilate, on the indictment of the principal men among us, had condemned him to the cross, those who had loved him at the first did not cease to do so, for he appeared to them again alive on the third

Jesus' miracles were intended to be a call to faith. He rejected the temptation to turn stones into bread, but used five loaves and two fishes to feed a crowd of 5,000 who had been listening to him all day.

Antiquities of the Jews
xviii 3.3

day, the divine prophets having foretold these and ten thousand other wonderful things about him. And even to this day the race of Christians, who are named from him, has not died out.'

This passage poses a certain problem, and scholars have different opinions as to how much of it was written directly by Josephus himself. The problem is that the passage says explicitly of Jesus that 'he was the Christ'. But of course we know that Josephus was not a Christian, and it would be remarkable for a Jew – even a renegade one – to make such an unequivocal statement. Perhaps this phrase has been inserted into Josephus's work by a later Christian editor. Or Josephus may originally have written that Jesus was 'called the Christ', and the text has subsequently been amended to make his reference more specific. But, in spite of this, most scholars have no doubts about the authenticity of the rest of Josephus's description of Jesus, which contains the statement that he was 'a doer of wonderful deeds'.

More evidence from a Jewish source is contained in the Babylonian Talmud (tractate *Sanhedrin* 43a) which reports that Jesus was executed because he practised 'sorcery' and misled the people. This is an interesting parallel to the evidence from the Gospels, which suggest that the Jews had no quarrel with Jesus over the *fact* of his miraculous power to heal, but only over the *source* of it. His Jewish opponents believed he was operating under the control of the devil, 'Beelzebul' – but they apparently had no reason to doubt the reality of what he was doing.

Matthew 12:22–28;
Luke 11:14–23

Early Christian preaching

A second source of information is the (admittedly slight) evidence provided by the *kerygma* of the early church, as reconstructed by Professor C. H. Dodd. One of the elements of this early statement of Christian belief was that the promises of the Old Testament had come true in the life, death and resurrection of Jesus. And in several places the ministry of Jesus is explicitly described in terms of miracle working. On the day of Pentecost, for example, Peter is reported as speaking of the 'mighty works and wonders and signs which God did through Jesus'. Again, in the sermon to Cornelius and his household, there is a mention of how Jesus 'went everywhere, doing good and healing all who were under the power of the devil, for God was with him'.

Acts 2:22

Acts 10:38

We need not enter here into the complex subject of the authenticity of these sermons attributed to Peter, for regardless of whether they come directly from him, they do suggest that at an early stage Christians believed that Jesus had performed miracles. They could also appeal to non-Christians on the basis of these miracles. If we take this together with the evidence from Jewish sources, it seems clear that most people who knew anything at all about Jesus' ministry believed that he had done remarkable deeds – and this belief was independent of whether or not they were themselves Christians.

Miracle stories in the Gospels

It is when we come to the Gospels themselves that we encounter some of the most formidable problems about Jesus' miracles. Three main questions need to be considered here.

● Some form critics, scholars who study how the Gospels were written, have shown that in their literary form the miracle stories of the Gospels are often similar to stories found in Hellenistic literature. A number of scholars have drawn particular attention to the parallels between the Gospel accounts and the stories of a first-century Cappadocian seer and wonder-

Jesus was out on the Lake of Galilee with his disciples when a storm arose. The disciples' fear turned to amazement when they saw Jesus calm the storm — his first miracle over the forces of nature.

worker found in the *Life of Apollonius*, written by the third-century author Philostratus. This of course is what we might expect, for the stories of Jesus' miracles were first written down by Greek-speaking people, who would naturally use the literary forms and conventions that were most familiar to them. It is hardly surprising that authors writing about the same kind of incidents in the same cultural situation should use similar language.

In addition, the 'parallels' drawn between Apollonius and Jesus favour the originality of the Gospel traditions. Not only are the Hellenistic stories of much later date than the New Testament, but they were published with the

express purpose of disputing the Christian claims about Jesus. If there is any question of 'dependence' by either account on the other, it could more easily be supposed that later writers consciously modelled their stories on the Gospel accounts than the other way round. In any case, similarity of literary form can really tell us nothing at all about the historical facts. (See the fuller discussion in section three.)

● It is a well-known fact of history that as time goes on, miracles tend to be attached to people who are highly regarded for other reasons. We can see this tendency at work in the legends that have been gathered around the lives of so many of the medieval saints. It is undeniable that the same thing happened to the stories of Jesus. We can see this from the so-called 'apocryphal gospels' which were written in the second century. They relate all kinds of bizarre miracle stories about Jesus. There are also certain miracle stories in the New Testament Gospels of Matthew and John that some scholars have compared with the stories in these apocryphal gospels. But on the whole there is compelling evidence to suggest that the central miraculous element of the New Testament Gospels does not derive from this kind of speculation.

In the first place, according to some recent datings of the Gospels, the earliest written records about the life of Jesus may be as early as AD 45, which is only fifteen years after his death. Even the more conventional dating of Mark to about AD 65–70 takes us only thirty-five years beyond the events recorded in the Gospels. A conscious mythologizing process would certainly need longer than that to develop, and at the time the Gospels were taking shape there must have been many surviving eye-witnesses of the events they describe. They could no doubt have corrected any stories that were out of character with Jesus as they remembered him.

Then there is also a striking difference between the miracle stories of the New Testament Gospels and the stories told about Hellenistic 'divine men', or medieval saints, or even about Jesus himself in the apocryphal gospels. There is, for example, nothing in the New Testament to compare with the grotesque tale told in the *Arabic Infancy Gospel*, according to which Jesus produced three children out of some goats he found in an oven. And even the story found in the *Infancy Gospel of Thomas* about Jesus turning twelve clay birds into real sparrows on the sabbath is of quite a different character from the stories told in the New Testament. Legendary tales of miracles are almost always concerned with the ostentatious display of special powers. But in the four Gospels there is none of this. Indeed it is made quite clear that the miracles Jesus performed were not concerned with satisfying idle speculation about the supernatural. When the Pharisees asked Jesus to perform a miracle to satisfy their curiosity, he told them in no uncertain terms that this kind of spectacle was quite alien to his work (Matthew 12:38–42; Mark 8:11–12; Luke 11:29–32).

It is also significant that Jesus is portrayed as a worker of miracles in even the very earliest strands of the Gospel traditions that we can trace. The Gospel source Q (see section three) is generally thought to have been an early collection of Jesus' sayings, but this material also reports one miracle, the healing of the Roman centurion's servant (Matthew 8:5–13; Luke 7:1–10). It also states that Jesus was in the habit of doing miracles. It is in Q that John's disciples are told to report the miracles they have seen (Matthew 11:1–19; Luke 7:18–35), and the cities of Galilee are condemned because they have not repented in spite of the miracles done in them (Matthew 11:20–24; Luke 10:13–15).

Perhaps the strongest reason for distinguishing the Gospel miracles from both pagan and later Christian stories is the fact that in the New Testament the miracles mean something. They are not just demonstrations of the supernatural for its own sake. Rather they are an essential part of Jesus' message about the arrival of God's new society.

● There is, however, yet another aspect. It is often pointed out by sceptics that in at least two of his temptations Jesus decisively rejected the temptation to perform miracles (Matthew 4:1–11; Luke 4:1–13). He was tempted to turn stones into bread and to throw himself from the temple without injury, and he refused to do either. Is it then likely that he would perform in the course of his ministry such a miracle as the feeding of the 5,000, which apparently resulted in the crowd trying to make him their king? (See John 6:1–15; Matthew 14:13–21; Mark 6:30–44; Luke 9:10–17.)

This is not such a problem as it appears at first sight. Indeed it only arises if we regard Jesus first and foremost as a wonder-worker. The ancient world was full of magicians who practised their art as a means of displaying their own special powers and significance. But the whole tone of the Gospel stories is quite different. Jesus' work is characterized not by a quest for power, but by humble service of God and man. In the temptations he rejected the possibility of commanding the obedience of men and women by working wonders, and the Gospels show how even

Jesus' ability to heal became so well known that crowds followed him wherever he went. Healing services and medical missions have remained an important part of Christian activity.

his miracles were subordinated to that intention. For the miracles, like his teaching and preaching, were a call for faith and obedience from those who experienced or witnessed them.

It seems therefore that the various pieces of evidence all have the same implication. Both Jewish and Christian sources suggest that Jesus did perform remarkable deeds. Though there is obviously room for making different judgements about different miracles, we cannot reasonably dispose of the whole of the miraculous element in the Gospel traditions. At the same time, we must resist the temptation to regard the miracles as an end in themselves. Like so many other parts of Jesus' ministry, their real importance lies in what they teach us about God.

The miracles and their meaning

To understand fully what the miracles mean, we have to set them in their proper context in the whole of Jesus' ministry. The Gospels view the life and work of Jesus against the background of God's promises in the Old Testament. These promises are being fulfilled in Jesus, and the long-awaited new society, or kingdom, has arrived.

This means that we need to begin our understanding of the precise significance of most of Jesus' teaching by looking at the Old Testament. For example, his self-designation as 'Son of man' would be difficult if not impossible to understand without our knowledge of its Old Testament meaning in the book of Daniel. Jesus' message about the kingdom of God would also be rather obscure if we did not link it with the Old Testament promises. The same is true of the miracles.

In the Old Testament, miracles invariably meant something. What God says is often associated with what he does. Indeed, in Hebrew the word *dabar* can mean both a word and an action, and the two were very closely linked together in Hebrew thought. God's actions could be regarded as an extension of his words. What he does is essentially identical with what he says. So, for example, at the time of the exodus the remarkable deeds performed by Moses before Pharaoh were not just wonders performed for effect. They were themselves the vehicle of God's message, living signs of the truth of God's words.

Exodus 10:1–2

This idea was taken up especially by the prophets of the Old Testament, who often performed symbolic actions to illustrate and enforce their message. Isaiah, for example, walked round Jerusalem naked and barefoot as a symbol of his belief that Judah's allies would soon be destroyed by their enemies. Ezekiel drew a picture of a besieged city on a tile, as a picture of what was going to happen to his own city of Jerusalem. Yet these actions were more than just symbols or illustrations. They were a part of God's message through the prophets, and were closely bound up with the meaning of God's activities in the history of his people.

Isaiah 20:1–6

Ezekiel 4:1–3

When the New Testament calls Jesus' miracles 'signs', it is probably this kind of 'dynamic illustration' that is in mind. Our English word 'sign' implies merely a symptom or an indication, and so it is easy for us to suppose that the miracles were nothing more than artificially contrived indications to prove that

Magdala was once a fishing town on the western shore of Lake Galilee. Mary Magdalene, one of many people whom Jesus released from the power of evil, came from this region.

Jesus was the Messiah, or that the new society had come. But they are more than that. Like the 'signs' given by the prophets, the miracles are part of Jesus' message. They are an extension in actions of the teaching given in the parables. Like that teaching, they describe God's new society and present its challenge to men and women.

When we consider the miracles in this light we can see that they draw attention to three aspects of the new society, or 'kingdom of God'.

The arrival of the kingdom

Mark 1:15

When Jesus began his teaching ministry, the main content of his message was the declaration that 'the kingdom of God is at hand'. The precise meaning that we give to the phrase 'at hand' will depend on our view of Jesus' eschatology. But most scholars agree that at least one implication of the statement is that the kingdom has already come into existence with the coming of Jesus himself. This is brought out quite clearly in Jesus' miracles, where the arrival of God's kingdom is both declared and explained.

On one occasion John the Baptist sent some of his disciples to ask Jesus whether he was indeed the Messiah who was to inaugurate God's new society. And the answer that Jesus gave was as follows: 'Go and tell John what you hear and see: the blind receive their sight and the lame walk, lepers are cleansed and the deaf hear, and the dead are raised up, and the poor have

Matthew 11:4–5; Luke 7:22

good news preached to them.' These words in which Jesus addressed John were a quotation from the Old Testament book of Isaiah, and were generally believed to be a reference to the

Isaiah 35:5–6

future messianic age. Jesus was telling John that his miracles were a sign that ancient promises were coming true.

In John's Gospel the miracles are actually called 'signs'. Through the miracles men and women realize not only that the new society has come, but that Jesus is its central figure. In the first miracle recorded in John (the changing of water into wine) Jesus 'revealed his glory, and his disciples believed in him'. Later on, the raising of Lazarus is 'the means by which the Son of God will receive glory'. Yet Jesus did not use miracles for personal gain. In the prologue to John's Gospel we are reminded that Jesus' glory was not his own. It was the glory of God, which he shared as God's Son. The same theme comes out in a number of the miracle stories, where Jesus requires praise to be given to God and not to himself. In the miracles, God was demonstrating his own power so that men and women would realize that his long awaited kingdom had arrived with the coming of Jesus.

John 2:11

John 11:4

John 1:14

Luke 17:11–19; John 11:4

The scope of the kingdom

The miracles not only announce the arrival of the kingdom in a general sense: their message also parallels Jesus' explicit teaching in many more detailed ways. It is not difficult to see how the various types of miracle that Jesus performed were meant to emphasize in a striking way the different things he said in the parables about the new society. The miracles fall into three main groups, each group expressing a different aspect of Jesus' teaching. They declare the meaning of the kingdom for individual men and women, for the world as a whole, and in the future.

● *The kingdom and the individual.* In one of his temptations, the devil had claimed that *he* was the master of the world's kingdoms. Many people in the time of Jesus would have agreed with him. As they looked at their own lives and the lives of other people, they saw suffering and illness and death as signs that their lives were influenced by the operation of evil forces in the world. It was commonly believed that disease was caused by the demonic members of an evil spiritual world operating in the natural, physical world. Sin and evil caused disease – not in the personal sense implied by those Pharisees who suggested that because a person was blind he and his family must be great sinners, but in a cosmic sense, so that human illness was seen as a part of the total fallenness of God's creation.

Matthew 4:8–10; Luke 4:5–7

John 9:1–12

We have seen that an important part of Jesus' teaching was that men and women could be set free from the mastery of sin in their lives. In the casting out of demons and in the other healing miracles, Jesus made this announcement in the most dramatic way possible. He also underlined another part of his teaching, for the miracles more often than not involved those who were the outcasts of society – lepers, whom no one would touch for fear of religious impurity; a Roman centurion, whom many Jews must have hated; those who were past helping themselves. Those were the people to whom Jesus' message and miracles were of most value.

Matthew 8:1–4; Luke 17:11–19 Matthew 8:5–13; Luke 7:1–10 Mark 5:21–43

● *The kingdom and the world.* If the healing miracles show Jesus releasing individual people from the power of sin, the 'nature miracles' show Jesus doing the same for the whole of creation. The devil's power had affected not just the lives of

John 12:31
Mark 4:39
Mark 1:25

individuals, but the life of nature as well. There was a real sense in which Satan *was* the ruler of the world, and Jesus had come to cast him out of every part of his dominion. So he 'rebukes' the wind and the waves in the same way as he 'rebukes' the demons that have such a harmful effect in the lives of men and women.

It was an important part of Jesus' message that he had come to save men and women in their whole environment, and in the nature miracles we have a striking declaration of the global scope of Jesus' work.

● *The kingdom in the future.* It is interesting that the future dimension of Jesus' teaching about the new society is also preserved in the miracles. In Jewish thought the future kingdom of God was often pictured as a meal, and Jesus himself described it in terms of a banquet. The miraculous feeding of the 5,000 and of the 4,000 are an acting out of this picture, in which Jesus showed himself as God's Messiah feeding God's people. According to one account of the feeding of the 5,000, the people were so impressed by what took place that they thought Jesus was meaning to imply that they should make him their king there and then.

Matthew 8:11; Luke 22:30;
14:15–24

Matthew 14:13–21;
Mark 6:30–44;
Luke 9:10–17;
Matthew 15:32–39;
Mark 8:1–10
John 6:14–15

Mark 5:21–43;
Luke 7:11–17;
John 11:1–44

There are also three instances in which Jesus restored to life people who were dead. These miracles are an expression in action of his teaching that his followers would have 'eternal life', by which they could anticipate in the present the future blessings of the messianic kingdom.

The challenge of the kingdom

When we dealt with the parables, we saw that they were a way of making people think out the full implications of God's new society in their own lives, and we noticed that without repentance

Bethany was the home town of Mary, Martha and Lazarus. Here Jesus brought Lazarus back to life – a miracle that caused such a stir that the Jewish leaders began plotting to kill Jesus.

and faith the full meaning of many of the parables would be hidden. The challenge of God's rule is presented in exactly the same terms in the miracle stories.

Faith seems to have been important in Jesus' cures. On three occasions Jesus says, 'Your faith has made you well' and according to Mark the absence of faith was a hindrance to performing miracles. Indeed without faith it was not possible to realize that the miracles were a sign of God at work, and unbelief led to the conclusion that Jesus was in league with Satan.

Mark 5:34; 10:52;
Luke 17:19

Mark 6:5

Matthew 12:24

Some students of the New Testament point out that in modern psychiatry 'faith' is often an important part of a cure, and they suggest that this may offer some sort of explanation of the healings Jesus performed. There is no doubt that observations of this kind have helped many people to accept the truth of the Gospel accounts. And there is equally no reason to suppose that Jesus, who knew what was in the heart of men, could not have anticipated some of the methods of modern psychology.

John 2:23–25

But the faith that Jesus required was really rather different from the kind of faith the psychiatrist asks for. What Jesus demanded was not a predisposition to be healed, but an unconditional acceptance of God's rule. To ask Jesus for healing was a sign of this kind of faith, that is, faith in the sense that it appears in the parables – implicit trust in God and in Jesus as his Son, so that we may share in the benefits of his new society.

Matthew 8:13; 15:28

The purpose of the miracles can therefore be helpfully compared with the purpose of the parables. To those who are willing to trust God they are the vehicle of revelation. But to those whose minds are closed not even a miracle will bring the possibility of enlightenment.

Luke 16:19–31

Chapter 9 God's society in action

Mark 2:27

Much of Jesus' teaching was in the open air, on the hills and in the crowded market places. Christians have often followed his example and proclaimed their faith in public places.

EVERY society, no matter how primitive or how civilized, has found it necessary to have rules and regulations to govern the conduct of its members. Often these rules are simply the result of what experience has taught about the best ways of doing things. Sometimes, as in a few of the law codes of the ancient Near East, the rules stem from a system of religious beliefs.

Occasionally, as in the Old Testament, we find a mixture of both. Not that the Old Testament seemed quite that simple to the people who were trying to follow it in Jesus' day. For by then the relatively straightforward laws of the Old Testament had been complicated by the addition of detailed interpretations and applications – so much so that one needed to be a theologian even to understand them, let alone to keep them.

Jesus' attitude to behaviour was quite different from that. On several occasions he directly challenged the rules laid down by the Pharisees. On the question of the sabbath day, for example, Jesus declared his belief that 'the sabbath was made for man, not man for the sabbath'. It was a day for men and women to use and enjoy rather than a dull and dreary day to be spent trying desperately not to profane it. The Pharisees were naturally distressed at this setting aside of their law, for after all its avowed purpose was to help men and women to please God – and how else could they do that except by obeying his requirements?

As we read the Gospels it is clear that Jesus, too, was intending to help people to know God. But the God of whom he spoke was pictured rather differently. He was not a God who required the observance of a lot of impossible regulations, but a God with whom one could have a personal relationship as Father. Jesus' Father was a forgiving God, one who cared about people even in their moral imperfection. But he was concerned that they should get to know him better so that his power might be set loose to transform their lives.

We have seen the implications of all this in the parables that Jesus told, and we have also noticed some of the ethical consequences of his teaching. Those who live in fellowship with God must also love their neighbours. They must care for the

The synagogue

Synagogues were the local centres of Jewish worship, and many were also schools. The drawing is an artist's impression of what such a building would have looked like in Jesus' time, based on the ruins at Capernaum. Many synagogues were not so lavish as this, however. The photograph shows the ruins of the synagogue at Capernaum. The building probably dates from the end of the second century AD, but is almost certainly on the same site as the synagogue in which Jesus taught.

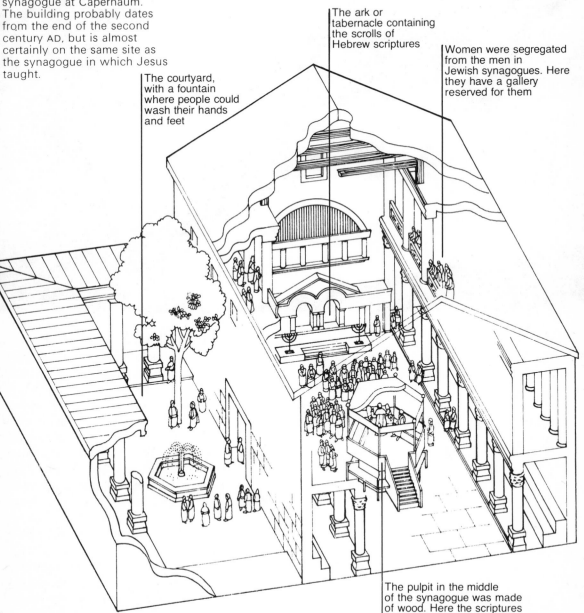

The ark or tabernacle containing the scrolls of Hebrew scriptures

Women were segregated from the men in Jewish synagogues. Here they have a gallery reserved for them

The courtyard, with a fountain where people could wash their hands and feet

The pulpit in the middle of the synagogue was made of wood. Here the scriptures were read and sermons preached

Jesus told his hearers to be careful of false teachers, who would betray themselves by the way they lived. 'A healthy tree cannot bear bad fruit, and a poor tree cannot bear good fruit,' he said. Fruit trees — these are figs — grow abundantly in Israel.

Matthew 5–7

outcasts of society, and be concerned for one another's welfare. But why should God's people act like this? What is the basis for the ethical teaching – the teaching about behaviour – that Jesus gave, and how can we understand it? These are the questions that we shall try to answer in this chapter.

It is of course not very easy to speak of Jesus' ethics in isolation from the rest of his teaching. All of his teaching about God and his new society has an ethical dimension to it. And the Sermon on the Mount, which is generally taken to be the most comprehensive collection of ethical teachings in the Gospels, is also full of theology. Nevertheless, this sermon does give us a good idea of the place of ethics in the new society that Jesus had come to inaugurate.

Before we look at the actual content of the Sermon on the Mount, we first need to consider the best way of understanding what Jesus says in it. This is an important question, for it is obvious that the way Jesus gives his teaching here is quite different from the approach of modern ethics textbooks, and even quite different from the ways ordinary people would express the same ideas. As a good teacher, Jesus naturally used forms of language and expression that would mean something to those who first heard him. There are at least three distinctive devices used in putting over his teaching.

● Much of the sermon is poetry, though until it is pointed out to us we probably would not recognize it as such. English poetry depends for its effect on rhyme or stress. But Hebrew poetry was rather different. It depended for its effect on a correspondence of thought, and there could be two basic kinds of poetry depending on whether the correspondence was one of similarity or of difference. Take, for example, the following statement from Matthew. This can be arranged poetically as follows:

Matthew 7:6

'Do not give dogs what is holy;
and do not throw your pearls before swine.'

What we have here is genuine Hebrew poetry, in which the second line repeats the thought of the first line, but using different imagery. This is called 'synonymous parallelism', and there are many examples of it in the psalms and other poetic sections of the Old Testament.

Another type of Hebrew poetry was what we call 'antithetical parallelism'. Again there is an example of this in Matthew:

Matthew 7:17

'Every sound tree bears good fruit,
but the bad tree bears bad fruit.'

A similar lesson is being taught in each line, but the thought is expressed by the use of exactly opposite concepts. This technique also occurs frequently in the Old Testament.

Matthew 6:9–13

Even the Lord's Prayer can be arranged poetically. Professor A. M. Hunter sets it out like this:

'Our father in heaven   hallowed be thy name,
Thy kingdom come;   Thy will be done;
As in the heavens,   so on earth.
Our daily bread   give us today
And forgive us our debts,   as we forgive our debtors;
And lead us not into
temptation,   but deliver us from evil.'

● Another common feature of Jesus' teaching is the use of pictures. Sometimes they take the form of story-parables; on other occasions they are simply vivid illustrations from everyday life. Many of the parables do of course teach moral lessons, but the Sermon on the Mount makes much use of pictures from real life. This is quite different from the way we tend to moralize today. We speak of ethics in an abstract way, but Jesus always dealt with concrete things. For example, we might say, 'Materialism can be a hindrance to spiritual growth'. Jesus said, 'No one can be a slave of two masters. . . . You cannot serve both

Matthew 6:24

God and money.'

● Jesus stated things in a vivid way. He often used extreme exaggeration to make his point. For example, he said that it is

Matthew 5:29

better to pull one's eye out rather than to commit adultery, or better to cut one's hand off rather than displease God. He was obviously not meaning to suggest that we should do either of these things, but he used this extravagant language to impress on his hearers the seriousness of his message.

As we read the Sermon on the Mount, we need to look out for these different techniques that Jesus used to put over his message. Recognizing the different forms will often help us to understand what Jesus was meaning to say.

What sort of ethic, then, did Jesus put forward? What principles of action should guide those who accept God's sovereignty in their lives? There are three things that distinguish the ethic of God's new society from most other ethical systems.

Jesus declares God's standards

Jesus' ethical teaching is quite inseparable from his teaching about God's sovereignty in the lives of men and women. Without understanding this, it is very difficult to make sense of the Sermon on the Mount.

All ethical systems have a basic premise from which everything else is developed. Jesus' ethical teaching is based on the declaration that the God who created all things and who acted in history in the experience of Israel recorded in the Old Testament can be known in a realistic and personal way. The behaviour of his followers is a natural outcome of their personal association with God, their Father.

This principle had always had a central place in Judaism. The Old Testament itself was based on two simple premises that are also basic to Jesus' teaching in the New Testament.

Human goodness takes its character from God

Leviticus 19:2

The central part of one section of the Old Testament law is the statement, 'You shall be holy; for I the Lord your God am holy'. The ethical standards which God's people were required to achieve were nothing less than a reflection of the character of God himself. One scholar sums it up by describing biblical ethics as 'the science of human conduct, as it is determined by divine conduct'. Men and women should behave as God behaves.

One of the most characteristic of God's activities in the experience of Israel had been his willingness to care for people who had no thought for him. Abraham was called from Mesopotamia and given a new homeland not because of any moral or spiritual superiority that he may have possessed, but simply because God's affection was centred on him. Israel subsequently emerged from the shattering experiences of the exodus and what followed, not because of their own moral perfection but simply through the care of a loving God. On the basis of these undeserved acts of kindness, God had made certain demands of his people.

The Ten Commandments begin with the statement, 'I am the Lord your God, who brought you out of the land of Egypt,

Exodus 20:2

out of the house of bondage . . .' This is the presupposition on which the commandments are based. Because God has done something for his people, they are to respond in love and obedience to him. The same pattern is found elsewhere in the law of the Old Testament: 'You shall remember that you were a slave in the land of Egypt, and the Lord your God redeemed you; *therefore* I command you today . . .'

Deuteronomy 15:15

The ethic of the New Testament has exactly the same basis of action. It is striking, for instance, that when Paul wanted to stop the quarrelling that was going on in the church at Philippi, he appealed not to ordinary common sense to solve the problem, but to just this very aspect of God's character that we have seen in the Old Testament. He takes the example of the way God gave himself for our salvation in Christ and makes this the basis of his moral appeal to his readers. Because Jesus gave up everything for us, we ought to be willing to sacrifice our self-centredness in order to please him.

Philippians 2:5–11

The fact that God's character as a holy God and as a loving Father underlies all the Bible's teaching on behaviour has at least three important practical consequences . . .

● It has given to both Jews and Christians a greater sense of the seriousness of sin. When people are faced with a holy God who was willing to give himself entirely in love for the benefit of those who neither cared for him nor respected him, they recognize how different their own character is from the character of their God. When Isaiah, for instance, had been impressed with the true meaning of God's holiness, his immediate reaction was to appreciate, perhaps for the first time, the full extent of his own sinfulness. The same must have been true of most people who met Jesus. In many cases Jesus forgave the sins of those who came to him – and he reminds us himself that only those who recognize their need can be forgiven.

Isaiah 6:1–8

Jesus said that his teaching was not intended to replace the Old Testament law but to make it come true. This Hebrew scroll is part of the Torah, or Law.

● Christian goodness has a numinous, other-wordly quality that goes beyond the demands of common sense. The character of God as revealed by Jesus shows his self-giving love, and this is recommended in practical action over and over again in Jesus' teaching. The rich man was told to '. . . go, sell what you have, and give to the poor . . .' In the Sermon on the Mount Jesus tells his disciples to go two miles if the Roman troops force them to carry their bags for one. They are to 'turn the other cheek' and return good for evil. These things often seem quite unreasonable to us, perhaps even absurd. But when we view them in the light of what God has been willing to sacrifice for us, they take on a different appearance.

Mark 10:21

Matthew 5:38–42

● The overwhelming desire of God's people should be to please God and to respond to his love in ways that reflect his own character. This is their motivation to obey Jesus' commands. We are to love our enemies not in order to draw attention to ourselves, but 'so that you may become the sons of your Father in heaven'.

Matthew 5:45

Christian goodness and the community

Matthew 22:34–40;
Mark 12:28–34;
Luke 10:25–28

The central theme of the Old Testament is the belief that God had acted decisively in the history of his people Israel and had entered into an intimate relationship with them through the making of a covenant. This meant that the individual Israelite was never simply an individual, but a member of the people of God. As a result of this the goodness that God required was to be demonstrated not simply in pious individuals but in the institutions of national life.

In the same way Jesus declared that he had come to establish God's kingship in the lives of his followers, and not only in their lives as individuals, but in their corporate life together. One of the two great commandments was that men and women should love their neighbour as themselves. And those who were willing to accept God's rule over their lives were given a new commandment that was to be the basis of the Christian community: 'that you love one another; even as I have loved you, that you also

'Do not save riches for yourselves here on earth, where moths and rust destroy,' Jesus said. His ethical teaching has been a source of inspiration to many people. The way of life of individuals and whole societies have been transformed by its application by dedicated Christians.

William Wilberforce was a nineteenth-century Christian politician who campaigned for many years for the abolition of the slave trade.

The Earl of Shaftesbury also campaigned during the last century for shorter working hours and better conditions in Victorian mines and factories.

John 13:34—35

love one another. By this all men will know that you are my disciples, if you have love for one another.'

Jesus' ethic demands commitment

Jesus' teaching was intended as a way of life only for those people who subjected their lives to God's rule. This is the point at which Jesus' ethic has most frequently been misunderstood. People who claim to be able to accept the Sermon on the Mount but not the claims that Jesus made about his own person have misunderstood the essential character of Jesus' teaching. It is quite impossible to isolate his theology from his ethics, and to do so destroys both.

In his introduction to the Sermon on the Mount Matthew tells us it was the disciples who formed the audience for the sermon; and the various elements of it are clearly directed to certain committed people, not to all and sundry. This was clearly

Mother Teresa has lived for many years in Calcutta caring for the sick and orphaned. Jesus specifically commanded his followers to care for the needy.

Jesus also warned his followers that some of them would be persecuted for their faith. Archbishop Janani Luwum is believed to have been murdered by the Ugandan authorities for speaking out against injustice.

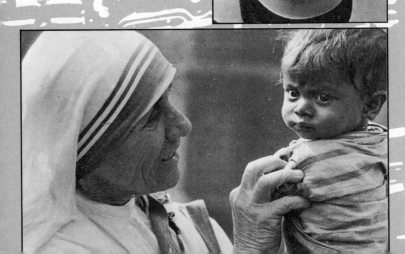

Jesus could be stern as well as thoughtful. On one occasion he said that if a man caused a child 'to lose his faith in me' it would be better for him 'to have a large millstone tied round his neck and be drowned in the deep sea'.

understood by the earliest Christians. The sermon was almost certainly used in the form we know it to instruct new converts in the churches with which Matthew was associated in the first century. Both in the context of Jesus' life and in the context of the early church, the ethical instruction of the sermon was preceded by the preaching and acceptance of the Christian message.

C. H. Dodd has demonstrated that two strands of early Christian teaching can be distinguished in the New Testament, and it is interesting to find that they correspond to the general pattern we have noticed in the ethics of the Old Testament. On the one hand there is the kind of teaching that he calls *kerygma*. This was essentially a declaration of what God had done for men and women in the life, death and resurrection of Jesus.

This was comparable to the way Abraham and his descendants had been called and established as a nation in the Old Testament. God had acted through Jesus not because of any moral value in the people who became his followers, but out of his own undeserved love – what Christians call 'grace'. As Israel had been called to obey the Law on the basis of what God had done, so too the early Christians could be given moral and spiritual exhortations.

Professor Dodd called this *didache*, or 'teaching'. We can see this distinction most clearly in some of the letters of Paul, which often deal with theological matters first and then make practical appeals to Christians on the basis of the theological arguments. But the distinction is not terribly important, and in reality both *kerygma* and *didache* tend to run into one another, for the ethic of the New Testament is not some rule imposed from outside, but a new quality of life given to Christians through what Jesus has done for them.

We can illustrate this from some of the individual sayings of the Sermon on the Mount, none of which can be understood apart from the belief that in Jesus God had broken into history in a decisive way. When Jesus says to his disciples, 'forgive others the wrongs they have done to you', it is because they themselves are receiving God's forgiveness. When they are called to love their enemies we call to mind the dynamic of God's own love, shown to them when they had no regard for him. In each case God's gift, his free grace, comes before his demand for action. Even the missionary work of the disciples was to be carried out on the same basis. Jesus told them that since 'You have received without paying, so give without being paid'.

Matthew 6:14–15
Matthew 5:44

Matthew 10:8

Jesus teaches an ethic of freedom

One of the greatest temptations to all readers of the Sermon on the Mount has always been to try to interpret it as a set of rules and regulations – a new law for Christians, to replace the old law of the Old Testament. This was something that emerged very early in the church's history, and some scholars believe that even Matthew himself considered it to be a 'new law' delivered by Jesus on a mountain in Galilee, comparable to the 'old law' delivered by Moses on Mt Sinai.

But the ethical teaching of Jesus was never intended to be a 'law' in any sense at all.

●The teaching of the Sermon on the Mount is quite different from what we normally understand by 'law'. Most laws are based on calculations of how the majority of people can reasonably be expected to behave. A law that cannot be kept is a bad law, and it is no use making a law to put pressure on men and

In the Sermon on the Mount Jesus spoke of those whose faith did not stretch to trusting God for everyday things. 'Look how the wild flowers grow,' he said. 'It is God who clothes the wild grass. Won't he be all the more sure to clothe you?'

women to become what they are not. But this, of course, is essentially what Jesus' teaching does: it asks us to be different from what we would naturally be. It is therefore inadequate to regard it as a 'new law', because its requirements are not the kind that anyone could keep simply by making the effort.

● Throughout the course of his ministry Jesus was in conflict with the Pharisees, the law-makers of the Jewish nation. They were concerned with actions that could be governed by rules. But Jesus had a different approach altogether. He was most concerned with people and principles. For him the secret of goodness was to be found not in obedience to rules, but in the spontaneous activities of a transformed character. 'A sound tree cannot bear evil fruit, nor can a bad tree bear good fruit.'

Matthew 7:18

Jesus' teaching is not a law. It is an ethic of freedom. Those who accept God's sovereignty within his new society enjoy the freedom to know him in the context of a living relationship as their Father. Jesus' Sermon on the Mount does not give rules and regulations. It sets out principles, and the principles are more concerned with what a person is than with what he does. Not that actions are unimportant. But Jesus realized that the way we behave depends on the kind of people we are. Without the right internal disposition and motivation, we cannot even begin to understand Jesus' ethical teaching. For, as T. W. Manson succinctly put it, Jesus' teaching is 'a compass rather than an ordnance map; it gives direction rather than directions'.

Did Jesus abolish the Old Testament Law?

One statement found in the Sermon on the Mount often causes some difficulty. This is the saying, in Matthew 5:17-18, 'Think not that I have come to abolish the law and the prophets; I have come not to abolish them but to fulfil them. For truly, I say to you, till heaven and earth pass away, not an iota, not a dot, will pass from the law until all is accomplished.'

Several explanations have been suggested for this statement.

● The simplest of them is to argue that this saying is not in fact original to Jesus, but has come into the sermon later and reflects a situation in the Jewish Christian churches for whom Matthew was writing his Gospel. Matthew may have had in mind the chaos that had been caused in some churches as a result of misunderstanding Paul's teaching about freedom from the restraint of the law, and perhaps he wished to pre-empt any similar movement by the Christians he knew. This may appear to be a drastic solution, but these verses are so out of character with the whole of the rest of Jesus' teaching

that many scholars believe it to be the best answer.

● It has also been suggested that when Jesus speaks of 'fulfilling the law' he may have meant something rather different from what we imagine him to mean. The new society that Jesus talks about is usually depicted as the fulfilment of the Old Testament, and an important element in the Old Testament was the belief that God's people could enjoy a living relationship with him. Though the scribes and Pharisees had externalized and legalized this relationship, Jesus could have been referring to its original intention, which called for a person's life to be right before God: 'what does the Lord require of you but to do justice, and to love kindness, and to walk humbly with your God?' (Micah 6:8).

● It is also possible that what Jesus says about the Law's permanence is not to be taken literally. Like so much of his teaching, it could be an exaggerated way of emphasizing that his whole mission and message were firmly grounded in the Old Testament revelation.

Section Three
Knowing about Jesus

Chapter 10   **What are the Gospels?**

Ruins of the forum in Rome (associated with Luke and Mark).

IN the first two sections of this book, we have said a great deal about the life and teachings of Jesus, but very little about how we have come to know about him. Naturally, our picture of Jesus has been based on those parts of the New Testament which tell of his life and work – the four books we call 'Gospels', and commonly associate with the names of Matthew, Mark, Luke and John.

Yet it must by now be obvious that in understanding the Gospels we have made a number of assumptions about them that, in one way or another, have coloured the picture of Jesus presented here. For example, we have assumed that the Gospels are not so much biographies of Jesus, as selective presentations of those aspects of his life and teaching which seemed most important to the people who first wrote them down. In addition, we have assumed that there is a good deal of overlap and repetition in the various accounts of Jesus' life, so that one Gospel may be used to elaborate or clarify the teaching contained in another. Then we have also implied that it is actually possible to know something about Jesus from the study of the Gospels – that, although they are indeed the products of the early church, they tell us not only about their writers but about Jesus himself.

The time has now come to examine some of these assumptions in greater detail, to explain the reasons for holding them, and to explore their implications.

What is a Gospel?

The modern reader approaching one of the Gospels for the first time may think it looks very much like a biography of Jesus. But a quick glance through any one of them will show that it is hardly that. A good biography usually begins with an account of the subject's childhood years, and progresses consecutively through adolescence and adulthood to show how the mature person has developed in response to the various influences of early life and environment. By contrast, the main emphasis in the Gospels is not on the course of Jesus' life, but on the events of the last week or so. This is prefaced by reports of Jesus' teaching and accounts of a few incidents from the three years immediately preceding his death, with virtually no mention at all of his childhood and adolescence. If this is biography, then it is certainly no ordinary biography.

We can most easily find out what it is by turning to the Gospels themselves. Rather than trying to classify them as a modern librarian would, we should ask what their authors thought they were doing as they wrote. Take Mark, for instance, the Gospel commonly thought to be the earliest of the four. The author describes his work in the opening sentence as 'The beginning

Mark 1:1 of the gospel of Jesus Christ'. This statement stands as a kind of title or heading to what follows, and two words are important here for an understanding of the purpose of the Gospel: the words 'beginning' and 'gospel'. 'Gospel' is simply the English equivalent of Mark's Greek word *euangelion*, and it was originally chosen because the two words had the same meaning: 'good news'. Mark, then, was writing about 'the beginning of the good news'.

What does this mean? Mark and the other Gospel writers had heard the 'good news' about Jesus. They had accepted its authority and recognized Jesus as Lord of their lives. Mark himself had subsequently become deeply involved in the work

Acts 12:25–13:13; 15:36–40; of the church, and an important part of this work was preaching
Colossians 4:10; and teaching the message that had changed his own life. This
2 Timothy 4:11 preaching and teaching is recorded in the New Testament. In its most basic form it consisted of the statements summed up by C. H. Dodd in his definition of the earliest *kerygma*. For Mark and his contemporaries this message was not just a bare statement of the facts about the Christian faith: it was also in an important sense the 'good news' of their faith, because as they accepted its challenge to repentance they found it a life-changing experience.

So when Mark describes his Gospel as 'the beginning of the good news', he is saying that his purpose is to describe the first stage in the development of the message to which he and others had responded. The story he tells was an integral and important part of their own story and experience as Christians. Luke had a similar intention: he writes so that his readers may know the full implications of the Christian message which they had heard so

Luke 1:4 often. Indeed, Luke felt it necessary to emphasize the continuity of the life of the church with the life of Jesus by writing a second volume (the Acts of the Apostles) to bring the story more fully up to date.

When we call the writers of the Gospels 'evangelists' we are therefore accurately describing their intention. For they were primarily concerned to deliver the message about Jesus to their own contemporaries, and only secondarily, if at all, with the normal interests of a biographer. This fact has at least three important consequences for our understanding of the Gospels they wrote.

● We must regard the Gospels as a *selective* account of the life and teachings of Jesus. In their preaching of the message the apostles and others no doubt spoke of incidents from Jesus' life in much the same way as a modern preacher may use appropriate illustrations to explain his theological points. Mark and the other evangelists had no doubt heard these incidents used to illustrate many a sermon, and they incorporated them into their Gospels for broadly similar purposes. Indeed Papias, one of the Fathers of the early church, claimed that Mark's Gospel consists of material extracted from the preaching of none other than Peter himself.

The fact that the information contained in the Gospels was first used to illustrate the message of the church also explains some of the difficulties we often feel about the apparent incompleteness of the Gospel accounts. All four of them put together would hardly contain enough information to document three years of anyone's life, let alone someone as active as Jesus. But when we realize that the information we have has been preserved because of its relevance to the life of the earliest churches, we can readily understand why so much that we would like to know has been left out.

This probably explains why we find no mention in the New Testament of the early childhood of Jesus, nor for that matter any descriptions of what he looked like, or the kind of person he was. Had the evangelists been writing merely to satisfy people's curiosity about Jesus, they would have included that sort of information. But that was not their intention. They were primarily concerned to win other people to faith in their Lord and Master, and for this purpose such details were quite irrelevant.

● If the Gospels are illustrations of the apostolic preaching, this means that we cannot regard their contents as simple stories about Jesus. They must be closely related to the theology of the evangelists. At one time it was fashionable to suppose that it was possible to recover from the Gospels a picture of a simple Galilean teacher which had later been altered by Paul and others into a theological message about the Son of God. But it is now widely recognized that the Gospels are themselves among the most important theological documents of the early church, and we can never in fact discover a picture of Jesus as a simple Galilean teacher. As far back as we can go, the Jesus whom we find in the pages of the New Testament is always a person who makes great claims for himself and utters definitive pronouncements on the relationship of men and women to God. All his teaching and every incident recorded in the Gospels has something specifically theological to tell us.

● If, as we have suggested, the authors selected their materials to serve their own purposes in writing, it follows that we can probably discover something about them and their readers by comparing their relative selection and use of information about Jesus. In the case of the first three Gospels we can do this quite easily, for they tell roughly the same story in the same order, and each of them repeats large sections of the material that is found in the others. By comparing the different ways that Matthew, Mark and Luke have used the deeds and teaching of Jesus in their narratives, we can readily learn something about them and the situation in which they lived and worked.

So to understand the Gospels fully is a rather complex business. We need to know why the evangelists wrote as and when they did. Then we need to try to understand the way they assembled their material, and why they used it in one particular way rather than another. And always we need to bear in mind that their Gospels were intended to serve the preaching ministry of the church: they were not written as biography, history, or even theology in the usual sense.

Preaching and writing

An obvious question to ask about the Gospels is: Where did the evangelists get their information, and what did they do with it? This may seem at first to be a rather irrelevant question, a kind of theologian's 'Everest', demanding to be conquered just because it happens to be there. But it is a helpful question for a satisfactory understanding of the nature of the Gospels. Tracing an author's sources and investigating his method of using them can be an important part of understanding what he is saying. If we know what he is doing, then we can understand more clearly what he may be getting at. And if we misunderstand his method, it is quite likely that we will also fail to grasp his essential message.

Ruins on the seashore at Caesarea (associated with Luke in its final form).

Since the Gospels almost certainly developed in the context of the preaching of the early church, we may expect to find some clues to their origin by examining the church's message. This essentially contains three major themes. First, the Christian gospel was connected with the promises of the Old Testament. Then came a series of statements about Jesus and his significance. Finally there was a challenge to men and women to repent and accept the message.

Old Testament texts

The message began with the statement that the promises of the Old Testament had been fulfilled in the life of Jesus. In the New Testament summaries of the preaching this statement is often made in a rather generalized way. But of course in real life situations it must have been a more specific declaration. For anyone familiar with the Old Testament would not be content until they had found out just which prophecies Jesus was supposed to have fulfilled. We know from other evidence that one of the favourite occupations of the Jews was the compilation of lists of Old Testament passages which the Messiah would fulfil when he came. The people at Qumran, for example, kept such lists, and so did other Jewish groups. These lists are generally referred to by scholars as *testimonia*.

There are a number of indications in the New Testament that these text-lists were probably in regular use amongst Christians from the earliest times. In both Matthew and John a great number of texts from the Old Testament are cited, with an indication that they were fulfilled in some particular incident in the life of Jesus. Yet it is striking that they hardly ever used the same passages. This may well have been because they were using different collections of *testimonia*.

In some of Paul's letters, too, we find Old Testament texts strung together in continuous passages in what often seems to be a rather arbitrary fashion. Again, it is reasonable to think that Paul originally found these grouped together under the same heading in his collection of Old Testament texts. It may well be that the collection of these texts from the Old Testament was the very earliest form of literary activity in the Christian church. They would be assembled for the convenience of Christian preachers, so that they could cite specific examples to support their claim that Jesus had fulfilled the Old Testament promises concerning the Messiah.

Words of Jesus

But the central element in the *kerygma* was the series of statements about Jesus himself. No doubt in the very earliest days of the church's existence it would be possible to proclaim the message with no more than a passing reference to Jesus' life and teachings. For most Christians were Jews and the church was still a local Palestinian sect, and many people in Palestine must have known something about Jesus, however little. But it was not very long before Christian missionaries were spreading out far beyond Palestine and carrying their teaching to parts of the Roman Empire where Jesus was quite unknown. It must have been essential at this stage for the preachers of the good news to include in their message some kind of factual information about Jesus himself, if only the account of the events of his death and resurrection.

Once people had become Christians they would require further instruction in their new faith. This instruction would include information about Christian beliefs, as well as the kind of advice about Christian behaviour often found in the New Testament letters. One obvious and important source of such teaching must have been the remembered statements of Jesus himself. This

A street in old Jerusalem (associated with John).

would not necessarily be given as information about Jesus, as we can see from Paul's advice in Romans 12 – 13. Much of what he says there is so close to Jesus' teaching in the Sermon on the Mount that it is hard to believe that the two do not derive from the same source. Yet Paul never identifies his advice with the teaching of Jesus himself. Other parts of Paul's writings also show that the traditions of Jesus' teaching were familiar to the

1 Corinthians 7:10–11   early Gentile churches.

It is therefore quite likely that long before the Gospels were written in their present form the sayings of Jesus would be collected together as a kind of manual for the guidance of teachers in the early church. No doubt there would be a number of such collections of Jesus' teaching, made for different purposes and occasions in the church's life. Scholars often call these collections of sayings by the name *logia*.

In addition to the general considerations already mentioned, there are several more substantial reasons for believing that this was one of the earliest types of Christian writing about Jesus.

● We know that there were later collections of this kind, even long after the writing of the New Testament Gospels. A number of papyrus fragments dating from the third century AD, found at Oxyrhynchus in Egypt, contain sayings of Jesus, some of them different from those found in the Gospels. A whole book of such sayings written in Coptic has also been found in Egypt. This is known as the *Gospel of Thomas*. It contains sayings of Jesus not found in the New Testament, but which may well be authentic. Whether or not they are genuine, however, these documents do show quite clearly that it was the custom of the early church to make such collections of the sayings of Jesus.

● About AD 130–40 Papias, the bishop of Hierapolis, wrote a five-volume *Exposition of the Oracles of the Lord*. Though most of this work is now lost, we do possess a few fragments of it in the form of quotations given in the writings of other people.

Nazareth was Jesus' home town. But he said the people's lack of faith there prevented him from doing many great works. This picture was taken looking across the valley of Jezreel from Nazareth. It shows the site of Megiddo where many Old Testament battles were fought. 'Armageddon' (the hill of Megiddo) became a symbol in apocalyptic literature of the final battle between good and evil.

Writing of Matthew, Papias says that he 'compiled the *logia* in the Hebrew language, and each one interpreted it as he could'. The precise implication of this statement is uncertain, but most scholars believe that the *logia* to which Papias refers is a collection of the sayings of Jesus rather than the book we know as the Gospel of Matthew.

● The organization of the material in the Gospels often seems to suggest that Jesus' sayings had been grouped together before they were placed in their present context. There are many groups of sayings which are only loosely linked together and do not form any kind of consecutive argument. For example, the sayings about salt in Mark really seem to be quite different from each other, and may well have been put together in a collection simply because they all mention salt.

Mark 9:49–50

Matthew 5–7

Then there is the whole of the Sermon on the Mount. Anyone who has ever tried to discover the argument of the sermon will realize the impossibility of the task, for there is no consecutive argument. What we have is a body of Jesus' teachings collected together because they all deal with ethical issues. But they hardly follow on in the same way as a modern sermon is expected to do. According to Professor Jeremias, the reason for this is that the sermon originally formed a collection of sayings of Jesus strung together to make them easily accessible to new converts to the Christian faith.

●A strong reason for assuming the existence of collections of Jesus' sayings early in the church's history is the fact that Matthew and Luke have a large amount of material that is common to both their Gospels, but which is altogether absent from Mark's Gospel. This material consists almost entirely of Jesus' teachings, but it also includes the story of his baptism and temptations and the story of one miracle, the healing of the centurion's servant. The generally accepted explanation of this common material is that Matthew and Luke both used the same collection of Jesus' sayings and incorporated it into their respective Gospels.

Matthew 3:13–4:11;
Luke 3:21–22; 4:1–13
Matthew 8:5–13;
Luke 7:1–10

Scholars call this supposed sayings collection Q. It may have been a written document, or perhaps a body of oral tradition. Its existence in some form is certainly credible, especially since its alleged contents are closely parallel to the collections of prophetic oracles that we find in the Old Testament. In addition to the prophet's words gathered together and edited by his disciples, the prophetic books also often contain an account of the prophet's call and one or two incidents in his life. This is precisely what we get in the tradition called Q: an account of the baptism and temptation of Jesus (which can reasonably be equated with his call), and an illustration of the most typical of his activities: a healing miracle. But the main emphasis is on his teaching.

From the evidence assembled so far, we may conclude that from the very earliest times the church's main interest was in two kinds of literature: the *testimonia*, and the *logia* of Jesus. They may also have had a commonly agreed outline of the course of Jesus' life and teaching. But before too long it began to be necessary to gather all this material together in a more permanent form. This process did not of course take place overnight. Indeed it may not really be a separate process at all, but just the natural extension and completion of the work already begun in making collections of *testimonia* and *logia*. But the end product was to be the four documents we now know as the Gospels of Matthew, Mark, Luke and John.

Putting the Gospels together

The first three Gospels are called the synoptics because they are so much alike; and the precise way in which their writers transformed *logia* into Gospel is at the centre of the 'Synoptic problem'.

These Gospels are in effect three different editions of what is more or less the same basic material. Much of their resemblance can of course be explained by the assumption that these evangelists may have been using the same collections of sayings that had been circulating among different groups of Christians. But the resemblances are more complex than that, for there are so many instances where the three Gospels use precisely the same language, vocabulary and grammatical constructions that most scholars believe they must have shared written sources.

The generally accepted explanation of these resemblances is the 'two document' hypothesis, which assumes that Matthew and Luke both used the same two source documents in writing their own accounts of Jesus' life and teaching. These were the sources we now know as Mark's Gospel and the hypothetical document Q. It is, of course, certain that Luke, at least, used a variety of sources in composing his Gospel, for he explicitly says that he has sifted through the work of other people, selecting those parts of their record that were suitable for his own purpose in writing. In view of the close literary connections with Mark and Luke, it seems certain that the author of Matthew used the same method in his work.

Luke 1:1-4

In reaching the conclusion that Matthew and Luke used Mark, New Testament scholars have analysed the text of the three synoptic Gospels using at least five different criteria.

● *Wording*. A comparison of the words used in different texts is a very simple way of determining their literary connections. More than half of Mark's actual vocabulary is contained in Matthew and Luke, and both of them have identical sections not found in Mark. So it is clear that there was one source known to them all, and another source used only by Matthew and Luke.

The closest followers of Jesus were mostly working men. Peter, who is believed to have supplied the author of Mark with stories of Jesus, was a fisherman, as were his brother Andrew, and James and John.

●*Order*. If the order of events in a narrative contained in more than one Gospel also corresponds with those sections that have the same wording, we can go a step further and assume a common source whose order as well as wording has been substantially reproduced by all three evangelists. Again, there is much evidence for this. Matthew, Mark and Luke all follow the same general order of events. They begin with John the Baptist's ministry, then go on to tell of Jesus' baptism and temptations. Following this comes a ministry of miracle working and teaching in Galilee, which begins to arouse opposition from the Jewish leaders. Then Jesus makes journeys in the north to give teaching privately to his disciples. Finally they go to Jerusalem, and we have the account of Jesus' last days there, his trials, crucifixion and resurrection.

Within this general framework, particular incidents are also often recorded in the same order.

Mark 3:13–19;
Matthew 10:1–4;
Luke 6:12–16

This feature of the synoptic Gospels is best explained if we suppose that Matthew and Luke were using Mark, and not the other way round. For it is striking that when Matthew departs from Mark's order, Luke has the same order as Mark; and when Luke departs from Mark's order, Matthew follows Mark. There is only one incident which both of them place differently from Mark: the appointment of the twelve disciples. Sometimes Matthew or Luke will leave the pattern of Mark's narrative in order to add something new, but after their addition they usually go back to the point in Mark at which they left off. This is one of the strongest arguments to support the belief that Matthew and Luke copied Mark, and not the other way round.

●*Contents*. An analysis of the contents of the narratives also reveals the use of different sources. If one writer records the same story in the same words and order as another author, then we can suppose either that both have used the same source, or that one has used the work of the other. This is what happened in the case of the synoptic Gospels; of the 661 verses in Mark, 606 are found in Matthew in a virtually identical form, and about half of them are also contained in Luke.

●*Style*. This is a very difficult criterion to use satisfactorily. An author's style can depend on so many things: the situation in which he is writing, the readership he has in mind, whether or not he uses a secretary, and so on.

There certainly are marked stylistic differences between Mark and the other two synoptists, and on the whole Mark's Gospel is written in a poorer Greek than the other two. For example, he very often describes incidents in the historic present tense (using the present tense to speak of something that happened in the past). Matthew and Luke however always have a past tense, which is, of course, the correct literary form.

It is often argued that this difference shows that Matthew and Luke were using Mark, and not the other way round – and it is certainly true that, if Mark had access to either Matthew or

Luke it would have been a very odd thing for him to change good grammar into bad. But this argument depends on the assumption that the evangelists used their sources in a rather wooden way, simply copying out word for word what they had before them. But not many authors would follow a source closely enough for its style to obscure their own. If Mark was poor at writing Greek, then his grammar would tend to be poor whether or not he was copying from some other source.

We are on firmer ground when we observe that in eight cases where Mark records sayings of Jesus in Aramaic there is no trace of this in Luke, and only one example in Matthew. It would certainly be more likely that Matthew and Luke have omitted the Aramaic sayings than that Mark had deliberately introduced them.

● *Ideas and theology.* If it could be shown that one Gospel narrative contains a more developed theology than another, then it may seem reasonable to regard it as the later of the two. This appears to be a simple test, but again it is not so easy to apply in practice. It is often hard to be sure that an apparent difference in attitude is a real one. And, in any event, who is to define what is a 'developed' theology, and how can we be sure that this must be later in time than a 'primitive' outlook? When we remember that the highly developed theology of Paul was certainly in existence at the time the Gospels were taking shape we can see that the definition of such differences, and their chronological relationship to one another, must be a very subjective matter.

There are, of course, a number of different emphases in the Gospels. But it is difficult to know for certain what their significance is for the composition of the Gospels. For example, Matthew and Luke appear to have modified or omitted certain statements in Mark that could be thought dishonouring to Jesus. Mark's blunt statement that in Nazareth Jesus 'could do no mighty work' appears in Matthew as 'he did not do many mighty works there', and Luke omits it altogether. Similarly, Jesus' question in Mark, 'Why do you call me good?' appears in Matthew as, 'Why do you ask me about what is good?'

Mark 6:5
Matthew 13:58
Mark 10:18
Matthew 19:17

Not all of these five points are of equal importance. There are difficulties in assessing the value of at least two of them. But taken together the cumulative effect of their evidence is most easily explained if we suppose that Matthew and Luke used Mark's account, rather than that Matthew was the original Gospel which Mark summarized and from which Luke made selective extracts.

Two sources or four?

What has been said so far about the way the Gospels came to be written can be taken as the almost universally held view of New Testament scholars. Though there may be differences of opinion on points of detail, by far the majority of experts are agreed on the broad outline of the facts.

But in addition to the idea that the synoptic Gospels depend mainly on the two sources Mark and Q, it has been suggested that these are not the only sources we can trace behind our Gospels. B. H. Streeter was one of the first British scholars to set out the arguments for the idea that Matthew and Luke both used Mark's Gospel. But he went further than that, and suggested that in order to understand every detail of the synoptic Gospels we need to have a slightly more sophisticated theory, dealing with not two but four basic sources. Besides Mark and Q, he defined sources which he called M and L. In effect this material is simply what is left of the accounts of Matthew and Luke when the Marcan and Q material has been removed. But Streeter believed that these two collections of material were themselves separate and coherent sources, of independent origin.

Proto-Luke

Streeter began his observations from the fact that Matthew and Luke each seem to use Mark in rather different ways. Matthew follows Mark's order and general framework very closely, though at the same time he frequently rewrites the actual material, and often condenses material from Mark to make more room for additional information. The result is that Matthew's Gospel looks rather like a new and enlarged edition of Mark. But Luke is rather different. Whereas Matthew makes use of almost all the material contained in Mark, Luke's Gospel contains only about half of Mark's material. What is more, Streeter discovered that if we remove all the Marcan material from Matthew, what is left has no coherence. The book simply falls to pieces. But if we do the same thing with Luke, we are left with a reasonably consistent and continuous story. This is particularly true of the stories of Jesus' death and resurrection in Luke, which seem to have been supplemented by information from Mark, rather than being based on Mark's story.

Streeter therefore suggested that before Mark was written, Luke wrote a first draft of his Gospel, based on the sayings collection Q and the material labelled L, which he had learned from the church at Caesarea where he stayed while Paul was in prison (Acts 23:23–27:2). Streeter called this first draft of the Gospel 'Proto-Luke'. Then, he suggested, when

Many of the incidents recorded in the Gospels are set around the Sea of Galilee.

Luke was living in Rome at a slightly later date he got to know of Mark's Gospel, which had been written in the intervening years, and he fitted extracts from it into his own already existing Proto-Luke. At the same time, he may also have added the preface (Luke 1:1–4) and the stories of Jesus' birth in chapters one and two.

There are a number of facts which fit well into this theory. For example, Luke often gives a quite different version of a story from Mark's. The story of Jesus' rejection at Nazareth is a good example (Mark 6:1–6; Luke

The first Christians travelled widely in the years after the death of Jesus, partly as a result of opposition in Jerusalem. They took with them the stories of Jesus which in time were written down.

4:16–30). It is obvious that both evangelists are reporting the same incident, but Luke's account is so much fuller that it is clear he must have had a different source of information. Then there is the way that small sections of Mark's narrative, often in Mark's exact wording, have been inserted into

the middle of other material in Luke – almost as if they had been put in later. It is also striking that a great deal of information contained in Mark is simply omitted in Luke. Streeter argued that if Luke had known of Mark's work when he made the first draft of his own Gospel, he would have included more of Mark's material in it.

It has also often been noticed that Luke's Gospel seems to have two beginnings. There is its present beginning at 1:1–4 but then, after the stories of Jesus' birth, it seems to begin over again in 3:1, with Luke's careful dating of the opening of Jesus' ministry, followed by the list of his ancestors in 3:23–38. Streeter explained this unusual feature by supposing that 3:1 was the original beginning of Proto-Luke, to which Luke later prefaced what is now chapters 1 and 2 of his Gospel.

The importance of Streeter's theory about the way Luke wrote his Gospel lies in the fact that if there was ever a Proto-Luke this would form another independent and early source of our knowledge of the life and teachings of Jesus. It has not, however, commanded anything like universal assent – though a number of recent writers on Luke have accepted it in some form or another.

Perhaps one of its weakest points is the assumption that is made about the nature of the Gospel traditions in the early churches. For Streeter assumed that we are dealing with a neatly definable literary process. He tended to think of the evangelists as newspaper editors, sitting down with a number of written sources in front of them and extracting various sections from the different documents. This was a popular concept at the time Streeter wrote (1924), and was widely applied to the study of both Old and New Testaments. But subsequent research has shown that this is an over-simplification of the matter, and it could well be that Luke was familiar with the Marcan material, but not through Mark's Gospel in its present form.

This is also a weakness in other suggestions that Streeter put forward. He argued not only that four identifiable sources can be traced behind our synoptic Gospels, but that each of them represented the traditions of the life and teaching of

Jesus as they had been preserved in the four most important centres of early Christianity: Mark was written in Rome, Q in Antioch, M in Jerusalem and L in Caesarea. There are, however, a number of difficulties with this view.

● Streeter assumed that M and L were coherent documents. But this is very hard to maintain. When the Marcan and Q material is taken away from Matthew, what is left is not a coherent collection at all. And the same is true to a lesser extent of L, which is just Luke's Gospel minus the Q and Marcan material.

● This theory seems to assume a kind of linear progression in the development of the Gospels, whereby the tradition proceeded from more or less primitive forms to the compilation of our present Gospels by a purely literary development. But it is now being widely recognized that we can no longer speak with much confidence of this kind of development from primitive accounts to more sophisticated ones.

New light on old problems

Much of the emphasis in New Testament scholarship is now moving away from a 'mechanical' analysis of the Gospels. Though the two-source theory of Gospel origins is still widely accepted, a number of new questions are being asked, some of which may well have a decisive influence on our understanding of the way the New Testament came to be written.

● From time to time questions continue to be asked about the two-source hypothesis itself. Was Mark really the first Gospel to be written? And is it really necessary to suppose that Q represents a fixed collection of *logia* rather than just a looser collection of traditions known by both Matthew and Luke? In view of the strength of the evidence for both Marcan priority and the fixed form of Q, very strong arguments would need to be brought forward to overthrow the general viewpoint. The close verbal and grammatical similarities among the three synoptic Gospels seem to demand that Mark was first, and that Q had a more or less fixed form. If we accept the suggestion that Q had a form similar to that of the Old Testament prophetic literature, then its form may well have been a written form too.

● The older idea of a linear development from *testimonia*, *logia* and *kerygma* through to a finished Gospel is now being questioned. What we know of the earliest churches suggests they were for the most part independent of one another. Churches in different parts of the Roman Empire would therefore develop at their own rate, and it is quite likely that Christians in different geographical locations would not be at the same stage of development at the same time. This means that it is unrealistic to suppose that in the collection of traditions about Jesus there was a period when all the interest was in collecting *logia*, and this was then followed by a period of intense literary activity during which the Gospels came to be written. It may well be that the type of information about Jesus current in any given church varied according to the needs of the particular congregation.

This has an important bearing on the question of dating the Gospels. If it is necessary to suppose a long history of development from *logia* to Gospel, then we need to allow time for this in our dating of the Gospels. But if *logia* and Gospel were both

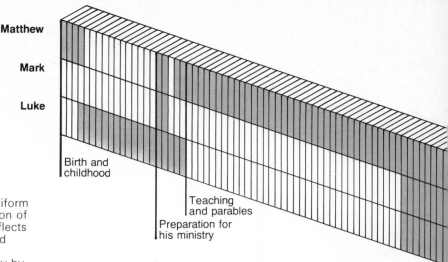

Matthew

Mark

Luke

Birth and childhood

Preparation for his ministry

Teaching and parables

The Gospels are not uniform documents. The selection of material in each one reflects its author's interests and intentions. This chart illustrates that selectivity by showing the relative proportions of the Gospels devoted to the major aspects of Jesus' life, and the degree in which their records overlap.

being formed at the same time, to meet the requirements of different churches, then there is no reason why we cannot date the Gospels somewhat earlier than is usually done.

● A similar point has been made with regard to the 'theological development' some suggest can be traced within the Gospels. In his book *Redating the New Testament*, Dr John Robinson has pointed out that a sophisticated theology does not necessarily indicate a later date than a primitive theology. For example, Mark's Gospel is undoubtedly less sophisticated than John's Gospel – and this has been one reason (though not the only one) why Mark has generally been dated first, and John last. But of course this assumes a direct evolutionary progression working through all the Gospels. If, however, the different Gospels were written to serve the needs of independent churches in different places, it is not difficult to believe that churches with a primitive theology could have existed at the same time as churches with a more sophisticated belief – and so 'theological development' is not necessarily a very useful concept in studying the Gospels we now have.

So there are a number of new questions being asked about the Gospels today, and they are of a rather different kind from those asked by earlier generations. It is now widely recognized that, wherever the information actually came from, each evangelist has written what is essentially an original work, distinctive in important respects from the work of any of the others. Much of our interest is now focussed on *what* the evangelists were doing, rather than on finding out *how* they were doing it. And that is a question that calls for a theological answer to supplement the earlier findings of the literary critics.

Form criticism

Once the two-source theory had been widely accepted as the most likely explanation of the 'mechanics' of Gospel writing, a whole series of new questions began to present themselves. For the isolation of the various sources used by the evangelists in composing their accounts of Jesus' life and teaching only answers the question, where did the Gospels come from? But there is also the further question, where did their sources come from? What was happening to the traditions about Jesus between his death and resurrection and their preservation in writing in the Gospels?

These questions had occurred to a number of scholars in Germany even before Streeter had published his great work on Gospel origins.

evangelists composed their Gospels had, they said, assumed particular literary forms according to the 'life situation' (*Sitz im Leben*) in which they were used in the early church. So, by examining the literary form of a story, they claimed to be able to discover the original use to which it was put in the teaching ministry of the earliest churches.

If this could be done successfully, it would of course be an invaluable aid to our understanding of the Gospels. For if we can know something of the use to which the Gospel traditions were put in the early church, we are in a good position to understand their relevance to the church's life, and hence

Miracles

The last week and crucifixion

Other narrative

Resurrection and ascension

In trying to answer them, they used a new method of analysing the Bible literature. They called it *Formgeschichte*, which literally means 'form history', but it is usually referred to in English as 'form criticism'. This technique was first applied to the Old Testament by the German scholar Hermann Gunkel, though some outstanding New Testament scholars were quick to appreciate its relevance to the study of the Gospels. The most prominent of these were K. L. Schmidt, M. Dibelius and R. Bultmann.

These scholars began from the observation that ancient literature generally assumed a particular literary form, depending on what kind of literature it was. This principle had been explored most thoroughly in the study of the traditional folk literature of northern Europe, which could be classified into fairy tales, history, biography, saga, and so on, simply by observing the way it was written. The form critics assumed that the same was true of the New Testament. The units of tradition from which the

to discover their essential meaning. Unfortunately, however, those who have studied the Gospels by this method have failed to agree at one crucial point. There is no widely accepted agreement on what formal types can actually be found in the Gospels. Martin Dibelius claimed to be able to distinguish five different forms, each corresponding to a specific situation in the life of the early church. But only two of these five forms have been at all widely recognized by other scholars: paradigms and tales.

Paradigms were called 'pronouncement stories' by the English form critic, Vincent Taylor. This term more accurately reflects their contents, for they are generally brief stories culminating in a striking statement made by, or about, Jesus. According to Dibelius this form originated in the earliest Christian preaching, in which such stories were used as examples and

illustrations. A typical pronouncement story would be the incident in
which Jesus picked corn on the
sabbath day, and explained his
actions to the Jews by saying,
'The sabbath was made for the
good of man; man was not made for
the sabbath. So the Son of man is
Lord even of the sabbath' (Mark
2:23–28; Matthew 12:1–8; Luke
6:1–5). Stories like this would often
have been told in preaching long
before they were written down in
the Gospels.

Form critics generally distinguish two main characteristics of
such stories:

● They always end with a striking
saying of Jesus. According to some,
this was a favourite device of early
Christian preachers. Whereas a
modern preacher usually begins
with his text, the apostles may have
kept theirs to the end, to serve as a
natural climax to what had gone
before.

● These stories contain very little
descriptive information. Just a bare
minimum of fact is given to set the
scene for the most important
element, which is the saying of
Jesus. When a story is handed on
by word of mouth, two things may
happen to it. Either it can be worn
down by frequent repetition, so that
nothing remains except the most
essential facts expressed in a
succinct and striking way. Or it can
be elaborated as it is told, with
extra details being added to make
it more realistic and interesting.
According to most form critics,
the pronouncement stories have
been worn down to their bare
essentials, rather than being
elaborated as they were handed on.

Tales were called 'miracle stories'
by Taylor, though not all of them
are concerned with miracles.
According to Dibelius the distinctive feature of these stories
is that they have been elaborated
rather than worn down in the course
of their transmission. Indeed he
suggested that these stories may
have been put into their present
form by a special class of person
in the early church – the story-
tellers, whose job was to cast stories
about Jesus into the same form as
the stories of the Greek gods. They
were stories designed to win
converts to the Christian faith by
demonstrating that Jesus was
superior to other deities.

There is of course no trace of
such people in the New Testament.

It is especially striking that Paul,
who gives more than one list of
people who have special functions
in the church, never mentions
story-tellers (1 Corinthians
12:1–11, 28–30; Romans 12:6–8;
Ephesians 4:11). It may well be
that the vivid details in these stories
derive from an entirely different
source. Perhaps they were told by
eye-witnesses, who actually
remembered all the details of the
incidents they were describing. In
view of the fact that the Gospels
themselves were written down in
something less than a generation
after the events they describe, it is
very difficult to believe that
professional story-tellers could have
freely invented fictitious details at a
time when many eye-witnesses of
the life of Jesus were still alive.

Dibelius identified three other
forms of story in the Gospels, but
not many other scholars have
accepted his opinion at this point.
These forms are:

Legends, which Dibelius compared with the stories often
connected with the medieval saints.
He defined them as 'religious
narratives of a saintly man in
whose works and fate interest is
taken . . . They are intended to
give a basis for honouring the
saint'. Such stories need not
necessarily be fabricated, though
according to Dibelius they most
often are. Their function is to
glorify the person they describe,
rather than to report any factual
information about him.

Myth was the name Dibelius
gave to any narrative involving
supernatural personalities or events.
Stories such as the baptism, the
temptations and the transfiguration
came into this category.

Exhortations were essentially the
teaching contained in the Gospels,
used to instruct converts in the
early church.

The study of the forms of the
Gospel narratives has been pursued
by others since the pioneering work
of Dibelius, and it has undoubtedly
shed some light on the origins of
the Gospels. There are a number of
outstanding insights which we now
take for granted that have been a
direct result of the work of the form
critics.

● We can now see that the
Gospels are not meant to be
biographies of Jesus. They are
selective accounts of certain parts of
his life and teaching, preserved

because of their usefulness to the ministry of the earliest churches.

● Because of this, it is now recognized that the interpretation of the Gospels is intimately bound up with our whole understanding of the early church. In order to appreciate the relevance and meaning of the Gospels we need to have a sympathetic understanding of the people who produced them.

● This process has in turn led to a positive, tentative, understanding of what was going on in the period before any of the New Testament documents were written, as the teaching of Jesus was applied and interpreted to new situations in the life of his followers.

Other stories besides those contained in the four Gospels were circulated during the first two centuries, most of which are probably legend and fantasy. This is a fragment of an unknown 'Gospel' from the second century.

These insights are undoubtedly valuable, and their importance must not be underestimated – especially the first one, which has radically affected our whole approach to the Gospels. There are, however, a number of points at which the work of the form critics has been less useful. Three major criticisms can be made of their work, especially in the early days.

● *Form and content.* Many of the classifications made by Dibelius really depended, not on literary form, but on content. For example, there is no purely formal reason why stories including supernatural persons should be put into a different category from other stories. In making distinctions of this kind some form critics were too often influenced by their own rationalistic presuppositions. As we have noticed, only two of Dibelius's forms have been at all widely recognized, and some scholars have doubted whether even these are really all that obvious. There are many instances where there is no very clear-cut distinction between paradigms and tales, and much of the Gospel material is difficult to categorize. When there is so little agreement on what the forms actually are, we cannot have much confidence in the constructions placed upon them.

● *Tradition and Gospel.* Another basic problem is that form criticism was based on the assumption that the development of New Testament literature was similar to the development of folklore in northern Europe. But there are important differences between the two. The early church saw its main job as the preaching of the good news about Jesus, not the handing on of traditional stories. They were more concerned with the present than with the past. And in so far as the past did concern them, it was the immediate past and not, as in the case of the European traditions, a long-forgotten past. The church's knowledge of Jesus did not come from traditional tales handed on for generations, but from the immediate experience of some of its own members. This means that the actual scope for the traditions to develop into standardized forms must have been very limited indeed.

● *Forms and facts.* Many form critics have not been content to make observations on the literary form of the Gospels, but have proceeded to make historical judgements about their contents on the basis of form criticism. Referring to the earlier form critics, Professor Ernst Käsemann writes that their main work 'was designed to show that the message of Jesus as given to us by the synoptists is, for the most part, not authentic but was minted by the faith of the primitive Christian community in its various stages'. This aim is clear even from the names given by Dibelius to some of the forms he discovered. 'Myth' and 'legend' are loaded terms – and even in his discussion of 'tales' it is almost a basic axiom that because there are literary similarities with stories told of pagan gods, this is the ultimate origin of the stories about Jesus.

But two important criticisms can be made of this procedure:

● Evidence drawn from literary 'form' is of no value at all in formulating historical judgements. This becomes quite clear if we take an example. Nowadays we do not generally distinguish different types of narrative by giving them special literary forms. Professor F. F. Bruce has drawn a helpful parallel with the one place where a story still usually does have a specified form. This is in the law court.

When a policeman gives evidence in court, he does not give an eloquent, literary account of what he has seen. Instead he sticks as closely as possible to a prescribed form – so much so that, apart from the alteration of various details, a description of one road accident will sound more or less the same as a description of any other. The hope is that by using a stereotyped formula the most important facts can be summarized as accurately as possible.

No sensible person would believe that because a policeman describes two incidents in identical language, he was giving variant accounts of one and the same incident; still less that neither of them actually happened, and the accounts had been fabricated out of a familiar legal formula. Whether or not the incident took place would depend on criteria of a totally different kind. And the same thing is true of the Gospels. We simply cannot make a judgement about their historical reliability on the basis of their literary form.

● There are also a number of other good reasons for doubting that the early church freely invented stories about Jesus, as some form critics have alleged.

First, there is the question of eye-witnesses, many of whom must have been alive at the time the Gospels were written, and who could have challenged the wholesale fabrication of 'events' in Jesus' life.

Second, a basic assumption of Dibelius and Bultmann was that the early church made no effort to distinguish its own teaching from that of Jesus. After all, they argue, Jesus' spirit was thought to be active in the church, and what the apostles said in his name was there-fore just as much a word of Jesus as anything he said during his ministry. But this inference is not supported by the New Testament itself. For in many instances its writers show that they did dis-tinguish between their own teaching and that of Jesus. The most striking example of this is in 1 Corinthians 7, where Paul goes out of his way to distinguish his own opinions from the words of Jesus. But even in the Gospels themselves there are instances where editorial comments made by the evangelists are clearly distinguished from the teaching of Jesus himself (Mark 7:19).

Another fact which points in the same direction is the difference between the Gospels and the rest of the New Testament. For example, Jesus is called 'Son of man' in the Gospels, though with one exception this title is found nowhere else in the New Testament. Moreover, the questions dealt with in the Gospels are not the same as those that troubled the writers of the letters. Take the question of the relationship between Jews and non-Jews, for example. This was a pressing problem in the early church, but it is not really touched upon anywhere in the Gospels. These facts suggest that the church did not feel at all free to place its own ideas into the mouth of Jesus, but was to a considerable extent consciously preserving traditions handed down from an earlier period.

More recent form critics have taken account of these problems in the work of their predecessors, and the discipline is now much more narrowly concerned with formal literary questions. The question of the Gospels' reliability is gradually being separated altogether from form criticism. Then there has been a further development which is in some ways the successor of the earlier form criticism. This is the discipline known as redaction criticism.

With the recognition that the history of the Gospels was not quite comparable with the history of European folklore, it became clear that the most useful question we can ask of the Gospels must concern the actual use the evangelists made of their source materials. What were these people doing as they wrote their Gospels? Why did they need to write four, instead of just one agreed account? And what were the special circumstances in their churches which led them to write in the particular ways they did? These are the questions that redaction criticism is trying to answer. It is a relatively recent development in the study of the Gospels, and there are by no means any agreed results as yet. But many of its insights will be of value in our next task, which is to discover the meaning and significance of the various Gospels.

Chapter 11 The four Gospels

Mark

MARK's Gospel is considered first because it is now recognized as a basic source for the other two synoptic Gospels. It is, however, only in fairly recent times that Mark has received careful attention. It was generally neglected by the church from quite early times, in favour of the longer accounts of Matthew and Luke. This is hardly surprising, for they contain most of Mark's information and a lot more as well, and so Mark soon came to be regarded as an abbreviated version of Matthew. But the situation has now changed and, with the knowledge that Mark's Gospel was almost certainly the first to be written, it has achieved an eminence it has probably never enjoyed since the time of its first compilation.

There is, however, some evidence to show that it was valued in certain Christian circles not long after its composition. Papias, for example, writing about AD 140 but quoting an earlier source, identifies Mark as 'Peter's interpreter', and says that 'he wrote down accurately, but not in order, as much as he could remember of the things said and done by Christ'. Irenaeus and Clement of Alexandria also associate Mark's Gospel with Peter's preaching, and in recent times the contents of the Gospel have often been

Quoted in Eusebius, *Ecclesiastical History* III.39.15
Irenaeus, *Against Heretics* I.1.1.
Clement of Alexandria, quoted in Eusebius, *Ecclesiastical History* VI.14.6ff.

Mark's Gospel was probably written in Rome, during the time the Emperor Nero tried to blame Christians for setting fire to the city. These ruins are of the Colosseum, the arena where Nero threw Christians to the lions.

thought to support the belief that Peter was the source of much of it.

A number of stories are told with such vivid detail that it is natural to regard them as first-hand accounts of the events they describe. The story of Peter's call and of Jesus' first sabbath in Capernaum, when Peter's mother-in-law was healed, are good examples of this. In addition, some of the references to the disciples, and to Peter in particular, are highly unfavourable. The disciples are consistently portrayed as ignorant, obtuse men who failed to understand what Jesus was trying to teach them. In Mark's Gospel the disciples are not at all the kind of people the later church liked to think they were. It is therefore unlikely that they would have been depicted in such an unfavourable light had Mark not had good information, perhaps coming from Peter himself, to support such a picture.

Mark 1:14–20

Mark 1:29–34

*Mark 4:35–41; 5:25–34;
6:37–38; 8:14–21, 31–33;
9:2–6, 32; 10:35–45*

The author

But who was Mark? Mark, or Marcus, was of course a very common name, and he could have been anybody. In considering this question we need to remember that none of the Gospels actually names its author. John's Gospel comes nearest to doing so, but even there we have only an enigmatic reference to a witness to the crucifixion. Though this person is often identified with the 'beloved disciple', it is far from clear who that might have been. In this respect the Gospels are quite different from most of the rest of the New Testament, for they are presented to us as anonymous writings. The traditional ascriptions to Matthew, Mark, Luke and John were of course added at an early stage, but they represent the opinions of the early church about the authors of the Gospels, rather than any sort of claim by the authors.

John 19:35

It is clear from the evidence that the author of the second Gospel was generally associated by the early church with a man called John Mark who is known from other parts of the New Testament. According to Acts, a group of Christians regularly met in his mother's house in Jerusalem, and John Mark himself is named as the companion of Paul and Barnabas in their earliest missionary work. Though Mark deserted them, Paul mentions him favourably in two of his later letters, so the two men must have patched up their differences. He is also spoken of with affection in 1 Peter and that (depending on one's view of the authorship of 1 Peter) may be taken as evidence for associating him with Peter as well as with Paul.

Acts 12:12

Acts 12:25; 15:37–41

*Colossians 4:10;
Philemon 24*

1 Peter 5:13

It is more difficult to be certain that this same Mark was actually the author of the Gospel. But in view of the tendency of second-century Christians to associate books of the New Testament with key figures in the early church, it may well be that the tradition connecting Mark with the second Gospel is not altogether untrustworthy. John Mark whom we meet in the New Testament is a very insignificant person, and not the kind of individual who would be credited with writing a Gospel unless there was good reason to believe that he did in fact do so.

The readers

It is generally thought that Mark's Gospel was written in Rome, to serve the needs of the church there. Irenaeus and Clement of Alexandria disagree on the precise circumstances of its composition, but both agree it was written in Rome. If the author of the Gospel was indeed John Mark, then references to him in the New Testament also place him in Rome.

The Gospel was certainly written for a non-Jewish readership.

Mark 5:41; 7:34

Aramaic phrases such as *talitha, koum* or *ephphatha* are translated into Greek for the benefit of Mark's readers. Jewish cus-

Mark 7:3–4

toms are also explained in a way that suggests they were unfamiliar. Then there are also a number of Latin technical

Mark 4:21; 12:42; 14:65; 15:19

terms in Mark, which suggests that the Gospel originated in a part of the Roman Empire where Latin was spoken. In view of all these pieces of evidence Rome certainly seems to be a plausible place of composition.

The first Christians in Jerusalem used to meet at a house owned by the mother of John Mark. He may have been the author of Mark's Gospel. The picture is of a street in old Jerusalem.

The date

Dating the Gospel, however, is not so easy, for a number of reasons.

● The evidence of the church Fathers is contradictory. Clement of Alexandria says that Mark wrote the Gospel under Peter's dictation, and that the final draft of it was approved by Peter himself. But Irenaeus says that the Gospel was not written until after the deaths of both Peter and Paul. This means that we have to try to decide from the evidence of the Gospel itself when it may have been written, and this is no easy task.

● It is often thought that the many references to trials and persecutions in Mark suggest that his readers were suffering for

Mark 8:34–38; 10:33–34, 45; 13:8–13

their faith in Christ. If this is so, it could date the Gospel somewhere between AD 60 and 70, during which period Nero tried to blame the Christians for the firing of Rome. But of course, persecution was such a common feature of church life in the first century that it is not essential to connect Mark's Gospel with one of the more well-known persecutions. There must have been many local persecutions that we know nothing of, though they would be real enough to those who had to suffer them.

● Then there is the question of whether the apocalyptic section in Mark presupposes that Jerusalem had already fallen to the Romans. Since this took place in AD 70, an answer to this question would at least date the Gospel on one side or the other of that event. But here again opinion is divided. J. A. T. Robinson has argued that Mark was certainly written before AD 70 (along with the rest of the New Testament), and in his view was in existence a long time before that date. He accordingly places its composition in the period AD 45–60. Other scholars, however, continue to date it between AD 60 and 70, and one or two later still.

Mark 13:1–37 (margin)

Mark's reasons for writing

Mark's intention in writing as he did is easier to define.

● If, as the early traditions suggest, Mark's Gospel has some connection with Peter, one reason for its composition could well have been the desire to preserve Peter's reminiscences as a lasting testimony for the church. This would be especially easy to understand if Mark wrote at a time immediately preceding, or just after, Peter's death.

● But this Gospel was also written with some specific situation in view. There are a number of striking and distinctive aspects to the portrait of Jesus in Mark. He is presented here as a very human figure. Jesus is angry on occasions; he is unable to perform miracles if the appropriate conditions of faith are absent; and he suffers physically in a way that might be thought incompatible with his position as the Son of God. At one time these things were thought to be signs of Mark's 'primitive' theology. But there may well be another explanation for them.

Mark 1:43; 3:5; 8:12; 8:33; 10:14 (margin)
Mark 6:1–6 (margin)

Mark 8:31–33; 9:31 (margin)

An idea put forward by Professor R. P. Martin is that many Christians found it difficult to reconcile the idea of Jesus' divinity with the fact that he was also fully human. So they suggested that the divine Christ only came into the human Jesus at his baptism, and left him again before the crucifixion. We call these people Docetists, because they held that Jesus only seemed to be human (from the Greek verb *dokeō*, 'to seem'). The writer of 1 John was concerned to correct such people, and John's Gospel may also have them in view. But Mark's Gospel too may well have been a corrective to this idea. In reply to those who were asserting that Jesus' humanity was illusory, Mark emphasizes its reality by depicting Jesus as the divine Messiah whose origin and significance is both hidden and revealed in the life of a truly human person.

Luke

Traditions associating the third Gospel with a person called Luke date from as early as the second century. The Muratorian Canon and the anti-Marcionite Prologue to Luke, as well as

Irenaeus, Clement of Alexandria, Origen and Tertullian, all identify Luke as its author. The exact value of these traditions is, however, uncertain, since most of what they contain could just as easily have been deduced from the New Testament itself, and so they are not necessarily of any independent worth. The evidence of the New Testament is in fact more useful in identifying the author of this Gospel.

● A distinctive feature of this Gospel is that it is not complete in itself: it is the first volume of the two-volume history of early Christianity which is continued in the Acts of the Apostles. The style and language of these two books is so similar that there can be no doubt that they are both the product of one writer. Both are addressed to the same person, whose name is given as Theophilus.

Luke 1:1–4; Acts 1:1

● In Acts there are certain passages known as the 'we passages'. They are given this name because at these points the narrative changes from using 'they' and 'he' to the pronoun 'we'. Though it is never clearly stated who the 'we' are, the use of this pronoun clearly implies that the writer was present on these occasions, and therefore was a companion of Paul. Since the style of these passages is the same as that of the book as a whole, it seems likely that the author has used his own travel diary as a source of information. A careful scrutiny of the narratives shows that Luke is the person who best fits in.

Acts 16:10–17; 20:5–15; 21:1–18; 27:1–28:16

● This Luke is identified as a doctor by Paul, and it has often been thought that the author of Luke-Acts displays a certain degree of specialized knowledge of medical language, and an interest in the diagnosis of illness. This point has often been given too much emphasis, and it is likely that the limited medical terminology used would be familiar to any intelligent person in the Roman world. But there are one or two points in the Gospel at which Luke seems to show himself to be more sympathetic than Mark to the work of doctors. This comes out very noticeably in the story of how Jesus healed a woman with an incurable haemhorrage. Mark records the fact that she had been treated by many doctors, and then comments, somewhat cynically, 'She had spent all her money, but instead of getting better she got worse all the time'. Luke, on the other hand, simply comments that 'no one had been able to cure her'.

A Roman corn ship similar to the ships Paul and Luke would have sailed in.

Mark 5:26
Luke 8:43
Colossians 4:14; Philemon 24; 2 Timothy 4:11

Luke is mentioned three times in the New Testament. On each occasion he is said to be a companion of Paul, and in Colossians Paul says that he was not a Jew. If he is indeed the writer of Luke and Acts he is probably the only non-Jewish writer of the New Testament. The Greek style of these writings certainly suggests that their author could have been a native Greek speaker.

Ecclesiastical History II.4.6

According to Eusebius Luke came from Antioch in Syria, and one ancient manuscript of the book of Acts implies that he was in Antioch when the church there received news of the impending famine. But the generally accepted text of Acts has Luke join

Acts 11:28

Paul when he enters Europe for the first time. He also accompanied Paul on his final journey to Jerusalem, and then on to Rome itself. According to Streeter and others, Luke may have collected some material for his Gospel during this period from the church at Caesarea – though his final version of it may well have been written in Rome.

The date

It is not possible to be certain of the exact date when Luke finished his Gospel. Since he incorporates in his own account some material from Mark, he must have written the final draft of his own book after the Gospel of Mark was written and in circulation. So the date we give to Luke will depend to some extent on the date we assign to Mark. It has been suggested that Luke displays a knowledge of the fall of Jerusalem to the Romans in AD 70, and if this is so we would need to date the finished Gospel some time after that. But others see no reason to support this idea, and date the Gospel earlier, some as early as AD 57–60.

Luke 21:5–24

Luke's reasons for writing

Why did Luke write his Gospel? This has been one of the more hotly debated issues in recent New Testament scholarship, and a large number of suggestions have been made. A few of the more important ones are worth mentioning.

Luke 1:1–4

● It must not be forgotten that Luke does tell us something of his purpose in the prologue to the Gospel. He says he is writing for a person called Theophilus, 'so that you will know the full truth about everything which you have been taught'. He also says that he did his work in a consciously literary manner: he studied the accounts written by other people, and on the basis of those decided to write 'an orderly account'.

A number of things are clear from this. On the one hand it seems obvious that Theophilus (whoever he was) was a Christian. Luke wrote his Gospel to help him and other believers to a better understanding of the Christian faith. But the author also suggests that in his view the best way to achieve this was to set out as much as could be known of the life and teaching of Jesus himself. So he also had a historical interest in discovering the facts about Jesus. Like the other evangelists, he did not set out to write a biography of Jesus in the technical sense. But at the same time, he realized that if his message to Theophilus was going to carry much weight then it needed to be firmly anchored to the facts of history.

● Because of this, Luke begins his story of Jesus with Judaism. In the first two chapters of his Gospel he demonstrates the continuity of Christianity with Judaism and the Old Testament. At the same time he emphasizes that Jesus is the fulfilment of all God's promises, and so the religion of the Old Testament is now redundant. The relationship of Jews and Christians was of course an important question in the earliest churches, as we can see from the letters of Paul. And Luke emphasizes at the very beginning of his Gospel that those who follow Jesus do not first need to become Jews in order to be Christians. Rather, Jesus

Luke 2:32

had come to be 'a light . . . to the Gentiles'.

● By the time Luke wrote, the events of Jesus' life were in the past. This fact has often led later generations of Christians to be more interested in the history of the first century than in the events of their own day. But in his account of Jesus' life and ministry, Luke emphasizes that there is an important connection between the events of Jesus' life and life in the contemporary church. He does this by stressing that the life-force of Jesus' presence in the church, the Holy Spirit, had also played a central role in the ministry of Jesus.

At many important points Luke draws out clearly what is

Luke is traditionally believed to have been a doctor because of the familiarity of his Gospel with medical terms.

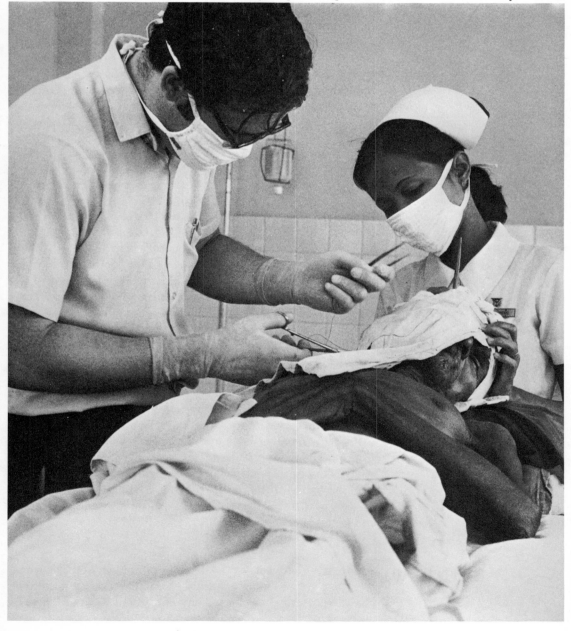

only implicit in Matthew and Mark. The Holy Spirit is involved

Luke 1:35; 3:22; 4:1, 14

in Jesus' birth, baptism and ministry. And at the end of the Gospel the disciples are told to wait in Jerusalem until they too

Luke 24:49

receive the gift of the Spirit. It may be that Luke emphasized the continuing presence of Jesus with his followers as a corrective to some of his contemporaries who were becoming impatient because the second coming of Jesus, the *parousia*, had not yet taken place. He reminds them that although his final appearance in glory is yet in the future, Jesus is with his people in a real way through the presence of the Holy Spirit in their lives.

● Another notable feature of Luke's Gospel is its emphasis on the fact that the Christian message is for everyone. This is something that is obvious to us today, but it was not at all obvious to the first few generations of Christians. One of the greatest contributions of Paul was to show that God's love extends to the very lowest classes of society. In his Gospel Luke demonstrates that this was also the message of Jesus' life and teaching. When he

Luke 2:32

tells the story of the infant Jesus, he includes the statement that he is to be 'a light to reveal your (God's) will to the Gentiles'. In tracing Jesus' ancestry, Luke goes back to Adam, the common

Luke 3:28–38
Matthew 1:1–17

ancestor of all men, whereas Matthew traces it back only to Abraham, the father of the Jewish race. In Luke's account of the sermon in the synagogue at Nazareth, Jesus' message is concerned

Luke 4:16–30

with the Gentiles. And Luke also tells of Jesus' special interest even in the Samaritans, whom the Jews hated more even than the

Luke 9:51–56; 10:25–37;
17:11–19

Romans. Throughout this Gospel Jesus is characteristically presented as the friend of the outcasts of society.

These are the people whom God is happy to welcome; and his pleasure in accepting people like this into his kingdom is also shared by Jesus' followers. The happiness of being a Christian is emphasized over and over again. Luke's account begins with the

Luke 2:10

angels telling 'glad tidings of great joy', and ends with the disciples returning to Jerusalem after the ascension 'with great

Luke 24:52

joy'. In between these events, many of the most appealing of Jesus' parables end on the same note of happiness. The lost

Luke 15:1–7
Luke 15:11–32

sheep, the lost son, and many others emphasize the joy that is given to Jesus' disciples – a joy based on God's forgiving love shown to them when they were themselves outcasts and sinners.

Probably no other book in the whole New Testament depicts Jesus so vividly as the friend and saviour of men and women. And this is exactly what Luke intended. For it was important that the church of his own day should realize how their own mission to the whole world was firmly grounded in the teaching and example of Jesus himself.

Matthew

Matthew's Gospel is very different from either Mark or Luke, and there are a number of special characteristics that need to be considered before we can say anything about its origin, date or authorship.

● This Gospel has a very well organized arrangement of the material, which is set out in topics. It is possible to divide it up in a number of different ways. One outline that has been widely used in the past treats the Gospel as a series of five blocks or 'books' of material, arranged between the prologue of the birth stories and the epilogue of the passion narrative. Each of these sections of the Gospel can be seen to have a well-balanced combination of narrative and teaching material, as follows:

Matthew 1:1 – 2:23
Matthew 26:1 – 28:20

Luke's Gospel emphasizes the concern of Jesus for the underprivileged. These people, victims of an earthquake in Guatemala, are queuing for food.

Matthew 7:28; 11:1; 13:53;
19:1; 26:1

1 The new law
Narrative (Galilean ministry)   3:1–4:25
Teaching (Sermon on the Mount)   5:1–7:29

2 Christian discipleship
Narrative   8:1–9:34
Teaching   9:35–10:42

3 The meaning of the kingdom
Narrative   11:1–12:50
Teaching (parables)   13:1–52

4 The church
Narrative   13:53–17:27
Teaching (order, discipline, worship)   18:1–35

5 Judgement
Narrative (controversies in Jerusalem)   19:1–22:46
Teaching (judgement on the Pharisees,
apocalyptic teachings)   23:1–25:46

It was suggested by B. W. Bacon that Matthew uses this scheme to present Jesus to his readers as the new Moses, and the five-fold division of his Gospel is a conscious parallel to the five books of the Law in the Old Testament. But this is difficult to prove. Nowhere does Matthew say that Jesus is the 'second Moses', nor do the individual sections of the Gospel really correspond to the five books of the Pentateuch. The only thing common to both is the number five.

Indeed it is not even certain that there are five sections in the Gospel. The main reason for dividing it up like this was the fact that the statement 'When Jesus had finished saying these things . . .' is found five times in the Gospel, at points corresponding to the alleged end of these sections. But if we analyse the Gospel according to its contents, rather than using this criterion of literary style, we may reach different conclusions altogether. Professor J. D. Kingsbury has suggested that there are not five divisions in Matthew, but only three. He argues that Matthew's main concern was to show how Jesus was God's Son and Messiah, and that the Gospel is arranged topically around this theme:

1 The person of Jesus as Messiah and Son of God (1:1–4:16)

2 The proclamation of Jesus' message (4:17–16:20)

3 The suffering, death and resurrection of the Messiah and Son of God (16:21–28:20)

A number of more speculative attempts have also been made to explain the structure of the Gospel by means of Jewish lectionaries, or various linguistic and mathematical formulae. It is of course true that the Gospel's teaching is often grouped in series of threes and sevens, but this may have been intended as an aid to Christians who wished to memorize Jesus' sayings, rather than as a cryptic clue to the organization of its material.

● Matthew also places a special emphasis on the Old Testament. The life and teaching of Jesus is presented as the fulfilment of the promises made by God to Israel. This is stated not just in the general sense that Jesus is 'the son of David', but more often with specific reference to Old Testament texts. The author was convinced that Jesus had fulfilled in his experience all that happened to Israel. To prove it he often quotes Old Testament texts in ways that to us may seem a little strange. For example, when Matthew tells of Jesus returning from Egypt to his homeland as a baby, he quotes Hosea's statement about the exodus of Israel from Egypt: 'Out of Egypt have I called my son.' But his message is clear: everything that was central in the relationship of God with his people Israel finds its true and final expression in the life of Jesus.

Matthew 2:15; Hosea 11:1

● It is therefore rather surprising to find that alongside this strong Jewish interest there is a great emphasis on the universality of the Christian message. The faults of Judaism are not passed over in silence. It is in Matthew that we find the most scathing criticisms of the hypocrisy of the Pharisees, and there are a number of indications that Israel's day as God's people has now passed. This is balanced by a striking emphasis on the missionary work of the church. It becomes most explicit in the great missionary commission given by Jesus to his disciples at the end of the Gospel. But it is implied right from the very beginning, when the non-Jewish wise men join in worship of the infant Jesus.

Matthew 23:1–36

Matthew 8:10–12; 21:43

Matthew 28:16–20

Matthew 2:1–12

● There is also a distinct interest in eschatology here, and the teaching on this subject in chapters 24 and 25 is considerably fuller than the corresponding sections of the other synoptic Gospels. Matthew has a number of parables on the subjects of the second coming and last judgement that are not found in the other Gospels. Most of them are concerned to encourage Christians to live in a state of constant readiness for Jesus' return, because 'you do not know the day or the hour'. Perhaps some members of Matthew's church were beginning to doubt that Jesus would return; parables like that of the ten bridesmaids emphasize that with such an attitude Christians can never be in a fit state to meet their Lord.

Matthew 25:13

● Another important characteristic of Matthew's Gospel is its concern with the church. Indeed it is the only Gospel where the

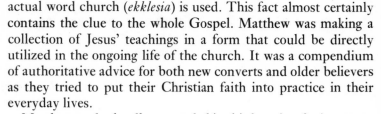

Matthew 16:18; 18:17

actual word church (*ekklesia*) is used. This fact almost certainly contains the clue to the whole Gospel. Matthew was making a collection of Jesus' teachings in a form that could be directly utilized in the ongoing life of the church. It was a compendium of authoritative advice for both new converts and older believers as they tried to put their Christian faith into practice in their everyday lives.

Matthew undoubtedly succeeded in this last aim, for it was not very long before his Gospel was the most widely used and respected. It contained Jesus' teaching in a form that could easily be understood by new converts, and so this Gospel could provide the basis of their instruction in the Christian faith. It also demonstrated the continuity between Jesus and the Old Testament in a very direct way, and so could be a useful handbook for dealing with questions raised by enquiring Jews. It had the added advantage of being the most comprehensive of all the synoptic Gospels. Since it contained almost all of Mark, and much of Luke, its position as the most important Gospel was soon assured in the early church.

The author

Matthew's Gospel reveals a strongly Jewish background and a concern with Old Testament law.

There is no widespread agreement on who wrote the Gospel, and when he did so. Many scholars today find no difficulty in accepting the early Christian traditions that identify Mark and Luke with the other two synoptics. But with Matthew the position is rather different. For the Matthew whose name is associated with this Gospel by the church Fathers was a disciple of Jesus, and therefore an eye-witness of the events he describes. It is not easy to see why one of the twelve disciples should have relied so heavily on the Gospel of Mark, which was written by someone who was not a witness of the events of Jesus' life.

The question of the actual authorship of the Gospel is of course not crucial for our understanding of it. The book itself is anonymous, and makes no claim at all about its author. He may well have been associated with the apostle Matthew, but at what stage or in what way is impossible to say with certainty.

The date

Matthew 22:7; 24:3–28

The date of the Gospel is also in doubt, and depends on the answer we give to a number of other questions.

● It must presumably have been written after Mark, and after the collection of sayings known as Q was in existence. But we have already seen the problems involved in giving firm dates to these materials.

● Many scholars believe that Matthew was written later than Luke, because the Gospel appears to contain direct references to the fall of Jerusalem in AD 70. Again, this does not necessarily mean that the Gospel was written after the event. The assumption that it was is largely based on the belief that there is no such thing as genuine predictive prophecy, and so if Jesus appears to have predicted an event in the future this means the early church must have rewritten the tradition in the light of later circumstances. But Robinson has rightly pointed out the naïveté of such an assumption, and argues for a much earlier date mainly on that basis.

● It has also been argued that the type of church organization envisaged in Matthew is well developed, and therefore reflects a stage very late in the first century. But this is not easy to substantiate. When we compare the details of this Gospel's teaching on the church with, say, Paul's letters to the church at Corinth in the mid-fifties of the first century, it is very difficult to see any real differences between the two.

Depending on how we answer these questions, the Gospel can be dated either in the period AD 80–100 (with the majority of scholars), or pre-AD 70, perhaps as early as AD 40–60 (with Robinson, Guthrie and one or two German writers).

John

With only one or two minor exceptions, almost everything that has been said here about the synoptic Gospels represents a consensus of opinion that has existed among New Testament scholars for a very considerable time. In most important respects relatively little has changed since Streeter's monumental work of fifty years ago. Here and there new and different emphases have been made as the newer disciplines of form and redaction criticism have been explored – though even this is a natural development from the work of previous generations.

But in the case of the fourth Gospel, John, matters are now very different. Streeter wrote of this Gospel that it derives 'not from the original authorities, but from the vivid picture . . . reconstructed by [the author's] own imagination on the basis of contemporary apologetic'. A majority of his contemporaries shared this view. They regarded John as a second-century theological interpretation of the life of Jesus using the language and thought-forms of Hellenistic philosophy. They thought of it as a kind of extended sermon, with no real connection with reliable traditions about Jesus as he actually lived and taught.

Recent developments, however, have shattered this picture of the fourth Gospel once and for all. Whereas twenty or thirty years ago John was often regarded as a fabricated misinterpretation of the synoptic Gospels, many competent scholars are now prepared to regard it as an early, independent source of knowledge about Jesus' life and teaching, and of equal value with the synoptic Gospels. We can trace three main reasons for this radical change of opinion.

John and the synoptic Gospels

John 6:1–15; Mark 6:30–44
Matthew 14:13–21;
Luke 9:10–17
John 12:1–8; Mark 14:3–9;
Matthew 26:6–13

Fifty years ago it was widely assumed that the author of John's Gospel knew the synoptic Gospels. The reason for this was the number of stories common to both. The story of how Jesus fed the 5,000 and the story of his anointing at Bethany are examples. It was therefore supposed that John was writing a kind of 'theological' interpretation of the 'factual' stories of the synoptic Gospels. This inevitably led to the conclusion that the fourth Gospel must be late in date and inferior in quality to the synoptic Gospels.

This assumption has, however, been questioned at two points. First of all, it is now widely recognized that it is not possible to set the 'history' of the synoptics over against the 'theology' of John. The synoptic writers were themselves theologians. They did not write their Gospels for purely biographical reasons, but because they had a message for their readers. It has also been demonstrated that the fourth Gospel is not really dependent on the other three, and indeed its author may well have written his work without any knowledge of the writings of the other evangelists.

The thought-forms used by John in his Gospel were those of the Hellenistic world. The author was associated with the city of Ephesus, now on the west coast of Turkey.

Closer examination of these stories found in all four Gospels shows that though there are similarities, there are also a number of differences in John's account, and these differences are not the kind that can easily be explained on theological grounds. John's variations are in fact much easier to understand if we assume that he had access to different reports of the incidents known also to the synoptic writers. When this hypothesis is tested in detail, it can be seen not only that John's account comes from a different source, but also that there are a number of pieces of information in John which can be used to supplement the information of the other Gospels. These help to make the whole story of Jesus' life and ministry more understandable.

For example, John tells us that some of Jesus' disciples had previously been followers of John the Baptist. This helps to explain the exact nature of the Baptist's witness to Jesus in the synoptics, and especially the emphasis placed there on his role in 'preparing the way of the Lord'. John's account also helps to answer the question (not obvious from the synoptics) of what Jesus was doing between his baptism and the arrest of John the Baptist. The synoptics report that Jesus began his ministry in Galilee after John's arrest. This is the only ministry recorded in the synoptic Gospels. But during his last visit to Jerusalem Matthew and Luke (Q) report that Jesus said of its inhabitants, 'How often would I have gathered your children together . . .'

John 1:35–42

Mark 1:14; Matthew 4:12; Luke 4:14–15

Matthew 23:37; Luke 13:34

This suggests that Jesus had visited Jerusalem on a number of previous occasions. John tells of just such an occasion, right at the beginning of Jesus' ministry, when he worked alongside John the Baptist in Judea before going back to Galilee when John was arrested.

John 2:13–4:3

John's Gospel fills out the synoptic material at a later point, when it records another visit by Jesus to Jerusalem some six months before his entry on Palm Sunday. John records how Jesus left Galilee and went to Jerusalem for the Feast of Tabernacles (September) and stayed there until the Feast of Dedication (December). Then, because of growing hostility, he returned to the area where John the Baptist had worked, and only made a brief visit to Bethany when he heard that Lazarus had died. A little later, six days before the Passover (April) he returned for his final visit to Jerusalem. This is the only one recorded in any detail in Mark, though the others are perhaps implied by Mark's summary statement: 'he left [Galilee] and went to the region of Judea and beyond the Jordan.'

John 7:1–10:42

John 10:40
John 11:1–54

John 12:1, 12

Mark 10:1

There are also a number of smaller details provided by John's Gospel which help to explain and clarify some points in the synoptic narratives. There is, for example, the feeding of the 5,000. At the end of the story in Mark we are told that Jesus compelled his disciples to escape on a boat while he himself dismissed the crowd. John's independent tradition fills in some of the detail, explaining that Jesus had to take this action because the crowd were eager to kidnap him and make him their king. We have already noticed in an earlier chapter how the stories of the Last Supper and of Jesus' trials can be fully understood only in the light of information contained in John's Gospel.

Mark 6:45

John 6:14–15

In view of evidence of this sort, it is now coming to be realized that John's Gospel is a source in its own right. The information it contains is independent of that in the synoptic Gospels, but at many crucial points John complements the other three.

The background of John in Judaism

It is also becoming recognized that the background of much of John's Gospel is Jewish, and not exclusively Greek. Early traditions place the origin of this Gospel in Ephesus. It was therefore natural that scholars should look for a Hellenistic background,

Medieval etchings represent some of the great scholars of the early church who wrote about the Gospels: (left to right) Tertullian of Carthage, Clement of Alexandria, Irenaeus of Lyons, Origen of Alexandria.

especially in view of the Gospel's prologue which explains the incarnation in terms of the word or *logos*. These church traditions are of course not always reliable. In the case of John's Gospel it is interesting to note that, if we remove the prologue from the Gospel, there is little in the rest of it that demands a Greek background. Quite the reverse, in fact. The evangelist states his purpose in writing in a very Jewish form: 'these things are written that you may believe that Jesus is the Christ (Messiah), the Son of God.' There is also an emphasis throughout the Gospel on the fulfilment of Old Testament sayings which again suggests a Jewish background.

John 1:1–18

John 20:31

This impression is confirmed by a closer analysis of the actual language of the Gospel, for at many points the Greek language shows a close connection with Aramaic sources. The writer often uses Aramaic words – for example, *Cephas*, *Gabbatha*, or *Rabboni*, and then explains them for the benefit of his Greek readers. Even the meaning of the word Messiah is given a careful explanation.

John 1:42; 19:13; 20:16

John 1:41

More significantly, there are also a number of points at which the Greek of the Gospel follows the rules of Aramaic grammar. An instance of this occurs when John the Baptist says of Jesus, 'I am not worthy *that I should untie* the thong of his sandals.' Though the distinction is not made in our English versions, the other Gospels have a different, and correct Greek expression, 'to untie'. But the unusual form of the statement in John is a regular idiom of the Aramaic language.

John 1:27

Then we also find Jesus' sayings in John expressed in the typical parallelism of Semitic poetry, and other sections of his teaching can be retranslated into Aramaic to form completely realistic Aramaic poetry.

John 12:25; 13:16, 20

John 3:29–30

It is not likely that John is a direct translation of an Aramaic document, though some have suggested this. But these facts do suggest that the teaching in John has the same Palestinian background as the material of the synoptic Gospels; and the curious use of Aramaic grammar in Greek writing may well suggest that Aramaic was the author's native language.

Archaeological discoveries

In addition to the internal evidence, there is also a considerable and important body of evidence drawn from archaeology which makes the old idea that John was a late Hellenistic Gospel now untenable. Three main pieces of evidence are important here.

● The Dead Sea Scrolls have shown that the odd combination of Greek and Jewish ideas which we find in John was current not only in Greek cities like Ephesus in the second century AD, but also in Palestine itself, in strict Jewish circles, in the pre-Christian era. Many phrases familiar from John are also found in the scrolls. 'Doing the truth', 'walking in darkness', 'sons of the light', 'the Spirit of truth' and many more expressions are as typical of the Qumran community as they are of John's Gospel. Moreover, the contrasts made in John between light and darkness, truth and error, are also typical of the Qumran scrolls. And in both contexts this dualism between light and darkness, truth and error is an *ethical* dualism, in contrast to the metaphysical emphasis of most Greek and Gnostic philosophies.

● Another discovery, of equal importance, and made at about the same time as the Dead Sea Scrolls, is the Coptic Gnostic library found at Nag Hammadi in upper Egypt. Prior to the discovery of these documents our knowledge of Gnosticism was based largely on information given by a number of church historians and theologians who wrote books to refute it. From their statements it was not too difficult to imagine that John's Gospel could have been written in the second century as a part of the battle between Gnostic and 'orthodox' Christians. But with our new knowledge derived from the writings of Gnostic teachers, it has become quite clear that there is a vast difference between the world of John's Gospel and the world of classical Gnosticism.

● Archaeological excavations in Jerusalem have also provided evidence to illuminate the traditions of John's Gospel. One of the unusual features of this Gospel is its proliferation of names and descriptions of places. It was widely thought at one time that these names were introduced either as a theological device (as symbols), or to give the impression of authenticity in otherwise fabricated accounts. But it is now clear that most of this geographical information rests on real knowledge of the city as it was before AD 70. In that year the Romans completely destroyed Jerusalem, and after that time it would have been impossible to observe the ruins and imagine what the city must have been like beforehand. Excavations in Jerusalem have now shown that descriptions of the Pool of Bethesda, for example, or 'the Pavement' where Jesus met Pilate are based on intimate knowledge of the city at the time of Jesus.

John 3:21; 12:35
John 12:36; 14:17

Archaeology has shown that John is more accurate than was once thought. The pool of Bethesda, a gathering place for the ill and disabled where Jesus once healed a man, was discovered only in this century.

John 5:1–18
John 19:13

The author and date of writing

The cumulative effect of all these converging lines of investigation has been to reinstate John's Gospel as a credible source of the life and teaching of Jesus. It has also re-opened the question of the authorship and date of this Gospel. The question of authorship has always been a rather confused one, not least because the church traditions mention two Johns in connection with the Gospel: the apostle, and a John whom they call 'the Elder'. Then there is the fact that the 'beloved disciple' seems to be portrayed in the Gospel itself as a source of some of the information. Here again it is far from clear who this person was. Irenaeus identifies the beloved disciple with John the apostle. But many scholars believe he may just be an ideal figure, symbolic of the true follower of Christ. He has even been identified with Lazarus who is, after all, the only person of whom it is consistently said that Jesus loved him.

John 21:24
Against Heresies I.1.1

John 11:5, 36

An attractive hypothesis that may explain the new facts now coming to light about John is the idea that this Gospel has gone through two editions. We have already seen that apart from the prologue the Gospel seems to be a very Jewish book, but with the prologue it takes on the appearance of a book more suited to the Greek world. It is therefore possible that the prologue was added after the completion of the original work, to commend the Gospel to a new readership.

This possibility is also supported by the odd connection between chapters 20 and 21. The last verse of chapter 20 appears to be the logical conclusion of the book, but this is then followed by the post-resurrection instructions of Jesus to Peter in chapter 21. This final chapter could also have been added at the time when the book was sent off to serve the needs of a new group of people, though its style and language is so close to that of the rest of the Gospel that it must have been added by the same person.

John 20:31

Another place mentioned by John is 'the pavement' where Jesus was tried before Pilate. It was part of the Antonia Fortress. The scratch marks on the ancient stones are part of a game played by Roman soldiers.

It seems possible that the Gospel was first written in Palestine, to demonstrate that 'Jesus is the Christ'. The author may have had in view sectarian Jews influenced by ideas like those of the Qumran community. Then, when the same teaching was seen to be relevant to people elsewhere in the Roman Empire, the Gospel was revised: Jewish customs and expressions were explained, and the prologue and epilogue added. The advice to church leaders in chapter 21 suggests that the final form of the Gospel may then have been directed to a Jewish Christian congregation somewhere in the Hellenistic world, perhaps at Ephesus.

The question of the date of the Gospel is really wide open, because we have no other evidence against which to set it. The church Fathers imply that it was written by John the apostle at the end of a long life, and most scholars continue to date it somewhere between AD 70 and 100. It must certainly not be dated later than the end of the first century, but there is no real evidence for dating it towards the end of that period. Robinson has argued with some force that it could well be the earliest of all the Gospels, and he places its composition in the period AD 40–65. If this is correct, John's Gospel could well be a contemporary of the synoptic Gospels, and such a date would effectively remove any barrier to viewing John the apostle as the author of the Gospel which now bears his name.

Chapter 12 Are the Gospels true?

IN OUR study of the life and teaching of Jesus, we have taken it for granted that we can actually learn something about him from the Gospels of the New Testament. We have recognized that the Gospels are not so much biographies of Jesus, as selective accounts of his words and actions compiled because of their usefulness in the preaching ministry of the earliest churches. But we have not taken that fact as a reason to doubt the general reliability of their account of Jesus' life and teaching. At most points we have felt justified in treating these records as a picture of Jesus as he really was, rather than regarding them as psychological case studies of the Christians who first wrote about him.

It must be frankly admitted, however, that this assumption has been called into question from a number of different directions. We do not need to take seriously those writers who occasionally claim that Jesus never existed at all, for we have clear evidence to the contrary from a number of Jewish, Latin and Islamic sources. But when people who have studied the New Testament for a lifetime claim that the Gospels reveal nothing of importance about Jesus, then we need to take serious account of their arguments.

Perhaps the most radical expression of this viewpoint in our generation has been associated with the name of Rudolf Bultmann. In a book first published in 1934, he made the remarkable statement: 'I do indeed think that we can now know almost nothing concerning the life and personality of Jesus.' The precise implication of what Bultmann meant by that must be decided in the light of some of his other writings, where he makes it clear that he does believe certain elements of Jesus' teaching as found in the Gospels to be original to Jesus himself. But to his dying day Bultmann remained sceptical about both the possibility and the value of knowledge about 'the historical Jesus'.

Not all Bultmann's followers have been quite as sceptical as he was. We can see this clearly enough from Gunther Bornkamm's book, *Jesus of Nazareth*, which shows that even from a radical form-critical standpoint there is still a good deal that can confidently be known about Jesus. But, for all that, those scholars who have been most influenced by Bultmann and his form-critical approach to the Gospels have generally taken it for granted that the Gospels are primarily a record of the beliefs of the early church about Jesus, rather than any sort of account of Jesus as he actually was.

Clearly, our knowledge of Jesus is not the same as our knowledge of, say, Winston Churchill, or Martin Luther, or even of Paul. For we can know these people through their writings and recorded utterances. Indeed, in the case of Luther and Paul, the main source of our information about them is the books that they themselves wrote. But Jesus did not write a book. He spent his brief life as a wandering teacher, working in a more or less remote corner of the Roman Empire, among people who were probably not very interested in literary matters.

It is quite unlikely that Jesus' words and actions had ever been written down, either by himself or by any of his contemporaries. Furthermore we know that Jesus lived in a society whose main language was Aramaic, and yet our knowledge of his teaching comes from documents written in Greek. It is possible that Greek may have been familiar to someone brought up in Galilee. But it is certain that most of Jesus' teachings were not originally given in this language, and that the Gospels are therefore a

There were no reporters with notebooks and tape-recorders following Jesus from place to place recording his words and actions. The story of Jesus was mostly passed on by personal conversation and public preaching for some years before the Gospels were written.

translation of the words of Jesus into the major language of the Roman Empire.

Moreover, one of the consequences of handing on Jesus' sayings in Greek is that we now have variant accounts in our Gospels of what is obviously the same basic tradition. If we take the Lord's Prayer, for example, we find that Matthew and Luke preserve different versions. The similarities are so close that there can be no doubt we are dealing with the same basic tradition. But the differences are too striking to be explained merely as variant translations. The same observations could be made at many other points in the Gospels, and they are the basic facts with which source, form and redaction critics are concerned.

*Matthew 6:9–13;
Luke 11:2–4*

We must not exaggerate the problems. Many generations of Gospel readers ignorant of the findings of modern scholars have found little difficulty in dealing with such matters. For all the distinctiveness of the various stories about Jesus and the reports of his teaching, there is clearly an inner coherence in the Gospels as a whole. It is not difficult to gather together an account of what the Gospels collectively present to us as 'the teaching of Jesus' – and the basic elements of that teaching are the same in all four Gospels.

Identifying the authentic words of Jesus

Jesus spoke Aramaic, and some Aramaic words are retained in the Gospels. But they were largely written in Greek. Left is an example of Aramaic from a fifth-century papyrus; right the Greek text of a first-century letter.

But how can we be sure that the Gospels contain the teaching of Jesus himself, and not the impressions of the early church about Jesus? This question has been the subject of a very considerable debate among New Testament scholars for the past decade or so, and it still continues. As a possible answer, a number of tests have been devised which are often claimed as a reliable means of identifying the authentic teaching of Jesus in the Gospels. These tests have been applied most comprehensively to the synoptic Gospels by Professor Norman Perrin. He outlines three separate tests, or criteria, and on the basis of these he argues that at least three areas of Jesus' teaching in the Gospels can be shown to be authentic: the parables, the teaching on the kingdom of God, and the themes mentioned in the Lord's Prayer.

The test of distinctiveness

The test of distinctiveness had already been used by Bultmann himself, in his book *The History of the Synoptic Tradition*. It is based on the assumption that anything in Jesus' teaching that can be paralleled in either the teaching of Judaism or the theology of the early church is of doubtful authenticity, for it could have come into the Gospels from either of those two sources rather than from an authentic reminiscence of Jesus. So at those points where Jesus' teaching is totally unique and distinctive we may be sure that we are in direct contact with Jesus himself. We could give as examples Jesus' use of the word *Abba*, 'Father', in his address to God, and his characteristic way of beginning important statements with the word

Amen. As far as we know, neither of these devices was used by the Jewish rabbis or by the early church.

Many scholars would agree with Professor Perrin when he claims that information retrieved from the Gospels by this means represents 'an irreducible minimum of historical knowledge' about Jesus.

But when we examine it more carefully, it is doubtful whether even this modest claim can be fully justified on the basis of this particular method. For its successful use depends entirely on the further assumption that our present knowledge of both Judaism and the early church is more or less complete. The fact is, however, that we know very little about the form of Judaism at the time of Jesus. New information is constantly being discovered and assessed – and with it new parallels to the teaching of Jesus are certain to emerge. As a method, therefore, the criterion of distinctiveness is a counsel of despair. It can only be a matter of time before the logical outcome is reached, that nothing certain can be known about Jesus. Besides this weakness in method, there are two other major problems with this particular approach.

● Even the limited picture of Jesus produced by this means is bound to be unreal and untrue to life, for it presupposes a Jesus who was completely isolated from his environment. The old adage that 'a text without a context is a pretext' is as true here as it often is in modern sermons. Jesus *must* have had a context – and it is certain that his context was Judaism. It is equally certain that there must have been *some* continuity between Jesus and the early church. A Jesus who is unique in the sense that his teaching is totally detached from both Judaism and the church is unlikely to be the real Jesus. And if this test cannot uncover him it must be judged to be a failure.

● There are large and important areas of the Gospels where this method is of no use at all. Take the question of Jesus' teaching about himself. On this subject the test of distinctiveness leads to completely negative results on all the major titles ascribed to Jesus. 'Messiah', 'Son of God', 'Son of man' were all used by some in the early church, and the application of this test therefore leads to the conclusion that Jesus gave no teaching about

his own destiny and person. The same happens with his eschatology, for that can be paralleled in Jewish and early Christian sources. Even the distinctive teaching of the Sermon on the Mount would have to be jettisoned for the same reasons, for Paul shows a clear knowledge of that in Romans 12–14. There is therefore a basic fault in the whole concept of this approach. It must inevitably lead, both theoretically and practically, to the claim that nothing useful can be known about Jesus from the Gospels.

The test of 'coherence'

Those who use these tests are not unaware of the problems involved with the test of distinctiveness. Perrin therefore puts forward another one which can be used in conjunction with it. This is the test of coherence. It is based on the assumption that any material in the Gospels that is compatible with the teaching which passes the distinctiveness test can also be counted as a genuine statement of what Jesus said and did.

On the face of it, this further test seems promising. But of course it is very heavily dependent on a successful application of the first test. We have already seen the difficulties involved in this, and if it leads to no sure results then this second test is also useless. In any case it is very difficult to judge what is 'coherent' and what is not. Even supposing we can make our own judgement on the matter, there is no guarantee that what seems coherent to us would have seemed so to the early church. So we are once more faced with serious practical difficulties in applying this test to the Gospel traditions.

The test of more than one source

A third criterion often used for assessing the traditions about Jesus is not directly dependent on the other two. It was widely used by T. W. Manson, who had little time for the approach of the form critics.

On this test, teaching mentioned in the Gospels is genuinely from Jesus if it is found in more than one Gospel source. This is a useful test as far as it goes, for if Mark and Q give us a similar impression of the content of Jesus' teaching, then it is reasonable to believe that it is an authentic impression.

But this test for authenticity also meets a number of difficulties, though they are not as great as the problems involved in operating the other two.

● It is not possible by this means to say anything about specific statements attributed to Jesus, for there are very few stories or sayings that are contained in more than one of the Gospel sources. Indeed this fact is one of the foundations of the whole source-critical approach to the Gospels. If the same teaching was represented everywhere, it would not have been possible for Streeter to formulate his hypothesis on Gospel origins. This means that the most this method can discover is the general tone of Jesus' teaching, rather than a detailed account of it.

● It also has another built-in limitation, for it would presumably dismiss as not authentic those parts of Jesus' teaching that are found in only one Gospel source. Yet this is the case with some of the most characteristic parts of Jesus' teaching. Using this test, stories such as the good Samaritan (Luke 10:25–37) or the lost son (Luke 15:11–32) would be excluded altogether from an account of Jesus' life and teaching, because they are found only in Luke's Gospel.

● When Manson and others applied this test to the Gospels, they could assume a fairly rigid distinction between the various Gospel sources, for at the time Streeter's hypothesis was widely held by British scholars in more or less its original form. But more recent study has shown that the question of the relationships between the Gospels and their sources is far more complex than Streeter thought. We can no longer assume as a matter of course the simple division into the four independent sources, Mark, Q, M and L.

A basic flaw

There are clearly many serious problems involved in using these tests to identify the authentic words of Jesus within the Gospels. So it is perhaps not too surprising that some scholars should have reached rather negative conclusions. It is hard to see how they could do otherwise. There is in fact a basic flaw in the

whole method represented by these tests. They all begin from the basic assumption that the Gospels mostly contain the beliefs of the early church, and only a very little, if anything at all, that comes directly from Jesus himself. Professor Perrin gives two main reasons to justify this built-in pessimism.

● 'The early Church', he writes, 'made no attempt to distinguish between the words the earthly Jesus had spoken and those spoken by the risen Lord through a prophet in the community, nor between the original teaching of Jesus and the new understanding and reformulation of that teaching reached in . . . the Church under the guidance of the Lord of the Church.'

The starting-point of this argument is the fact that the earliest Christians clearly believed that the risen Jesus was present and active among his followers in the church. He was, of course, no longer physically present, and so his word could be communicated to Christians only indirectly. An example of how this could happen is said to be found in the first three chapters of the book of Revelation. There the Christian prophet John delivers messages from the heavenly Christ to seven churches in Asia Minor. Paul also mentions prophets working in the church (1 Corinthians 12:27–31), and it is often argued that their main function was to issue 'sayings of Jesus' to meet some specific need in the church's life.

Though this argument is widely accepted by New Testament scholars, it is highly questionable. A number of very serious objections can be made against it.

First, it is based on very precarious evidence. Though it is often confidently stated that the role of the Christian prophet was to invent sayings of Jesus, we have in fact no real evidence to show what the prophets did in the early church. The messages to the seven churches in the book of Revelation are quite irrelevant, for a clear distinction is made there between the experience and words of the writer of the book and the message of the risen Christ. In any case he claims to have received them in a vision, and we can say that he made them up only if we make the further questionable assumption that visions never happen. The only direct evidence in the New Testament of the function of these prophets is in Acts 13:1–3 where they give instructions regarding the missionary work of Paul and Barnabas. Even these instructions are given, not in the name of Jesus, but with the authority of the Holy Spirit. This kind of evidence is so slight that it can give us only the vaguest indication of the precise work of the prophets in the life of the church.

A very early fragment of John's Gospel, dating from about AD 130.

Secondly, the assumption that prophets could freely invent 'sayings of Jesus' also assumes that the first Christians made no clear distinction between Jesus' teaching and their own. But this is quite untrue. Paradoxically, our evidence for this is clearest in the writings of Paul, and for that reason it is all the more striking. For, of all the New Testament writers, Paul is the one most often accused of sitting loosely to the teachings of Jesus. He also claimed more than once to have a greater measure of God's special gifts than most of his contemporaries (1 Corinthians 14:18–19; 2 Corinthians 12:1–10). These two facts alone would make him an ideal candidate to have been a purveyor of 'sayings of Jesus'. We would expect his letters to be full of such sayings, manufactured by himself under the influence of the Holy Spirit for the purpose of giving advice to his readers. But in fact we find quite the opposite. In 1 Corinthians 7, for example, he goes out of his way to distinguish between his own opinions and the teaching of Jesus.

Thirdly, another problem with the assumption that the early church freely manufactured sayings of Jesus is its illogicality. The only

'evidence' that the prophets formulated such sayings is the notion that the Gospel traditions had their origin in the early church and not in the ministry of Jesus. A hypothetical life-setting has been imagined for the Gospels; then the Gospels are interpreted in the light of the hypothesis. This is a very uncertain procedure, not least because it is a circular argument with no external support. It is not surprising that on this basis the Gospels can be demonstrated to be products of the pious imagination of the early church; the evidence has been put into them at the outset of the investigation.

● Professor Perrin's second reason for scepticism has a firmer foundation. He asserts, quite correctly, that the primary aim of the Gospels was not to give historical or biographical information about Jesus, but to edify their readers. Everything in the Gospels is there because it served a particular purpose in the church's life. But he goes on to say that this fact of itself excludes the possibility that the Gospels contain historical reminiscences of Jesus as he actually was. This is another argument that is often asserted but seldom supported.

There is, however, no logical reason at all why a story or piece of teaching that conveys a practical or theological message has to be historically false. For example, I have often preached sermons on Paul's statement that in Christ 'There is neither Jew nor Greek, there is neither slave nor free, there is neither male nor female; for you are all one . . .' (Galatians 3:28). No doubt many sermons have been preached on that theme, relating it to our modern problems of inequality and injustice. It is certainly highly relevant to such issues. But the fact that I preach a sermon on that text and relate it to twentieth-century problems would not normally lead people to conclude that I made it up myself and Paul never wrote Galatians, or even that he never existed at all. That would be absurd. Yet this is precisely the kind of reasoning that some scholars apply to the Gospels when they argue that, because their contents were relevant to life in the middle of the first century, they can have had no historical context in the of Jesus himself. It is an assertion that simply does not make sense.

A positive approach to the Gospels

Many scholars find the scepticism of Bultmann and his followers quite unacceptable. They argue instead that there are a number of good reasons for starting from the assumption that the Gospels are reliable, rather than unreliable, as records of Jesus as he actually was. A number of important arguments point in this direction.

● To begin at the most general level, we must not forget that ancient writers were not on the whole either fools or frauds. Many modern theologians (though not as many historians) speak so disparagingly of the historians of the Roman world that we are often given the impression that the concept of accurate history writing was quite unknown to them. It is of course true that the ancient historian did not have at his disposal all the modern aids we have today. But that is not to say he simply invented his stories. Both Latin and Greek historians had high standards, and though they did not always keep to them, it was certainly not for lack of trying. The principles outlined by people like Lucian and Thucydides make it quite clear that they operated within guidelines that would not be out of place even today.

Whatever else may be said about the people who wrote the Gospels, it is clear that they thought they were working within this kind of historical tradition. Luke explicitly says that he sifted all his sources of information and carefully compiled his story on that basis. Since the other synoptic writers used a more or less similar technique in dealing with their sources, it is natural to suppose that they also worked on the same lines. Certainly they all thought they were giving actual information about a person who had really lived in the way they described. They were not conscious of reporting sayings made up by their contemporaries and attributed to Jesus. They believed that their risen Lord was actually a Galilean rabbi, and that as a wandering teacher he lived and spoke as they depicted him.

Luke 1:1–4

● This argument is of course not very strong by itself, for the evangelists could have been mistaken and deluded. But it gains considerable added force when we discover that the details of their accounts do actually give an authentic picture of life in Palestine at the time of which they purport to write. When we recall that they all wrote in Greek for a more or less non-Jewish readership, and that at least two of them were not living in Palestine when they wrote, this is all the more remarkable. At point after point we find that the background of the Gospels is authentic. Moreover, at places where their record was once believed to be mistaken (as in the case of John's Gospel), subsequent discoveries of new information have often shown that the Gospels preserve reliable accounts of a number of important geographical and social details.

● The Gospels have also been firmly rooted in a Jewish context by the work of two Scandinavian scholars, Harald Riesenfeld and his pupil Birger Gerhardsson. Gerhardsson has put forward the view that the teaching of Jesus was very similar in form to that of the Jewish rabbis, and in an extended analysis of their teaching methods he has shown how the rabbis took great pains to ensure that their sayings were accurately remembered and passed on by word of mouth to their followers. Gerhardsson suggests that Jesus adopted the same methods, and that he formulated his teaching with a view to his disciples learning it by heart so that they could pass it on to their own followers in the same easily memorized form. It is suggested that the teaching of Jesus was handed on in this way as 'holy word' in the early church, and that the Gospels represent the writing down of accurately transmitted traditions going right back to Jesus himself.

We have no evidence that the early Christians regarded themselves as the transmitters of tradition, however. They were preachers of the good news, explaining how the life and message of Jesus was relevant to the needs of their own generation. We also have the unanimous testimony of the Gospels that Jesus was quite

Mark 1:22 different from the Jewish rabbis. He taught 'with authority', and did not simply hand on memorized sayings from one group of disciples to another.

Yet, though the case of Riesenfeld and Gerhardsson may be exaggerated, they have reminded us that Jesus' teaching was given in a Jewish context, and in that context the teaching of an authoritative leader was treated with great respect. Even if the earliest disciples did not learn Jesus' sayings by heart, they would certainly have a high regard for them.

There is also ample evidence for the reliable oral preservation of stories in the wider Hellenistic world. Take the *Life of Apollonius of Tyana*, which we have mentioned in an earlier chapter.

The Bible has been subjected to close scholarly scrutiny over the past two centuries. This group of people organized the translation of the New English Bible. Their task took twelve years.

This man Apollonius was a contemporary of Jesus, though he lived on into old age and died towards the end of the first century. The account of his life, however, was not written down until the beginning of the third century. Though the author collected the stories of his life from a number of different sources, and though he was not an impartial biographer, very few ancient historians would have serious doubts about the reliability of the main outline of his account. In the case of the Gospels we are dealing with documents that were written down very shortly after the events

Mark 5:41; Matthew 27:46;
John 19:13

The Gospels — and most of the
Bible — have been translated
into many languages. Some
tribal languages first have to be
reduced to writing before the
translation can begin.

of which they speak. To most ordinary people it would seem absurd to assume that such accounts are useless for the purpose of knowing something of Jesus himself.

● According to the German scholar Joachim Jeremias, the Gospels do indeed bring us into close contact with Jesus as he actually was. Jeremias has scrutinized the linguistic and grammatical features of the Gospels, and argues that in them we can discover the authentic voice of Jesus.

Occasionally we come across actual Aramaic words, even in the Greek text of the Gospels. In many other cases there are passages where an idiomatic Aramaic construction has been used in the writing of the Gospels in Greek. Jeremias also outlines a number of ways of speaking which he says were characteristically used by Jesus. Much of his teaching is given in the form of Aramaic poetry, recognizable even in an English translation. At other points, as we have already said, it has been shown that when sayings attributed to Jesus are translated back into Aramaic, they often assume a typically Semitic form, and even display alliteration and assonance that could have had meaning only in Aramaic. Then there are the parables, which are quite different from the teaching of the rabbis; and Jesus' special use of the words *Amen* and *Abba*.

Features such as these do not themselves prove that the Gospel traditions go back to Jesus. Strictly speaking, the most they can show is that they go back to a form in which they were preserved by Aramaic-speaking Palestinian Christians. But when we get

back into that context we are also back to a time shortly after the events of Jesus' life, death and resurrection. At this time many eye-witnesses must still have been alive to challenge any accounts which were pure fiction.

These facts therefore favour the authenticity of the Gospel accounts of Jesus' teaching. Jeremias for one has no doubt that they place the burden of proof squarely on those who would dispute their accuracy: 'In the synoptic tradition it is the inauthenticity, and not the authenticity, of the sayings of Jesus that must be demonstrated.'

●Another consideration that gives us confidence in accepting the Gospels as generally authentic records of Jesus' life and teaching is the fact that they are so different from what we know of the life and concerns of the early non-Jewish churches. It is wrong to imagine that, because the Gospels were written to serve the needs of the churches, they are little more than a mirror reflecting the life of the early church. The rest of the New Testament shows that the church had many needs that are not even remotely met in the Gospels.

There is, for example, no real teaching on the church itself in the Gospels. This is so obvious a gap that we found it necessary to ask in an earlier chapter whether Jesus was interested in founding a church at all. It was suggested there that the emergence of the church was by no means incompatible with Jesus' teaching, but we still need to admit that there is virtually no specific guidance on the subject in the Gospels. Even baptism, which very soon became the rite of initiation into the Christian fellowship, is never mentioned by Jesus, apart from one isolated instance. Jesus himself did not baptize, nor did he make baptism a central part of his teaching. Yet this was a matter of great importance to the early church. If they did indeed make a regular practice of manufacturing 'sayings of Jesus' to meet their needs, they certainly missed an important opportunity here.

Matthew 28:19

We find the same lack of specific guidance on other crucial topics. The question of Jews and non-Jews, for example, is not really dealt with in the Gospels, though we know from the rest of the New Testament that it soon became one of the most important matters of all.

In other places the Gospels make quite a different emphasis from the rest of the New Testament. The term 'Son of man', for instance, is the most widely used name for Jesus in the Gospels, but it hardly appears anywhere else. Likewise, 'the kingdom of God', which was the heart of Jesus' teaching, is hardly mentioned in the rest of the New Testament.

The fact is that if we were to try to reconstruct the church's life-situation from the Gospels, we would never arrive at the kind of picture we know to be true from the New Testament letters. For there are so many features of the Gospel stories about Jesus that are quite different from the life and concerns of the early church.

In the light of facts such as these, it seems reasonable to conclude that there are good reasons for supposing the Gospels preserve authentic reminiscences of Jesus as he actually was. The whole character of their picture of Jesus is such that we would need very strong and coherent arguments to show that they are fundamentally mistaken.

This assumption does not of course mean that we can adopt a naïve and uncritical attitude. The evangelists were not mere recorders of tradition. They were interpreters of the facts handed on to them, and we need to scrutinize their work carefully in order to understand the precise nature of what they were doing. But it does give us confidence in thinking that the tradition they interpreted for their first readers was itself authentic, and that in general terms they have preserved a realistic account of the life and teaching of Jesus. Whether they have done so in specific instances must naturally be determined by a literary and historical approach to particular sections of their work.

God's revelation and history

In view of the many reasons that lead us to presume the authenticity of the Gospels as records of Jesus' teaching, we might well be surprised that so many scholars have adopted such a negative attitude towards them. One basic reason for this is almost certainly to be found not so much in their historical and literary approach to the Gospels themselves, as in their total understanding of the whole question of revelation and the knowledge of God.

To understand this, we need to go back to the work of Friedrich Schleiermacher (1768–1834), the so-called 'father of modern theology'. In trying to deal with the great upsurge of rationalism that came with the European Enlightenment, Schleiermacher reasoned that if religious belief was to retain any validity for modern Western people, it would need to be removed altogether from the realm of rational investigation. For the historical science of his day was totally sceptical of the whole idea that God could make himself known in history through the kind of events recorded in the Bible.

Schleiermacher therefore aimed to rescue religious belief from what he thought would be its inevitable suffocation in this sceptical atmosphere. He argued that the essence of faith is quite different from the essence of either morality, which directs the practical side of life, or science, which is concerned with rational thought-processes. Faith, he said, is pure feeling, and this means that religious belief can be valid quite independently of anything that can be interpreted scientifically.

This idea has been challenged and modified at many points by later thinkers. But Schleiermacher's general distinction between religion and reason has been decisive for the subsequent development of theological thought in much of the Western world. In the study of the Gospels it is expressed by the acceptance of two

Friedrich Schleiermacher
(1768–1834), the German
thinker, was the father of one
school of modern theology.

principles which dominate the thinking of many scholars.

● *The supernatural and history.* Many theologians, especially those who, like Bultmann, stand in a German Lutheran tradition, believe that the universe is a closed system, operating according to rigidly structured 'laws of nature' which cannot be broken. When taken to its logical conclusion, this belief means that it is impossible to accommodate any kind of miraculous or unique occurrence in our concept of history. If the workings of the world are totally predictable then, by definition, the unpredictable cannot take place. On this view it therefore becomes inevitable that the Gospels should be seen as something other than history, for they do contain accounts of a number of unique happenings which appear to violate the 'laws of nature' as they are known to us.

Various arguments may be brought against this kind of view of the world and its workings. For one thing, it is outdated. It is interesting to note that, at this point, the assumptions of some philosophers and theologians are much less flexible than the views of many modern scientists. The discoveries made by twentieth-century physicists, for example, have shown at many points how tenuous the concept of the universe as a closed system really is, and many scientists now recognize that there is more to its workings than just the mechanical operation of laws of cause and effect.

Then, from another standpoint, the belief that the universe is a closed system can too easily become a means of avoiding the need to take serious account of the actual evidence of history. If we are to allow ourselves room to consider the full implications of the Gospel accounts, or indeed of history as a whole, we must in principle be prepared to operate on a wider definition of history and reality than is allowed by many modern theologians. To say that unique events cannot happen, or that the supernatural does not exist, is no kind of answer to the questions raised by history. It merely begs larger and more important questions.

● *Facts and faith.* Another assumption often made by theologians is that facts and faith are unconnected, and that religious belief cannot be founded on the facts of history. There is a problem with Christianity at this point. For no matter what we say about Christian belief it is somehow connected with the Jesus who lived and died in first-century Palestine. In some sense, therefore, it must be a 'historical' faith. But what do we mean when we say that?

When we speak of 'history' or of 'historical events', we can mean two things. On the one hand, 'history' can mean 'the past'. It is what really happened on a given occasion: what we would have seen with our own eyes and heard with our own ears had we been there. This is the kind of 'history' the nineteenth-century rationalists were trying to discover in their quest for the historical Jesus. But we can also use the word 'history' to mean 'referring to the past' – what we might call 'history-as-story' rather than 'history-as-fact'. In the one case we are dealing with the actual things that happened, and nothing else. In the other, we consider the events in their proper context and in the light of their ultimate significance for our own existence.

A number of German theologians have seized upon this technical distinction as a means of separating the Jesus of Christian faith (the risen Lord) from the Jesus of history. They use two different German words to describe the two kinds of history: *Historie* to denote 'history-as-fact', and *Geschichte* to denote 'history-as-story'. And, they say, it is only the latter that is really important to Christian faith. It is the *significance* of history as it affects us that matters, not the history itself. This means that knowledge of Jesus himself as a historical person is irrelevant to faith. What really matters is the Christian's beliefs about Jesus.

This kind of assertion is gravely inadequate, both as a statement about theology in general, and as a statement about the Gospel accounts of Jesus' life and teaching. The sharp distinction made between *Historie* and *Geschichte* is based on a misunderstanding of the true nature of history-as-fact and history-as-story. For the two things are very closely related, and it is quite impossible to think of one of them without also presupposing the other. Nobody would ever write history-as-story unless he was convinced that something had actually happened that was important enough to be worth writing about. And, similarly, we can gain access to 'what actually happened' only through the medium of stories and records that tell of them in their context and over-all significance.

It is therefore logically inevitable that when we speak of 'history', whether in general or in relation to the New Testament, we should include something of both meanings. It is also highly desirable that we should do so. If we confine our attention to the meaning of history we are in a very precarious position, for if an event did not actually take place then any interpretation we place upon it is bound to be completely meaningless. It would, for example, be pointless to convince myself that Jesus died for my sins if, as a matter of historical fact, he never died at all. To say that faith is important and facts are not is naïve. It leads away from objectivity in historical understanding, and represents a religious faith that is both irrational and subjective.

The writers of the New Testament were not unaware of these questions, and they provide their own answers to them. In his important account of the resurrection of Jesus and its meaning, Paul emphasizes very strongly the importance of facts as an indispensable element in his own Christian faith. Though he himself became a Christian through a direct encounter with the risen Christ, he sets his theology very firmly in the context of a historical event that he believed could be verified in the normal way by the report of witnesses. And he has no hesitation in saying that if the witnesses were wrong, and 'if Christ has not

1 Corinthians 15:17

been raised, then your faith is a delusion . . .'

The various accounts of the early Christian preaching also emphasize that history is important, and much of the *kerygma* as outlined by C. H. Dodd is a recital of facts about Jesus. The Jesus who confronts us in the New Testament, and supremely in the Gospels, is not a phantom figure whose only importance is his meaning. He is a real person who can be relevant to our world because he has lived in it.

But the good news does not demand that we become ancient historians in order to be Christians. The facts require us to take action, to exercise faith. If Jesus rose from the dead, then we must face the implications, the need to submit to the risen Lord and his demands over our lives. But it also assures us that both his demands and his promises are reasonable, fair, and true because they can be vindicated by reference to the events of history.

In the final analysis, the Jesus of history can only be the Jesus of the church's faith. For it was in the events of the life, death and resurrection of this person that God was at work, revealing his own character and reconciling the world to himself.

Although the Gospels have presented scholars with many questions, people of every race and generation have found in them a source of inspiration and hope.

Sayings of Jesus outside the New Testament

At various points in this book we have referred to traditions about Jesus' life and teaching that are not found in the New Testament. A number of 'gospels' written in the second century purport to tell of the early childhood of Jesus. Then we have also mentioned collections of Jesus' sayings, such as the *Gospel of*

Thomas. A very considerable number of such traditions about Jesus are known to us (see the book list).

These documents are not the only sources which contain information about Jesus not found in the New Testament Gospels. Some of the church Fathers preserve a few fragments of teaching which they say was first given by Jesus, and of course in other parts of the New Testament itself we occasionally find references to sayings of Jesus not found in the Gospels. For example, at the end of his message to the elders of the Ephesian church, Paul sums up by quoting what he says are the words of Jesus, that 'It is more blessed to give than to receive' (Acts 20:35). Yet no such saying of Jesus is recorded anywhere in the Gospels.

The material preserved in the second-century sources is of a remarkably varied character. Much of it, especially in the infancy stories, is clearly legendary. It was written to fill in the gaps that are left by the New Testament Gospels, for they tell us nothing at all of Jesus' childhood. Many of the stories of these apocryphal infancy gospels are so unreal and pointless that one only need read them to realize that they are of a quite different character from the New Testament accounts of Jesus.

Other questions are raised, however, by the collections of Jesus' sayings found in such documents as the Gospels of Philip and Thomas, or the various papyri discovered at Oxyrhynchus in upper Egypt. Most of these documents were written for sectarian purposes, and many of them emanate from the various Gnostic groups that were prevalent in the second century and after.

The *Gospel of Thomas* in its present form was compiled for the purpose of supporting the life of an esoteric group in the church. Scholars are uncertain as to whether it was a Gnostic group, or perhaps some other kind of group connected to Jewish Christianity, but they are unanimous in regarding it as a document produced to uphold the beliefs of a particular sect. Many of its sayings are taken from the New Testament, but presented with a Gnostic slant. Others have probably come in direct from some other Gnostic source.

But, besides these, there are still some others which appear to be of independent origin. For example, logion 82 of *Thomas* reads as follows: 'Jesus said, He who is near me is near the fire; he who is far from me is far from the kingdom.' This particular saying was also known to the church Father Origen (AD 185–254), and there may be allusions to it in other early Christian writers. It is certainly characteristic of the kind of sayings of Jesus recorded in the New Testament and, in addition, it has the form of Aramaic poetry, which again is a regular feature of Jesus' teaching in the four Gospels.

There are a number of such sayings scattered about in the literature of the early church. When they do not teach any specially sectarian doctrine, and when they are in general agreement with the teaching of Jesus found in the New Testament, there seems to be no real reason for doubting that they could go back to authentic traditions about Jesus. If, as in the example we quoted, they also have the form of Semitic poetry, that is a further indication of their primitive character.

In his book *Unknown Sayings of Jesus*, Professor Jeremias has isolated a number of such fragments of teaching, and a few stories told about Jesus, that he considers may be genuine reminiscences of the life and teaching of Jesus himself. Some of them undoubtedly do have the marks of authenticity. The fact that such information should have been preserved outside the New Testament need not surprise us. The writer of John's Gospel mentions many accounts of Jesus' life and teaching known to him, but which he did not use in his own Gospel (John 20:30–31). But we can be sure that they would not be entirely lost to the church. No doubt they were remembered and repeated, and perhaps some of them ended up in the various documents we have mentioned here.

But it is important to notice that by comparison with the vast number of apocryphal traditions about Jesus, only a tiny proportion have even a slight claim to being genuine. The vast majority of the material is quite worthless as a historical source for knowledge of Jesus. Professor Jeremias is undoubtedly correct when he comments that 'The real value of the tradition outside the Gospels is that it throws into sharp relief the unique value of the canonical Gospels themselves. If we would learn about the life and message of Jesus, we shall find what we want *only* in the four canonical Gospels. The lost dominical sayings may supplement our knowledge here and there in important and valuable ways, but they cannot do more than that.'

Glossary of special terms

apocalypse	Literally means 'a revelation of secrets' – a special kind of literature claiming to reveal God's plans and purposes in future history. It was very popular in certain Jewish circles before and after the time of Jesus.
Diaspora/Dispersion	Jews living outside Palestine.
didache	Moral and spiritual teaching given to new converts in the early church.
eschatology	Traditionally, teachings concerning the end of the world. But the word is often used with a much wider meaning, to include God's activity in the lives of men and women, in the past and the present as well as the future.
form criticism	The study of the literary forms of the stories contained in the Gospels.
Judaism	The Jewish religion.
kerygma	The pattern of statements about Jesus which make up the Christian message in the 'sermons' recorded in Acts.
logia	Early collections of sayings of Jesus.
parousia	The second coming of Jesus.
Pentateuch/*Torah*	First five books of the Old Testament – Genesis to Deuteronomy.
redaction criticism	The study of the way the Gospels were put together by their individual writers, trying to discover their purpose in writing and to understand the way they dealt with their source materials.
Sanhedrin	The Jewish supreme council of seventy members.
synoptic Gospels	Matthew, Mark and Luke: the three Gospels which are very much alike.
testimonia	Collections of Old Testament texts which seem to predict some aspect of Jesus' life.

Other books on Jesus

*Books marked with an asterisk are recommended for more advanced study

General

G. Bornkamm, *Jesus of Nazareth*, Hodder and Stoughton, 1960/Harper and Row, 1975. An account of Jesus' life and teaching by a noted German scholar involved in the 'New Quest for the historical Jesus'.

F. F. Bruce, *Jesus and Christian Origins outside the New Testament*, Hodder and Stoughton/Eerdmans, 1974. An interesting discussion of what is known about Jesus and the early church from sources outside the New Testament. Includes Josephus and the apocryphal gospels, as well as Islamic traditions about Jesus.

C. H. Dodd, *The Founder of Christianity*, Collins, 1971/ Macmillan, 1970. An award-winning account of the life of Jesus by one of the great British New Testament scholars of this century.

A. M. Hunter, *The Work and Words of Jesus*, SCM Press (second edition)/Westminster Press, 1973. A simple account of the main problems encountered in under-standing the Gospels.

*J. Jeremias, *New Testament Theology*, volume I, SCM Press/ Scribner, 1971. A comprehensive account of the message of Jesus, by a leading conservative German theologian.

B. Vawter, *This Man Jesus*, G. Chapman/Doubleday, 1973. A readable discussion of New Testament Christology by a Roman Catholic scholar.

W. G. Kümmel, *Theology of the New Testament*, SCM Press, 1974/ Abingdon Press, 1973. A lucid discussion of the whole of the New Testament, with many helpful insights on the message of Jesus, as well as that of Paul and John.

Section One. God's promised deliverer

Chapter 1. The world of Jesus

E. Lohse, *The New Testament Environment*, SCM Press/Abingdon Press, 1976. A readable, compre-hensive account of the religious background of the New Testament.

W. S. LaSor, *The Dead Sea Scrolls and the New Testament*, Eerdmans, 1972. A judicious and thorough survey of the implications of the Dead Sea Scrolls for study of the New Testament.

M. C. Tenney, *New Testament Times*, Inter-Varsity Press/ Eerdmans, 1965. Lays more emphasis than Lohse on the Jewish and Roman history of the period, showing how it helps our understanding of the New Testament.

Chapter 2. Jesus' birth and early years

C. H. H. Scobie, *John the Baptist*, SCM Press, 1964. A survey of all that is known of John the Baptist, and an examination of his sig-nificance.

Chapter 3. Who was Jesus?

*O. Cullmann, *The Christology of the New Testament*, SCM Press, 1959/Westminster, 1964. Discusses the various titles applied to Jesus, not only in the Gospels but throughout the New Testament.

*A. J. B. Higgins, *Jesus and the Son of Man*, Lutterworth Press, 1964. An account of various approaches to the Son of man problem, together with a reassessment of the evidence.

*M. D. Hooker, *Jesus and the Servant*, SPCK, 1959. A study of the importance of the Old Testament concept of the Servant of the Lord.

I. H. Marshall, *The Origins of New Testament Christology*, Inter-Varsity Press, 1977. Discusses the rela-tionship between the church's beliefs about Jesus, and his own beliefs about himself.

*H. E. Tödt, *The Son of Man in the Synoptic Tradition*, SCM Press, 1965. A radical, though com-prehensive study of this subject.

H. E. W. Turner, *Jesus the Christ*, Mowbray, 1976. A study of Christology and the atonement, tracing its development from the New Testament through to the later beliefs of the church.

*W. Wrede, *The Messianic Secret*, Cambridge University Press, 1971/Attic Press, 1972. The classic study referred to in our discussion of the subject.

Chapter 4. Why did Jesus die?
On Jesus' trials

J. Blinzler, *The Trial of Jesus*, Westminster, Md., 1959. A helpful guide to the complexities of the New Testament stories.

*A. N. Sherwin-White, *Roman Society and Roman Law in the New Testament*, Oxford University Press, 1963, pp. 24–47. A study of Jesus' trials from the legal point of view.

The Last Supper

*J. Jeremias, *The Eucharistic Words of Jesus*, first edition 1955; SCM Press, 1970/Allenson, 1966. Perhaps the most comprehensive study of the meaning and signifi-cance of the Last Supper, arguing that it was the Jewish Passover.

*A. Jaubert, *The Date of the Last Supper*, Alba House, 1965. Finds the answer to the chronological problems by arguing that Jesus used a different calendar from the Pharisees.

L. Morris, *The Gospel according to John*, Eerdmans, 1971, pp. 774–86. A balanced discussion of all the issues involved in dating the Last Supper.

M. H. Shepherd, Jr, 'Are both the synoptics and John correct about the date of Jesus' death?', in *Journal of Biblical Literature* 80 (1961), pp. 123–32. Argues that the different emphases in the Gospel accounts are to be explained by the calendars used by the evangelists.

The cross

J. Denney, *The Death of Christ*, London (many reprints). A classic study of the subject, though now somewhat dated in parts.

L. Morris, *The Cross in the New Testament*, Paternoster Press/Eerdmans, 1964. A comprehensive study of the meaning of the atonement throughout the New Testament.

F. M. Young, *Sacrifice and the Death of Christ*, SPCK, 1975. A helpful study of the use of sacrificial language in the New Testament and the early church, together with an interesting discussion of the continued usefulness of the imagery in expressing the meaning of the atonement in the modern world.

Chapter 5. The resurrection

*D. P. Fuller, *Easter Faith and History*, Tyndale Press, 1968/Eerdmans, 1964. Considers the philosophical problems raised by belief in the resurrection.

*R. H. Fuller, *The Formation of the Resurrection Narratives*, SPCK, 1972/Macmillan, 1971. Examines the Gospel narratives and their composition.

S. H. Hooke, *The Resurrection of Christ*, Darton, Longman and Todd, 1967. A study by a notable Old Testament scholar. Includes helpful discussion of the background of the concept, the accounts of Jesus' resurrection, its meaning in New Testament theology, and its relevance for the church today.

Section Two. God's new society

Chapter 6. The Nature of the New Society

C. H. Dodd, *The Parables of the Kingdom*, first edition 1935; Nisbet, 1955/Scribner. Dodd's classic study in which he put forward the idea that Jesus had a realized eschatology.

*W. G. Kümmel, *Promise and Fulfilment*, SCM 1961 (second edition). Argues persuasively that Jesus held an eschatology in the process of being realized.

G. E. Ladd, *Jesus and the Kingdom*, SPCK, 1966. A survey of the various understandings of Jesus' eschatology, and a re-examination of the evidence.

*A. Schweitzer, *The Quest of the Historical Jesus*, first edition 1910, Black, 1954/Macmillan, 1968. The classic study referred to in our discussion.

Chapter 7. Pictures of the new society

A. M. Hunter, *Interpreting the Parables*, SCM Press, 1960/Westminster, 1976. A readable account of the history of their interpretation (up to 1960), and an exposition of their meaning, largely based on Dodd and Jeremias. There have been a number of new developments since the book was published, but it is still useful.

*J. Jeremias, *The Parables of Jesus*, SCM Press/Scribner, 1972 (third edition). A helpful survey of the meaning of the parables, trying to understand them against their historical background in the life of Jesus and the early church.

G. V. Jones, *The Art and Truth of the Parables*, SPCK/Allenson, 1964. Examines the parables as an art form, and emphasizes their direct appeal to the human situation.

*T. W. Manson, *The Sayings of Jesus*, SCM Press/Allenson, 1949, reprinted 1971. An older exposition of the non-Marcan material in the Gospels of Matthew and Luke.

D. O. Via, *The Parables*, Fortress Press, 1967. Also emphasizes the aesthetic nature of the parables, rather than their historical life setting.

Chapter 8. The power of the new society

R. H. Fuller, *Interpreting the Miracles*, SCM Press/Allenson, 1963. Considers the meaning of the miracles in the New Testament, and their value to Christians today.

*E. and M.-L. Keller, *Miracles in Dispute*, SCM Press, 1969. An account of the way the miracles have been understood down the ages by Christian theologians and others, and a consideration of some of the philosophical problems involved in understanding miracles.

C. S. Lewis, *Miracles*, 1947 (and many reprints). A readable study of the problem of what is meant by a miracle.

*H van der Loos, *The Miracles of Jesus*, Leiden 1968. An encyclopedic examination of the Gospel narratives, and the issues raised by them. Easily the most comprehensive study of the subject, though not a book for the fainthearted.

Chapter 9. God's society in action

*W. D. Davies, *The Setting of the Sermon on the Mount*, Cambridge University Press, 1964. A massive and scholarly study of the meaning of the Sermon in its first century context.

A. M. Hunter, *Design for Life*, SCM Press, 1965 (second edition). A clear, concise and helpful exposition of the meaning of the Sermon on the Mount. Hunter's interpretation has been followed fairly closely in our own discussion of the subject.

J. Jeremias, *The Sermon on the Mount*, Athlone Press/Fortress Press, 1963. A short account of the sermon and its use in the early church.

R. Schnackenburg, *The Moral Teaching of the New Testament*, Search Press/Seabury Press, 1975. Includes a section on the ethics of Jesus, as well as covering the rest of the New Testament.

Section Three. Knowing about Jesus

Chapter 10. What are the Gospels?

*R. Bultmann, *The History of the Synoptic Tradition*, Blackwell, 1972. Bultmann's form-critical analysis of the synoptic Gospels.

G. B. Caird, *St Luke*, Penguin, 1963 (Pelican New Testament Commentaries). A recent study of

Luke which adopts a form of Streeter's Proto-Luke hypothesis.

M. Dibelius, *From Tradition to Gospel*, Cambridge University Press, 1971 (first German edition 1919). Dibelius's pioneering work on form criticism.

C. H. Dodd, *The Apostolic Preaching and its developments*, third edition Hodder and Stoughton, 1963/Harper and Row. Dodd's classic study of the form of the *kerygma*.

*I. H. Marshall (editor), *New Testament Interpretation*, Paternoster Press/Eerdmans, 1977. Includes articles on source, form and redaction criticism, as well as dealing with other aspects of New Testament studies.

R. P. Martin, *New Testament Foundations*, volume I, Paternoster Press/Eerdmans, 1975. A helpful introduction to the study of the Gospels. Includes a section on the historical background as well as detailed consideration of the writing and interpretation of the four Gospels.

N. Perrin, *What is Redaction Criticism?* SPCK, 1970/Fortress Press, 1969. A useful introduction to a relatively new discipline.

*J. A. T. Robinson, *Redating the New Testament*, SCM Press/Westminster, 1976. Argues for an early dating of the Gospels, and includes valuable surveys of academic study of the New Testament, especially the Johannine literature. A more popular presentation of parts of the argument is in the same author's book *Can we trust the New Testament?* (Mowbray, 1977).

*B. H. Streeter, *The Four Gospels*, Macmillan, 1924. Streeter's classic study of the origins and composition of the Gospels.

V. Taylor, *The Formation of the Gospel Tradition*, Epworth, 1949. A form-critical study of the Gospels by an English scholar which makes a number of points differing from those of Dibelius.

Chapter 11. The four Gospels
General

D. Guthrie, *New Testament Introduction*, Tyndale Press, 1970 (second edition)/Inter-Varsity Press. The section on the Gospels contains useful accounts of the

history of their interpretation, and the main points at issue.

Matthew

B. W. Bacon, *Studies in Matthew*, Macmillan, 1930. Suggests the five-fold division of Matthew, paralleling the five books of the Pentateuch.

H. B. Green, *The Gospel according to Matthew*, Oxford University Press, 1975 (New Clarendon Bible). A simple, straightforward commentary on the Gospel.

*D. Hill, *The Gospel of St Matthew*, Oliphants, 1972 (New Century Bible). A slightly more technical commentary.

*J. D. Kingsbury, *Matthew: Structure, Christology, Kingdom*, SPCK, 1976/Fortress Press, 1975. Puts forward an alternative view to Bacon's on the structure of Matthew's Gospel.

E. Schweizer, *The Good News according to Matthew*, SPCK, 1976/John Knox Press, 1975. A readable and helpful commentary by a noted German scholar.

Mark

*R. P. Martin, *Mark: Evangelist and Theologian*, Paternoster Press, 1972/Zondervan, 1973. Puts forward the idea that Mark was written to counteract some kind of Docetic Christology in the early church.

D. E. Nineham, *St Mark*, Penguin, 1963 and reprints (Pelican Gospel Commentaries). A readable commentary, taking full account of the work of the form critics.

E. Schweizer, *The Good News according to Mark*, SPCK, 1971/John Knox Press, 1976. A companion volume to the author's work on Matthew.

Luke

*E. E. Ellis, *The Gospel according to Luke*, Oliphants, 1974 (second edition) (New Century Bible). A useful commentary on Luke.

G. H. P. Thompson, *The Gospel according to Luke*, Oxford University Press, 1972 (New Clarendon Bible). A more elementary book offering a critique of the proto-Luke hypothesis, and dating Luke's Gospel before AD 65.

John

*C. H. Dodd, *Historical Tradition*

in the Fourth Gospel, Cambridge University Press, 1965. A massive study of John's Gospel, arguing that it preserves reliable and independent historical traditions about Jesus.

A. M. Hunter, *According to John*, SCM Press, 1968/Westminster, 1969. A short and lucid account of the background and contents of the Gospel.

*L Morris, *Studies in the Fourth Gospel*, Paternoster Press/Eerdmans, 1969. A series of studies on the recent interpretation of John's Gospel.

L. Morris, *The Gospel according to John*, Eerdmans, 1971 (New International Commentary on the New Testament). Probably the most comprehensive recent commentary on this Gospel. It could be hard going for the beginner, but rewarding in the end.

*J. N. Sanders, *John*, Black/Harper and Row, 1968 (Black's New Testament Commentaries). Shorter than Morris, though more technical in parts.

Chapter 12. Are the Gospels true?

R. S. Barbour, *Traditio-historical Criticism of the Gospels*, SPCK/Allenson, 1972. A helpful examination of the various techniques used for discovering the authentic words of Jesus in the Gospels, and a consideration of the issues raised by them.

C. Brown (editor), *History, Criticism and Faith*, Inter-Varsity Press, 1976. A series of essays by conservative scholars on the question of history and theology in Christian belief. Includes chapters on myth in the New Testament, and the authenticity of the sayings of Jesus in the Gospels.

*B. Gerhardsson, *Memory and Manuscript*, Lund 1961. A thorough examination of the teaching traditions of the Jewish rabbis, setting the teaching of Jesus in that context.

A. T. Hanson (editor), *Vindications*, SCM Press/Morehouse-Barlow, 1966. A collection of essays by five leading English theologians, affirming the importance of the historical basis of Christian belief. Includes a detailed examination of the issues raised by the Gospels.

*V. A. Harvey, *The Historian and the Believer*, SCM Press, 1967/

Macmillan, 1969. An extended account of the dichotomy between faith and history made by some contemporary theologians, and an examination of the validity of their arguments.

J. Jeremias, *Unknown Sayings of Jesus*, SPCK/Allenson, 1964. A comprehensive account of sayings of Jesus outside the New Testament, and a consideration of their character as authentic utterances of Jesus himself.

*H. Palmer, *The Logic of Gospel Criticism*, Macmillan, 1968. A critical analysis of the methods applied to the understanding of the Gospels by New Testament scholars, written by a philosopher. A most useful book for clarifying the issues involved in the debate about the Gospels and the historical Jesus.

*N. Perrin, *Rediscovering the Teaching of Jesus*, SCM Press, 1967. An investigation into what can be known about Jesus and his teaching by the use of the criteria of dissimilarity, coherence and multiple attestation.

H. Riesenfeld, *The Gospel Tradition*, Blackwell, 1970, pp. 1–29. An essay by a Scandinavian scholar claiming that Jesus himself took care to ensure the reliable transmission of his teachings to future generations.

T. F. Torrance, *Space, Time and Resurrection*, Handsel Press/Eerdmans, 1976. A helpful discussion of the consequences of divine revelation for our understanding of the world and its workings, with special reference to the resurrection of Jesus. Argues strongly against the idea that the universe is a closed system that cannot accommodate the supernatural.

Index

References to pictures are in *italics*